THE ROMAN REPUBLIC IN
POLITICAL THOUGHT

THE MENAHEM STERN JERUSALEM LECTURES

sponsored by the Historical Society of Israel
and Published for Brandeis University Press by
University Press of New England

Carlo Ginzburg, *History, Rhetoric, and Proof*

Anthony D. Smith, *The Nation in History:
Historiographical Debates about Ethnicity
and Nationalism*

Peter Brown, *Poverty and Leadership in the Later
Roman Empire*

Fergus Millar, *The Roman Republic in Political Thought*

THE ROMAN REPUBLIC IN POLITICAL THOUGHT

Fergus Millar

THE MENAHEM STERN JERUSALEM LECTURES

Brandeis
University
Press

Historical
Society of
Israel

PUBLISHED BY UNIVERSITY PRESS OF NEW ENGLAND

Hanover and London

Brandeis University Press/Historical Society of Israel

© 2002 by Historical Society of Israel

All rights reserved

Printed in the United States of America

5   4   3   2   1

Library of Congress Cataloging-in-Publication Data

Millar, Fergus.
The Roman Republic in political thought / Fergus Millar.
    p.   cm.—(The Menahem Stern Jerusalem lectures)
Includes index.
ISBN 1-58465-198-9 (cloth : alk. paper)—ISBN 1-58465-199-7
(pbk. : alk. paper)
    1. Rome—Politics and government—510–30 B.C. 2. Political
science—History. I. Title. II. Series.
JC88 .m55 2002
320.437'07'204—dc21   2001008177

For Chava Stern

Contents

Foreword by Joseph Geiger   ix

Acknowledgments   xiii

1. Introduction   1

2. Greek Observers: Aristotle, Polybius, and After   12

    Introduction   12
    What Aristotle Might Have Seen   15
    Polybius and the Roman Constitution   23
    Later Greek Narrators   37

3. Looking Back on the Republic: The Empire,   50
   the Middle Ages, Machiavelli

    Roman Reflections   50
    The Republic in Medieval Thought   54
    Florence and Machiavelli   64

4. Three Views from Seventeenth-Century England   80

    Introduction   80
    Marchamont Nedham   84
    Harrington's *Commonwealth*   86
    Milton's *Commonwealth*   96

5. From Restoration to Revolution: England, France,   100
   and America

    England   100
    France   108
    America: The Debate on the Constitution   120

6. Some Contemporary Approaches   135

   Introduction   135
   Recent Political Studies   142
   The Crowd and the Mob   153

7. Cicero's Rome: What Aristotle Might Have Thought   157

   Introduction: The Historical Context   157
   Aristotle's Criteria   168

      Notes   183

      Subject Index   196

      Index of Passages Quoted   200

Foreword

Joseph Geiger

"It is, moreover, a historical fact worth dwelling on in its own right, that perhaps the finest expression in the twentieth century of what was best in the German scholarship of the nineteenth should have come from a man born in Poland, but writing in English in Jerusalem." Thus we have Fergus Millar's summing-up of his appreciation of the first volume of Menahem Stern's magnum opus, *Greek and Latin Authors on Jews and Judaism* (1974).[1] The praise, by no means excessive, is significant. By now, Stern's outstanding achievement as a leading historian of the Second Temple period hardly needs additional highlighting. Yet it is not superfluous to emphasize one of the rock-solid foundations on which his scholarship was built: the strict philological acumen of a man, who, for many years, started his day with an hour of reading Greek texts, often of the more obscure sort. The great work in which the evidence for the acquaintance of the classical world with the Jews is collected and evaluated—but other works as well—is a constant reminder that at the root of historical judgment lies the philological examination of the evidence. Yet it was not only what was best in German scholarship, but it was equally the Jewish tradition of the study and exegesis of texts of great linguistic complexity, which was at its peak in eastern Europe before the Holocaust, that helped forge the formidable armory of Stern's mind. His scholarship was so impressive precisely because it was devoid of any trace of sensationalism and because it did not feature great "discoveries" and "innovations," let alone "revolutions of method." Rather, it presented and weighed the information with the modesty of the truly learned. To appreciate the scholarship of this great work, there are no grandiose conclusions to read, only the small print of fine philological argument.

The three volumes of *Greek and Latin Authors on Jews and*

Judaism constitute one of the indispensable tools available to the student of Jewish history in the classical world; another being the three volumes (in four) of the *New Schürer*,[2] which is, perhaps, the most useful twentieth-century updating of a great work of nineteenth-century German scholarship.[3] Yet it was more. Although strictly adhering to the standards of scholarly objectivity, the editors added a last sentence to the first volume: Schürer ended his book with Jerome's gleeful description of the lamentations of the miserable Jews in Jerusalem on 9th Ab, the date of the destruction of the Temple. And the editors added: "Yet the tears of mourning concealed hope, and hope refused to die." But for this short, but important, departure from academic aloofness, the *New Schürer* shares with Stern's collection the pursuit of the most up-to-date and exact state of research.

Fergus Millar's participation in that project first signaled the importance he accorded to the history of the Jews as part of the history of the Roman Empire. Indeed, this was only one aspect of his wider vision of the history of Rome, a view from the periphery rather than from the center of the Empire, thus giving the various regions, ethnicities, and cultures of the Roman world their due.

History from below came into its own in Roman history with a relocation of attention from Rome and the center of power to the fifty to seventy million inhabitants of a vast empire. A culmination of this approach is *The Roman Near East 31 B.C.–A.D. 337* (1993). One critic's words may be repeated here: "[O]ne of the most powerful, and most convincingly demonstrated conclusions of the book [is] the uniqueness of the Jews and the Jewish community. This has of course been asserted on endless occasions, both as part of a religious and national(istic) credo and in works of scholarship with claims to objectivity, but it seems that the case has very rarely been so convincingly argued, and against the background of such an impressive wealth of comparative material."[4]

This approach had to be based on a shift of emphasis in the source material. Ronald Syme remarked famously in the preface to his first great masterpiece that there was much in it that would make Hugh Last (whom he was to succeed as Camden Professor of Ancient History at Oxford) raise his eyebrows.[5] No doubt the author of *Tacitus*, a work that secured his place as the greatest contemporary historian of Rome with a study of the man he regarded as the greatest of Rome's ancient historians, must have raised his eyebrows at the statement of his most prominent pupil and eventual successor to his chair, when he described in his Inaugural Lecture Josephus' *Jewish Antiquities* as a book that could enter "a claim to be regarded as the most significant single work written in the Roman Empire."[6] The realization of the importance of Josephus and the ongoing study of his text certainly associates Fergus Millar more closely with Menahem Stern than with the conventional Oxford ancient historian. Indeed, despite deriving all that is best from a traditional classical training, conventional is the epithet less suited to describe the scholarship of Millar, who not only broke new ground in the study of Roman history, but whose wide reading brought in the influence of disciplines and subjects traditionally far removed from the classics.

The emphasis of this preface on Fergus Millar's interest in Jewish history does him a serious injustice because it disregards the majority of his works from *A Study of Cassius Dio* (1964) to *The Crowd in Rome in the Late Republic* (1998), including the highly influential *The Emperor in the Roman World (31 B.C.–A.D. 337)* (1977), from which the words "the Emperor was what the Emperor did" became a catchphrase for a generation of students—and scores of major papers and other publications, soon to appear in three volumes of his collected papers, *Rome, the Greek World and the East*. Indeed, Millar's growing interest in the history of the Republic, after decades of research devoted mainly to the Empire, is now to receive a new slant in *The Roman Republic in Political Thought*. And nothing has been said yet of Millar's influence as a teacher, of the dozens of former research students spread all over the world, not the least in Israel, of the man whose advice is sought, never in vain, by younger colleagues as well as by established scholars.

There is a curious mixture of sadness and joy over the occasion of welcoming in Jerusalem a friend, a friend of the late Menahem Stern, and a friend of many lesser men and women and lesser scholars in this country as well. It is not only his towering distinction as a scholar but also his personality, combining as it does the moral rectitude of his Scottish forebears with his human warmth and kindness, that make Fergus Millar the ideal person to deliver a series of Menahem Stern Jerusalem Lectures.

Acknowledgments

I owe a great debt to the Historical Society of Israel, and, above all, its chairman, Professor Yosef Kaplan, and its Secretary, Mr. Zvi Yekutiel, for the privilege of giving the Jerusalem Lectures in History in Memory of Menahem Stern; and to many friends in Jerusalem for their hospitality to my wife and myself during our stay; but most of all, as ever, to Hannah Cotton and Ari Paltiel.

My greatest intellectual debt, in pursuing a topic that has taken me far outside the limits of my normal subject matter, is to Mogens Herman Hansen, both for the example he has set of seeing the Athenian democracy in a wider intellectual framework of analysis and comparative study and for much advice on bibliography over the last few years. A further debt is to Quentin Skinner, both for his own exceptionally stimulating published work and for much advice, not least to the effect that the Roman Republic had in fact attracted more attention on the part of more thinkers of various periods than I had originally supposed. I also have gained enormously, during his periodic visits to Oxford, from conversations with Paul Rahe.

I am much indebted to those who have read the text at a late stage and have done their best with its many imperfections. Vernon Bogdanor, Andrew Lintott, and Quentin Skinner have saved me from various errors and misapprehensions, while generously accepting that the book's patent limitations were already determined.

Anyone with the slightest acquaintance with my handwriting will know that it is no mere formality to thank Priscilla Lange once again for the skill, patience, and good humor shown in converting the manuscript into an intelligible text.

Finally, and all the more so because the text was composed following a spell in hospital in February 2000, I would like to say that everything is made possible only by Susanna's love and support.

Oxford   F.M.
June 2001

1 Introduction

The Roman Republic, whose citizens had the right to meet in assembly to pass laws and to elect all the annual office-holders, made a momentous impact on the history of the world. In the lifetime of Cicero, who was killed in 43 B.C., its forces reached southern England to the northwest, and the Caucasus, the Tigris, and northern Arabia to the east. One need not feel the least admiration for the ingrained militarism of Roman tradition to think—as Polybius had a century earlier, when the bounds of Roman military activity had been far narrower—that the nature of Rome's constitutional and political order deserves both detailed empirical examination and (as Polybius gave it) interpretation by comparison with other known examples of political systems. The word *empirical* needs to be stressed, for much of what the Romans themselves wrote about their own political order was polemical, ideologically loaded—and to a significant degree directed to periods in the remote past, hundreds of years before the writer's own time. As will appear repeatedly in the course of this book, it is impossible to exaggerate the importance for later Western political thought of the literary image of the early Republic of the fifth and fourth centuries B.C. contained in the first ten books of Livy's *History*, which was written under Augustus, at the end of the first century B.C. For it was this literary image of an earlier Rome that was to be the subject of Machiavelli's *Discorsi sopra la prima deca di Tito Livio*.

By "political thought," I mean a loose range of interconnected approaches, from descriptive or historical studies of particular constitutions or political systems, to sociological studies of participation, patronage, or voter behavior, to comparative evaluations, to philosophical discussions of terms such as *law*, *rights*, *sovereignty*, or *democracy*. The tradition of combining detailed empirical reporting of particular systems and the use of comparative examples drawn from a wide variety of places with philosophical reflections on political structures goes back to Aristotle's *Politics* and to the collection of 158 different examples of *politeiai* which his school made. Both works seem to date to his final stay in Athens between 335 and 323 B.C.

As we will see in chapter 2, it seems certain that, although Aristotle knew of Rome, its *politeia* did not form one of the 158 examples. But it will become clear there how close Rome's connections with the Greek world were, and indeed always had been, how near the political studies by Aristotle and his school brought them to Rome, and how significant an example Rome would have been for them. Greek "political" thought, as is well known, always focused on the nuclear *polis*, or city-state, to the relative neglect of the larger political formations, which were becoming ever more important in the fourth century, namely, leagues of cities on the one hand and monarchies (above all, Macedon and Persia) on the other. Rome was just such a city-state, with an urban center having monumental temples and open-air political meeting places for the citizens, a surrounding territory, and a citizen army commanded by elected political leaders. In many ways, Rome of the fourth century B.C. could have been fitted without much discomfort into Greek conceptions of a *polis*, just as Polybius was to do some 170 years later.

One of the most significant aspects of the Roman system and its evolution, however, is that, precisely at the moment when Aristotle's school might have attempted to describe it, it began to acquire an expanded structure, both by colonization and by the absorption of other Italian city-states (many of which Greeks could easily have seen as *poleis* of a familiar type), progressively generating a citizen body living far away—even hundreds of kilometers—from the political center. Yet this process of expansion proved from the beginning, from Aristotle's own lifetime, to be compatible with the continued existence of self-governing city states, whose inhabitants could be seen as enjoying a dual citizenship, that of their native city and of Rome. To take only the most familiar example, in 304 B.C., eighteen years after Aristotle's death, the Romans granted the "citizenship without the vote" to the small hilltop city of Arpinum, following it with full citizenship in 188 B.C., eighty-two years before the birth of its most famous product, Cicero.

One of the most interesting, but relatively neglected, aspects of the Roman republic as a political system is thus, on the one hand, the *nature* of citizenship as exercised by persons living several or even many days' journey from the political center and on the other, the relation between the functioning of that political center and the local city-state structures, several hundred in number, all over Italy.

As will be seen, it is his failure to take account of the spatial extension of the Roman citizen body (and its sheer size, some 300,000 adult males in his time) that constitutes the greatest limitation in Polybius's otherwise powerful and penetrating analysis of the political system. It is all the more regrettable, since he does pay due attention (more than do most political analysts) to military service. Furthermore, he was quite aware of the fundamental feature of Roman military resources in the second century, namely, that all adult males in the Italian peninsula were liable to serve. Whereas Romans all were enrolled in the legions, the other two categories, "Latins" and "allies," served in units organized, officered, and paid by their own communities.

By the time Cicero's career as an elected officeholder had begun, in the 70s B.C., a colossal change had taken place as a result of the "Social War" (the "War of the Allies") of 90 to 87 B.C.: The entire population of the Italian peninsula up to the Po River were now Roman citizens, local military units had disappeared, and all were now enrolled in the legions. We can see local political structures and the wider Roman citizenship intersecting in a famous document from southern Italy, the "Tabula Heracleensis," which shows that Roman legislation laid down the qualifications for the holding of local elective office, one of which was service in the Roman army; and that, when a census was held, the local magistrates were obliged to construct lists of citizens and deliver them to Rome (pp. 162–63 below).

In certain important ways, therefore, what we call the Roman Republic had by the middle of the first century B.C. become a nation-state—after 49 B.C. closely coterminous with the modern Italian state, minus Sicily and Sardinia—with a single register of citizens, universal liability to legionary service (although erratically activated), a universal formal right to vote in Rome, and a common private law. But within that structure, several hundred local city-states, with assemblies, elected magistrates, public properties and finances, and local legislation, persisted. This remarkable balance between the center and the subordinate city-state structures is certainly one aspect of the republic that would deserve attention in comparative political studies.

Within this wider structure, which from some angles could properly be thought of as that of a nation-state, Rome itself remained, as has always been recognized, an anachronistic anomaly, retaining to the end the fundamental institutions and political practices of an archaic, nuclear city-state. Neither the elected annual magistrates (consuls, praetors, and so forth) nor the Senate, in which ex-magistrates now held seats for life, were in any sense representative of constituencies or of regions of Italy. The very real and important rights that adult male citizens enjoyed, of electing the annual officeholders and above all of voting on legislation (*all* legislation, because the Roman Senate was not a legislature), could be exercised only in person in Rome. It was in Rome that political speeches were made and voting took place, both on legislation and in elections.

The question of how we should understand this curious and anomalous political system is hotly debated among specialists. Can the Senate properly be regarded as the true governing organ of the Republic? In terms of political behavior, was the great mass of potential voters dominated by a restricted number of aristocratic families exercising power through patronage? Did the voters from the numerous local communities of Italy ever really make the journey to Rome to vote, and, if so, what influence did they exercise? Or was effective voting confined to those citizens who lived either in the city or near it (perhaps some 300,000 out of a total of 1,000,000 or so)?

Some particularly significant aspects of the evolution of the Rome that Aristotle might have seen and that Polybius did so brilliantly analyze more than a century and a half later are discussed in chapter 2. Cicero's Rome, another century later, will the subject of chapter 7, and these chapters also attempt to spell out in more detail some reasons why this evolving structure might deserve more attention than it has received in comparative political studies.

Two points, however, should be made in advance. One is the crucial dependence of all comparative political thought and reflection on the availability of coherent preexisting texts relating to the political structure in question. Athens owes its primary place in the history of democracy above all to a concentration of historical, rhetorical, and philosophical texts written in the fifth and fourth centuries, crowned by the publication a little more than a century ago of the Aristotelian *Athēnaiōn Politeia,* the "Constitution of Athens," a detailed empirical or analytical study of how the system worked in the fourth century, preserved on a papyrus from Egypt. That prominence is of course deserved, and it cannot be denied. But there were literally hundreds of small Greek "republics" or city-states, nearly all with a council (*boulē*) and assembly (*ekklēsia*), stretching from the Black Sea to Spain, and lasting into the Roman Imperial period. And for that matter, apart from the Greek cities of Italy themselves, many of the other numerous non-Greek communities of Italy were also "republics" with constitutions. But in the canonical history of democracy, these worlds of small, self-governing republics have no place.

The place of Rome in that history is more controversial. One crucial factor is, again, that although the Rome of Cicero's time is illuminated both by a mass of contemporary evidence (all too largely from Cicero himself) and by later narratives (mainly Greek), there is no empirical description of its system to match the *Athēnaiōn Politeia* and no analysis and comparative valuation to match that of Polybius. There is therefore no central ancient text to which political thinkers from the Renaissance to the present have been able to turn. In consequence, although it is clearly not true, as I had earlier supposed, that the Republic has played little part as the source of material for comparative political thought, it is certainly true that many significant aspects of its political character have not attracted wider attention.

One further reason for the relatively low level of attention that the Roman Republic has attracted during the last century from students of political systems is the conviction that has reigned among ancient historians themselves that the workings of Republican politics can be explained systematically in terms of the operation of a "top-down" system of patronage, or *clientela*. In consequence, the formal structures of voting or law-making or elections have seemed of no real interest. The relevant issues are pursued elsewhere in this book (pp. 139–40). But the reader should be warned that the question of the historical interpretation of the middle and late Republic is currently controversial, and that I myself, in a series of studies culminating in *The Crowd in Rome* in the Late Republic,[1] occupy the extreme end of the spectrum in arguing that precisely what was distinctive about the Republic was that the crowd, which met in the Forum to hear speeches and then to vote, was itself, once formed into voting units, the *sovereign* body, and the only one that could legislate.

It therefore follows, I would argue, that we cannot properly deny the Roman Republic *a* place in the history of democracy. The subject of this book is both what place the Republic has occupied in analyses of political systems written both in the ancient world and since and what place (or places) it *should* occupy, if proper attention were first paid to its distinctive features. One of these features, in my view (but not in that of many other experts), is that republican Rome was a direct democracy, in which persuasion through the vehicle of oratory played a central part, and in which the sovereign power really was held by "the Roman People" (*populus Romanus*), both in elections and (even more important) in legislation—or, rather, if we speak in terms of voter participation, by those members of the *populus* who could and did present themselves at the right time and place in Rome.

To make this claim is not in any way to deny the manifold anomalies that marked the system; but it is to say that the Republic should be seen as *a* form of democratic system. It is also to suggest that there might be room for a different sense of the word *representative* in considering political systems, namely, one in which it applies not to elected representatives sitting in a legislative chamber but to those of the citizens themselves who participate, that is to say, those who come to witness formal acts, to listen to speeches, and to vote. In the Roman case, behind the right of the citizen to vote lay a broader concept, the requirement of publicity, namely, that a range of public acts should be performed "under the gaze of the *populus Romanus*." It is in this sense that whoever was present in the Forum at the relevant moment did "represent" the Roman people as a whole.

This book is therefore intended as a dialogue between what I conceive to be the "real" Roman Republic as it evolved from the fourth century B.C. to the first, including the interpretations and representations of it, and the arguments derived from those conceptions by outside observers from the Republican period itself until now. As regards the political system of the Republic, the standard treatment is now contained in an excellent book by Andrew Lintott, published in 1999, two years after the delivery of the lectures on which this book is based. Furthermore, Lintott's book ends with a very fine chapter, "The Republic Remembered," which in some thirty pages deals with later interpretations of it up to the present.[2] Our two studies are mutually independent; but reading his makes me regret all the more keenly the narrowness of my historical culture. For it hardly needs saying that, when I move out of the ancient world and begin to explore such representations as are found in political thinkers and students of comparative political systems, from Machiavelli to the present day, I cannot rely on any significant knowledge of the historical background or of the mass of political writing, say in the later Middle Ages or in Florence of the later fifteenth and early sixteenth century, or in England during the Commonwealth or in America in the years before the Revolution or after it in the intense debate that surrounded the adoption of the Constitution in 1787–88. All that I can claim to offer are my reflections on, and reactions to, the presumptions about the Roman Republic made, first, in the canonical works of Western political thought and second, in some contemporary studies in political science. Among contemporary works, it is a pleasure to acknowledge the truly remarkable achievement represented by the posthumous work by the late S. E. Finer, *The History of Government* I–III (1997).

This has thus been a voyage of (inevitably rather superficial) discovery for me, embracing great intellectual masterpieces like the *Federalist Papers* and giving some impression of the intense contemporary debate about (for instance) different conceptions of rights, liberty, and republicanism that are conducted above all in the United States (far more so, it seems to an outside observer, than in Britain, where they are so badly needed). It is impossible not to be impressed by the moral commitment and the high intellectual level of much of this writing, including instances when it takes the form of introductions to paperbacks for students. I note two outstanding examples, R. F. Stalley's introduction to the *Politics* of Aristotle in Oxford University Press's World's Classics (1995) and Isaac Krammick's introduction to the *Federalist Papers* (Penguin Classics, 1987). In these areas I, too, am in the position of a student and therefore owe an enormous debt above all to various volumes in that wonderful series, *Cambridge Texts in the History of Political Thought.* I cannot and do not advance the slightest claim to be able to contribute to the understanding of these and other major works. All that I claim to be able to contribute is to see how (if at all) the Roman Republic is represented in them, what lessons are drawn from those representations, and to suggest that the "real" Roman Republic is both a more interesting case of a political system than has been realized and represents a radical example of popular sovereignty untrammeled by constitutional safeguards, as well as being a "republican" system corresponding very well to Paul Pettit's criterion that issues of policy should be publicly contested.[3] It is paradoxical, but in my view unquestionably true, that the Roman Forum, from which Finer derived the notion of a "Forum polity" was, in strict constitutional terms, the setting for a far more democratic, or populist, system than Finer's own definition of this type allows: "The Forum polity, though not necessarily democratic, is 'popular': that is, authority is conferred on the rulers from below" (vol. I, 43). The Roman *populus*, when voting in elections, did indeed confer authority, for strictly limited periods, on their "rulers." But the people in the Forum also retained in their own hands the exclusive right to pass legislation.

As is well known, Aristotle in the *Politics* characterized the selection of public officials by *direct election* (as opposed to the use of the lot) as an "aristocratic" (competitive or meritocratic) feature of a political system. This point has not been forgotten even in modern works, which see election, or political representation, as the defining feature of democracy.[4] Aristotle still offers profound conceptual challenges to political thought. So, even if at the beginning we are able only to speculate as to how Aristotle might have described and analyzed the rapidly evolving Roman *res publica* of the 330s and 320s B.C. (pp. 15–23), at the end I will allow myself a further thought-experiment and ask how far the Roman Republic of Cicero's time, which I firmly claim to have been significantly more "democratic" than generally supposed, in fact lived up to Aristotle's criteria for a democratic system (chapter 7).

My active interest in the Roman Republic, as opposed to the Empire, began nearly two decades ago, with a period spent at the British School at Rome and what was (regrettably) my first occasion to explore in detail the topography of the ancient city. The intervening years have also posed profound political and conceptual problems for anyone living in Britain, beginning with basic changes to the political structure of the United Kingdom, following the devolution of powers to the Scottish Parliament, the Welsh National Assembly, and (precariously) the Northern Ireland Assembly. Equally important, British membership in the European Union, and the significance of European Union law, poses fundamental questions about sovereignty, citizenship, and national identity. In this situation, it is not only the intense debates about the need for effective central government embodied and reflected in the *Federalist Papers* that give food for thought;[5] so also does contemplation of the complex constitutional structure of republican Italy, first before and then after all its inhabitants came to add the Roman citizenship to that of their local community.

Closer to home, the citizen of Britain, and not least any such citizen who teaches in a university, has had ample cause to acknowledge the truth of Rousseau's conception of English government as a system of slavery punctuated by occasional moments of liberty, namely, at elections.[6] Traditionally, there have been no constitutional bounds whatsoever on the power of a government with a parliamentary majority to legislate in whatever terms it wishes. There are no entrenched clauses, for there is no constitution for them to be entrenched in; a fortiori there is no supreme court with the capacity to rule on the constitutionality of legislative acts. There is perhaps no other country where the structure of local government is wholly subject to the whims of a parliamentary majority, and in which the local authority governing a capital city of several million people, as it was in 1986 (the Greater London Council), could simply be abolished by Parliament.

Nor, as it turns out, is there any statutory protection for what the citizen might suppose to be fundamental legal principles, such as the avoidance of retrospective legislation. It is a striking instance of the unfettered power of Parliament that in November 1987 the then government published an education reform bill, one of whose purposes was to make British universities, uniquely in the developed world, legally incapable of conferring tenure. In the scale of human suffering, this is of course a minor step; in the context of intellectual freedom, however, it is most certainly not. But legally, and in the framework of considerations about the rights of

individuals and of semipublic corporations, what is significant is
that this clause of the bill, which became law in 1988, came into
effect not from the date on which it was passed but retrospec-
tively, from when it was promulgated. As the then Lord Chancel-
lor wrote to me when I protested, "Parliament may legislate with
retrospective effect if it so chooses." So much for legal principle or
individual rights. And, as Rousseau would no doubt have predicted, a subsequent election, producing a different government
with another large majority, has not, with regard to academic freedom, made the slightest difference. At all levels, from the future of
the national state to the nature of law, to the possibility of a written constitution, to the positive or negative freedom of the individual citizen, a reconsideration of principles and structures is
urgently needed. In that context, there may be benefits in looking
again at a variety of historical examples, even distant, alien, and
much misunderstood ones like the Roman Republic.

I may add that I write in the context of a university which in
constitutional form perfectly exemplifies the Aristotelian ideal of
a self-governing *polis*. The academic "citizens" all enjoy the right
to vote, are by definition highly educated, control their own time
even if they are certainly not leisured, and all work, if they do
not live, within a small radius. Collectively, they have a sovereign voice in the affairs of the university, and there is nothing to
prevent them from attending and speaking in its debates and
from voting. Yet, in the current climate, academic citizenship
and academic democracy are completely dead. Each goes about
his or her business without a thought for common issues, and
most would no more offer an opinion on a controversial matter
of policy than if they were the subjects of a totalitarian state.
There is painful material for reflection as to how this state of
affairs came about.

This book owes its immediate origins, however, to what was, in
one sense, the happiest of occasions, when I was invited by the
Historical Society of Israel to give the Jerusalem Lectures in History in memory of Professor Menahem Stern. The three lectures
were given at the Israel Academy and the Van Leer Institute in
April 1997 before a large and well-informed audience of friends
and colleagues. Our stay in Jerusalem, lodging in Mishkennot
Sha'ananim, from which we could look across the Valley of Hin-

nom to Mt. Zion and the Ottoman walls of the Old City, remains the most rewarding of memories. As the date 1997 all too clearly indicates, the lectures should have been turned into book form much more promptly than they have been. But, as indicated, the book from which they spring, *The Crowd in Rome in the Late Republic*, was published only in 1998. In any case, there was a need to find the time at least to reduce somewhat my profound ignorance of political thought from the Middle Ages onward.

One possibility, at any rate, was not open: namely, failing to produce the book at all. Menahem Stern was, in my eyes, the ideal of a scholar and a man, with a straightforward devotion to, and love of, learning and a fundamental innocence and unworldliness that did not in the least inhibit him from ironical views of human ambition, pretension, and self-deception. It was characteristic of him that he could take one of the most emotionally loaded of subjects—perceptions of Jews and Judaism in the Ancient World—and turn it into a paradigm of calm, objective, and thorough scholarship.[7]

At any rate, I had one advantage over the three distinguished historians who preceded me in giving the Menahem Stern Lectures—Carlo Ginzburg, Emmanuel Le Roy Ladurie, and Anthony Grafton.[8] I had met Menahem Stern quite often, in both Jerusalem and Oxford, and will carry with me always the image of him walking contentedly toward the Bodleian Library, with his head in the air, his hat on the back of his conspicuously bald head, and his mind evidently already absorbed in the books that awaited him. It is a treasured memory but also a painful one. For it is all too easy to imagine that he will have been similarly abstracted, on the walk between his home and the university library in Jerusalem, when he was brutally murdered in June 1989.

2 Greek Observers

Aristotle, Polybius, and After

Introduction

Thought about political systems, in particular thought about how a city (*polis*) should be organized, how power should be exercised within it, and how decisions should be made, is as old as Greek literary culture itself.[1] So also was Greek emigration and colonialism, leading to the formation of new Greek *poleis* in the eighth and seventh centuries around much of the Mediterranean and later the Black Sea.[2] One consequence, which is becoming increasingly clear in modern work, is that there was never a time in the history of Rome, from the alleged date of its legendary foundation (in our terms, 753 B.C.) onward, when the population who lived there was not influenced by Greek culture, importing Greek pottery, later imitating Greek art, and establishing the cults of Greek gods and goddesses.[3] Indeed, what may be the earliest known scrap of writing in the Greek alphabet, apparently of the first half of the eighth century B.C., comes from Osteria dell'Osa, ancient Gabii, a few kilometers from Rome.[4]

With the passage of time and the growing importance of Rome in the Greek world, an immense variety of legendary accounts of the origins of Rome grew up, all relating Rome in some way to Greek myth or mythological history. Of course, the version that became canonical was that Aeneas, a fugitive from Troy, had founded a dynasty at Alba in Latium and that, after generations of kings there, two brothers, Romulus and Remus, members of the royal house, founded a new city on the site of Rome. That was (it was later agreed) in 753 B.C., and after a succession of a mere seven kings, the last of them, Tarquin "the Proud," had been ejected and a republic founded. Now, in place of the kings, there were two annually elected *consules* (perhaps originally called *praetores*). At any rate, later tradition assented categorically that even the Rome of the kings had been a sort of constitutional monarchy, with popular assemblies, a senate apparently recruited by the king, and procedures for appointing a king.

Later tradition also claimed to know the names of the annual pairs of consuls from the very moment of the foundation of the Republic onwards—509 B.C.—and therefore, apparently, exactly contemporary with the establishment of all the basic institutions of the Athenian democracy by Cleisthenes. This date, like the chronology of the progressive emergence of the institutions of the Roman Republic, some of which indeed may have preceded the Republic itself, may be a later construct. But what cannot seriously be doubted is that Rome in the fifth and fourth centuries B.C. was indeed a nuclear city-state, with an urban center, a citizenship, a citizen army, popular assemblies (as it happens, two different ones, constructed on different principles), laws that were passed by an assembly of the citizens, and annual office-holders who all normally gained office by election. In short, and (as is obvious) leaving out many disputed details, Rome was a constitutionally structured community that the Greeks would not have had difficulty in characterizing as a *polis*. Indeed, one Greek writer of the fourth century, Heraclides, referred to it not just as a *polis*, but as a Greek *polis*.[5] That was going too far, for although no Latin literature appears until the middle of the third century, there are enough scraps of documentary evidence to confirm that the language of the inhabitants of early Rome was Latin.[6] Whether they already spoke of themselves as the *populus Romanus*, when the expression "Senatus Populusque Romanus" came into use, and when people began to speak of their *res publica*, we cannot know. But, for all the difficulties with the portrayal of the evolution of Rome in the early Republic, which we owe to later tradition (Livy's *History* above all), it would be hypercritical to deny that it was already a republic with a constitution that was progressively altered, added to, and adapted by legislation.[7]

For the first century or more of its existence, the republic does not seem to have attracted much attention from Greek observers. Even the later tradition of telling a story of repeated internal strife and endless wars against neighbors does not suggest that there was much reason why it should have. Rome, however, was a city of significant size, with a major temple of Jupiter on the Capitol and, at least by the fourth century, an eleven-kilometer circuit of walls (of which some is still clearly visible near the Stazione Termini). It also seems to have lived in an uneasy and fluctuating state of alternate collaboration and conflict with a league of other places in Latium, had repeated contacts with the nearest Greek city (Cumae in Campania), and is recorded as forming treaties with Carthage, a Phoenician settlement in North Africa.

Significant change began only in the early fourth century, first with territorial expansion and an increase in the number of the territorial subdivisions of the Roman population, called *tribus*, of which more later. It will suffice to say here that the apparently obvious (and indeed unavoidable) translation, *tribes*, gives quite the wrong impression; rather, *tribus* were artificial constructs created by legislation. Second, there was a disastrous setback, which did attract Greek attention, when Gallic invaders occupied the city in 390 B.C. It was to this event Heraclides referred in calling Rome a "Greek city." More important, Aristotle himself also referred to it and mentioned the name of the Roman commander who saved the day, Camillus.[8]

In the second half of the fourth century, Rome had recovered, and it was then that truly momentous changes began. The other members of the league of communities in Latium were defeated. Some were absorbed into the Roman citizenship, a momentous step to which we will return. Others retained "Latin" rights, which conferred a degree of common citizenship with Rome. It was now, moreover, that Rome began to settle colonies of its own with the "Latin" right, the first according to tradition being Cales in northern Campania. In the same period, a series of wars were conducted against the Samnites of south-central Italy, and Rome formed its first alliance with a Greek city, Neapolis (Naples), in 326 B.C.

In short, Rome had arrived on the map of the Greek world, still on a scale that was minute in comparison with the contemporary conquests of Alexander (336–323 B.C.) but with even greater long-term consequences. Whether, as some later sources say, the Romans sent an embassy to Alexander in Babylon must remain uncertain, but the prominence that Rome had just achieved makes the idea plausible.[9]

What Aristotle Might Have Seen

At this moment, the 330s and 320s B.C., there was already a long
tradition of Greek thought about the proper running of the *polis* —
expressed in poetry, in histories, in tragedies, in pamphlets (such
as the "Old Oligarch"), and in rhetorical and philosophical works,
of which Plato's *Republic* and *Laws* are the most famous. It was
precisely now, during Aristotle's final period of residence in
Athens between 335 and 323 B.C., that argument and reflection
(and in many instances outright civil strife) over the best form of
the *polis*, and the distribution of power within it between different
social classes, also took on the form of systematic empirical observation of different examples. Aristotle's *Politics* itself, the foundation of Western political thought, makes extensive use of allusions to events or institutions in many different Greek *poleis* (i.e.,
communities or regions). Indeed, more than a hundred, and they
covered much of Greece proper, the Aegean, western Asia Minor,
the Black Sea, Sicily and Southern Italy, and as far west as Massilia
(Marseilles), which had been founded in about 600 B.C.: "Sometimes an oligarchy is undermined by people who, though wealthy
themselves, are excluded from office. This happens when the
holders of office are a very limited number, as for example at Massilia, at Istros, at Heraclea, and in other cities."[10]

The two other places mentioned were Greek colonies on the
Black Sea: Istros on the west coast not far south of the mouth of
the Danube and Heraclea on the south coast. Non-Greek communities are brought into consideration also, for instance, the Carthaginians and the Etruscans. Some episodes from Roman history
(such as the story of Camillus, which he knew) might equally have
been brought in as an example. But in fact none is.

Aristotle's comparative studies of political institutions and behavior did not stop at the use of passing examples, however. Later
tradition recorded that he had put together surveys of the *politeiai*
of 158 *poleis*, dividing them into democracies, oligarchies, tyrannies, and aristocracies.[11] With the exception of Athens, to which
we will return, only fragments remain of this collection of studies,
but there are enough to show that once again the Greek west was
well represented: There were *politeiai* of the Massilians; of Gela,
Himera, Akragas, and Syracuse in Sicily; and Sybaris, Kroton,

Taras, and Kyme in Italy.[12] This place was the nearest Greek city to Rome, and Aristotle later referred to the tyrants there. Later sources record in great detail how one of these, Aristodemos, had played a major part in Rome at the moment of the fall of the kings and in the early years of the Republic.[13]

We can take it as certain that Aristotle's school never compiled a *Constitution of the Romans* (*Rōmaiōn Politeia*), for it seems clear that this collection confined itself to unambiguously Greek places. It is worth noting, however, that Aristotle's interests did in fact extend outside the sphere of purely Greek institutions and that his *Barbarian Customs* (*Nomima Barbarika*) covered Rome's immediate neighbors to the north, the Etruscans. The one fragment that survives from this section of the work is of rather an engaging character, and what Aristotle says finds an echo on the large number of Etruscan sculptures showing couples reclining together: "The Etruscans dine with their wives, reclining under the same covering."[14]

It is still worth speculating about what an Aristotelian *Constitution of the Romans* might have been like, for a variety of reasons. First, no extended text of his *Constitution of the Athenians* was known until a papyrus containing it was published in 1892.[15] So the limits of the knowledge we might one day recover are quite uncertain. Second, the *Athēnaiōn Politeia* as we now have it, the only one of the 158 *politeiai* that is available in extended form, provides a model of how each of them may have been treated: a historical, or narrative, section giving the earlier evolution and, in the case of Athens, taking the story down to 401 B.C. (chapters 1–40), and then a second half (chapters 41–63) describing and analyzing the (in fact, quite stable) democratic constitution as it was throughout the fourth century and until the year of Aristotle's death, 322 B.C. It is this remarkably detailed description and analysis, along with the evidence of contemporary orators, that makes the fourth-century Athenian democracy easily the best known of ancient political systems.[16]

It is therefore likely that a *Rōmaiōn Politeia*, if there ever had been one, would equally have begun with a historical section (just as we know that Polybius's account of the Roman constitution was to do).[17] It might have proved very difficult, however, assuming that any narrative of the evolution of the Roman republic was available, to know where to bring the historical section to a close.

Perhaps the most likely point would have been 367 to 366 B.C., the years that, according to later narratives, saw the restoration of the consulship (and election of the first nonpatrician consul) and the creation of the praetorship.

Any attempt to envisage how Aristotle might have conceived of the Roman political system of his own time is made extremely difficult by our dependence on narrative histories written three centuries later by Livy and Dionysius of Halicarnassus (more on whom later). It is absolutely uncertain whether they were in a position to understand either the sequence of steps by which the system in the late Republic had evolved, or could have had any real idea about how the system had worked at any one moment, or how power was distributed among the discordant and competing elements within Roman society. It is perhaps worth repeating that the "Roman Republic" that was to have the greatest influence on later political thought was that on which Machiavelli was to meditate, namely, that covered in the first ten books of Livy (see chapter 3). Book VIII of Livy, which ends in the year of Aristotle's death, 322 B.C., was written almost exactly three hundred years later.

The Aristotelian *Constitution of the Athenians*, in its opening section, makes a couple of references to Athenian "aristocrats" (*eupatridai*); but in the second half of the work, no such descent group plays any part at all. So (if, once again, we can use Livy's narrative as a guide at all) an Aristotelian observer would have been struck by the centrality in fourth-century Rome of the "struggle of the orders," in fact, a conflict over whether, first, tenure of elective office and, second, membership of the "colleges" of public priests, filled by co-optation, should be limited to members of a quite small number of families with the designation *patricii*. To cut a long story very short, neither our sources nor we can offer any convincing explanation of the basis on which the distinction between *patricii* and *plebeii* (namely, everyone else) had arisen. Suffice to say that it persisted into the historical period, and that the "struggle," which is so prominent in accounts of the fifth and fourth centuries, was solved essentially by compromises opening public or priestly office to plebeians while keeping some places for patricians.

That would not, however, have been the most difficult feature of the contemporary Roman political system with which an

Aristotelian observer would need to come to terms. First, as noted earlier, Rome had just entered on a fundamental phase of development involving the expansion of citizen settlement from beyond the area that naturally would have been associated with a nuclear city-state. That is to say, far beyond the territory of the earlier four "urban" and seventeen "rustic" tribes occupying the area around the city, new "tribes" of Roman citizens had been progressively created and occupied territory farther away (according to Livy's narrative, four new tribes in 387, two in 358, and two in 332 B.C., making twenty-nine "tribes" in all so far). Along with that went the absorption of existing city-states into either full Roman citizenship or citizenship without the vote (*sine suffragio*), the foundation of Roman colonies (whose citizens, unlike those of Greek colonies, retained the citizenship of the mother city) and the creation—even after the dissolution of the Latin League in 338 B.C.—of "Latin" colonies, self-governing city-states with their own citizenship but whose citizens enjoyed certain private-law rights in Rome and might gain the Roman citizenship by settling there and could vote in one of the Roman "tribes."

Any attempt to analyze all this probably would have brought out two significant weaknesses, or rather, perhaps, limitations, of Aristotelian political thought as regards *poleis*: first, a relative lack of attention to their geographic extension and the local subdivisions within them (although some remarks of his on the possible scale of a *polis* are discussed on pp. 160–61 below) and, second, an even more marked lack of attention to inter-state, or inter-*polis*, relations. So adequate attention to the spatial distribution of Roman citizens, or to the various grades of association with Rome that now marked communities of different types, would have required a considerable expansion of the normal frame of reference.

So also would the very distinctive structures within which Roman citizens voted, structures that would have been then, and were to remain throughout the history of the Republic, crucial to the question of what citizenship meant and of how far, if at all, Rome had a claim to be regarded as a democracy. Central to that issue are the two interlinked questions of who had the formal right to vote, in elections or on legislation, and who could exercise that right effectively.

Again, it will be necessary to summarize drastically. In broad terms, it is beyond reasonable doubt that in Aristotle's time two wholly distinct forms of assembly existed in Rome: the assembly of centuries (*comitia centuriata*) and the assembly of tribes (*comitia tributa*). The ordinary citizen could vote in either, depending on the occasion and the context. What has always attracted attention, and presumably would have attracted the attention of a Greek observer, is that both were based on a group voting system, with the voters organized in units. The majority vote within each unit determined "its" vote, and the majority of units determined the result (whether electoral or legislative). We might be tempted to see the voting by *tribus*, which were subdivisions of the population by locality, as being something like a constituency system, in which a series of separate local majorities is determinative. But, in fact, in Roman voting there was no trace of local representation, and in both forms of assembly, and for both electoral and legislative voting, the unit votes contributed to a single result.

What has not attracted similar attention is the underlying principle that every citizen (meaning every adult *male* citizen) had a vote, if within a voting subunit of the citizenry, and that the collective majority votes cast in each subunit, when collated, determined the result. There is no trace in the standard narratives of Roman history of any specific moment when the right to vote on the part of all citizens or the principle of the (segmented) majority vote was established. There is no trace either of a property qualification for voting or even of a requirement of citizen birth. Another feature of the Roman system that would have surprised a Greek observer is that the slaves of Roman citizens, if freed following a regular procedure, themselves became Roman citizens and could vote.

These underlying principles are never stressed in the standard ancient narratives, which is precisely why they have not generally found a place in subsequent reflection on the nature of the Republic as a system. Instead, what we encounter are narratives of the institution of the two forms of assembly. The older of the two was the "assembly of centuries," said to have been created by the second-last of the kings, Servius Tullius. We shall come later to the account of this invention by one important later Greek observer, Dionysius of Halicarnassus. So it will be sufficient here to state that, given the underlying (and unstated) principle of the right to vote for all, the assembly of centuries is agreed in all accounts to have been intended to give priority in voting to the rich and to have done so by mirroring the structure of the archaic citizen army (Greek or Roman) in which a man's role on the battlefield depended on the level of the weaponry and armor that he could afford to provide. So the cavalry (*equites*, or *hippeis*, in Greek) voted first, in 18 *centuriae*, followed by 170 *centuriae* of infantrymen (*pedites*, in Greek *hoplitai*), eventually subdivided into five *classes*. There followed five *centuriae* of persons too poor to provide any armor.

Social priority, based on the principle that those who were richer and had more stake in society should have the determining vote, was achieved first by the fact that the *centuriae* were of unequal size, with smaller numbers in the highest ranks and the vast mass of the population in the lowest; second, that they voted in order and discontinued voting when a majority of the 193 *centuriae* had agreed. So, in principle, if unanimous, the 18 *centuriae* of the cavalry and the 80 *centuriae* of the first *classis* of the *pedites* could determine the result before the others even voted.

It is largely the accounts of this structure, as it is recorded to have been in the early Republic, that have determined later conceptions of Rome as a firmly class-stratified, hierarchical, society. But, as we will see later, by the historical period this structure had changed again, and in any case its sphere of operation had been very sharply reduced. If we return to what would have confronted a Greek observer in the 330s or 320s B.C., however, there is no serious reason to doubt that this was the standard form of assembly, which elected the two *consules* and the one *praetor* and (every five years) the *censores*, which voted on legislation, and also met as a communal criminal court to hear capital charges.

Aristotle was familiar with the idea of assessing constitutions in terms of the place they gave to various socioeconomic groups and with the notion of characterizing those groups in terms of their military role (cavalry, heavy-armed infantry, light infantry, or rowers in the fleet).[18] Equally, the two oligarchic revolutions in Athens in 411 and 404 to 403 B.C., as recorded by the *Athēnaiōn Politeia* and other sources, had been based on the notion of giving power to "those providing arms."[19] The social effect of the structure of the *comitia centuriata*, as it seems to have been in the later fourth century, will have been to make Rome a *politeia* in the special sense that Aristotle uses on occasion in the *Politics*, namely, a system that was broadly based but still kept power in the hands of the middle classes rather than the mass of the population.[20] There is nothing to suggest, however, that he or his school will have encountered a precisely graduated voting system of this type anywhere in the Greek world.

What would have made Rome seem even more anomalous is that an alternative voting structure had evolved in the course of the fifth and fourth centuries. This, as mentioned earlier, was the "assembly of tribes," in which voting was channeled through the originally twenty-one and now twenty-nine *tribus*, artificial subdivisions of the people based on locality. In the longer term, as we shall see, this body was to become the normal vehicle for the passage of legislation. So it cannot be emphasized too strongly, first, that its origins, as recorded in later narratives, lay in violent protest on the part of the *plebs*; second, that there is no evidence to suggest that the exercise of the vote in this context was structured in any way by social class; and, third, that it both produced annual officials by direct election and eventually passed legislation by direct popular voting via the segmented system of majorities within each of now twenty-nine and eventually thirty-five tribes.

We need not dwell on the complex and uncertain details of the evolution of this counterassembly in the fifth century. It is enough to say that it seems clear that by Aristotle's time it elected annually ten Tribunes of the Plebs, invested with "sacrosanctity" (so that it was an offense to impede or injure them), and with the power to veto actions taken by the normal elected magistrates. We shall see later how their role and evolution were assessed by a major Greek historian of the Imperial period, Cassius Dio (p. 47 below).

What remains highly confusing in later accounts is that the standard narratives on the one hand record repeatedly through the fifth, fourth, and early third centuries B.C. that Tribunes of the Plebs carried legislation (by proposing it to the "assembly of tribes") and on the other report that it was only by a law of 287 B.C., the Lex Hortensia, passed by a *dictator*, Hortensius, that "votes of the *plebs*" (*plebiscita*) became binding on the whole community (except this step is also recorded for 339 B.C.).

Given the fundamental difficulties presented by later tradition, it is hardly worth speculating further as to exactly what an Aristotelian observer would have encountered in the 330s or 320s B.C. or how this observer would have analyzed it. It does seem certain, however, that there was constant constitutional tension and adjustment within the Roman system and that there were two radically different structures within which the ordinary citizen could vote. Looking at participation, or potential participation, we can see that the citizen body was already very large by the standards of any known Greek *polis* (about 150,000, it seems);[21] that it was spread over a wide area, with the most distant territory allocated to tribes lying some eighty kilometers from the city; that all voting took place in or near Rome in the Campus Martius by the "assembly of the centuries" and in the Forum by the tribes; that votes were delivered orally; and that (unlike Athens) there was no pay either for holding political office or for attending the assembly.

Finally (and still leaving aside many complex questions), we have to ask what a Greek observer would have made of the Senate. Here, too, the basic facts are quite remarkably and surprisingly obscure. Our standard narratives speak of the enrollment of senators from the very beginning, indeed from Romulus onward.[22] But who had the power to create senators in the early Republic, what the qualifications for enrollment were, and what the powers of the Senate were are all questions that are entirely uncertain. It is probable, however, that down to the fourth century senators were enrolled by the consuls, and as a body it bore throughout its history the mark of a basic principle that its votes were merely advisory to the elected officials. At any rate it seems to have been a *plebiscitum* that gave the power of enrolling senators to the pair of *censores* elected every five years, and that this law was passed some time before 312 B.C. (when we find *censores* carrying out this role) and perhaps not very long before. In short, there is a good chance that an Aristotelian observer, who (if there had been one) certainly would have expected a city-state to have a *boulē*, or council, might have found that the Senate (perhaps already of 300 members?), as a formally constituted body, with a public procedure for the nomination of members, was a very recent innovation.[23] Or so it seems. How, then, do we understand Livy's report that the same *dictator* of 339 B.C., Publilius Philo, who supposedly passed legislation making *plebiscita* binding on all (see preceding), also passed a law that the *patres* (the Senate) should ratify laws passed by the *comitia centuriata* before voting took place. If that has any validity, and if (as it seems) the *patres* ("fathers") were the

Senate, that implies a much more central and established constitutional role for the Senate in the early Republic.

In other words, to ask what a contemporary Greek observer would have made of the Roman political system of the later fourth century is to reveal all too clearly just how many fundamental puzzles and contradictions are presented by the later accounts. Many features of the Roman system were always to remain anomalous, unclear, and controversial, and not least the Senate itself, and these later controversies have also left their mark in the tradition. In any case, no actual analysis by a contemporary Greek observer is available until we come to the central figure in all discussions of the Roman system, Polybius.

Polybius and the Roman Constitution

Polybius spent some seventeen years in Rome as a hostage, from 167 to 150 B.C., and his great *History* in forty books was intended, first, to record and explain the rise of Rome to domination of the Mediterranean in the fifty-three-year period from 221 to 168 B.C.; and, second (as a subsequent change of plan), to analyze how the Romans had used their power between 168 and 146 B.C., the year in which both Corinth and Carthage were destroyed.[24]

The notion that an important part of the explanation, designed for a Greek readership, would lie in an analysis of the Roman political system (*politeia*) was integral to the project from the beginning (Polybius III.2.6), and the famous analysis that he duly provided in *Book VI* will have been written before 150 B.C.

Before we look at it, however, it is necessary to sketch in very broad lines the evolution of Rome from the later fourth until the middle of the second century B.C., for we need to gain some sense of how Polybius focused his account and what he left out.

Starting from externals, Roman domination had extended by the earlier third century all over central and southern Italy and also to the north, covering Etruria and Umbria and bringing Rome into recurrent conflict with the Celtic population inhabiting the Po River valley. The First Punic War (264–261 B.C.) against Carthage produced the first overseas provinces, Sicily and Sardinia, and the second (218–202 B.C.) produced two provinces in southern Spain. The great victories against Hellenistic kings that followed, over Philip V of Macedon in 197 B.C., Antiochus III of Syria in 190 B.C., and Perseus of Macedon in 168 B.C., provided the subject matter of Polybius's question about how domination had been achieved so quickly and unexpectedly but did not lead to an expansion of direct rule. Instead, there were control and manipulation from a distance, backed by threats of force and assisted by conflicts between and within Greek states. Polybius's own earlier career was a reflection of this period of unstable hegemony by Rome. For Polybius, born not long before 200 B.C., was the son of a leading figure in the Achaean league, a confederation of cities in the northern Peloponnese, which sided with Rome in 198 B.C. and, thereafter, was wracked by conflicts with neighbors, by divisions as to how to behave toward Rome, and in the end by social revolution that precipitated Roman military intervention, the destruction of Corinth in 146 B.C., and the attachment of Greece to the new province of Macedonia.

This background is of central importance to understanding Polybius, first because of his high social and political status, which enabled him to be treated as an equal by the highest senatorial circles when he came to Rome as a hostage; second, because he had belonged to the group in the Achaean League that had argued that they could and should behave toward Rome as free allies, and not as humble subordinates; and, third, because the glowing account of the institutions of the Achaean League, which he included in *Book II* (37–42), represents one of the very few systematic accounts of a confederation in Greek political thought:

For while many have attempted in the past to induce the Peloponnesians to adopt a common policy, no one ever succeeding, as each was working not in the cause of general liberty, but for his own aggrandizement, this object has been so much advanced, and so nearly attained, in my own time that not only have they formed an allied and friendly community, but they have the same laws, weights, measures and coinage, as well as the same magistrates, senate, and courts of justice, and the whole Peloponnesus only falls short of being a single city in the fact of its inhabitants not being enclosed by one wall, all other things being, both as regards the whole and as regards each separate town, very nearly identical.[25]

Moreover, as so often, it was the existence of this literary portrait that was to be the necessary precondition for reflection on the nature of this league to play a significant part in the debates on the American constitution, specifically in the *Federalist Papers*.[26]

Polybius thus arrived in Rome not only with extensive political experience but also with a detailed knowledge of Greek history and an intellectual basis in Greek political thought.[27] In setting out the principles on which the Achaean League operated, indeed, he was going beyond what Plato or Aristotle had covered. That would have been an important advantage in looking at the complex structure of Roman Italy as it now was; instead, it has to be admitted that he allowed himself to drop back into the categories of analysis appropriate to a nuclear city-state, in other words, those of Plato and Aristotle.

To a large degree, the structure of Roman control in Italy could be seen as a system for calling out troops, and military service in the interests of Rome was the common factor in the situation of all the communities of second-century Italy. Those least closely related to Rome were the *socii* ("allies") or *foederati* ("peoples with an alliance," *foedus*) who had made treaties with Rome under which they provided troops or ships, when required. Then there were the, by now, numerous "Latin" colonies, whose relation to Rome was briefly described earlier, and which were scattered from Valentia or Brundisium in the south to Placentia, Cremona, or Aquileia in the north. They, too, provided their own military contingents. The rest were Roman citizens, either occupying *coloniae* (in which case their military obligations were fulfilled locally) or occupying two broad bands of territory stretching out from Rome, one southeast into Campania and the other north across Italy to the Adriatic Sea. With that expansion had come an increase of the tribes to thirty-five; the final total was reached in 241 B.C. As a result, therefore, Roman voters belonging to one or other of the thiryt-five voting units (*tribus*) might be living as far as two hundred kilometers from the city, which was the only place where their votes could be cast. Roman citizens were liable (as we know from Polybius himself) for a period of service in the legions, perhaps sixteen years.[28]

The category of citizens without the vote had by now apparently disappeared, being last heard of in Livy's account (XXXVIII. 36) of the year 188 B.C., when the people of Fundi, Formiae, and (significantly) Arpinum, Cicero's hometown, were granted full citizenship and enrolled in *tribus*.

Polybius's analysis of the Roman political system in *Book VI* is in fact distinctive in devoting a substantial section (chapters

19–42) to military arrangements, beginning with the procedure for enrolling the legions: The consuls announced before an assembly the date on which men of military age should present themselves, and on that day, they appeared on the capitol and were divided into legions (chapter 19). He then turns to the allies: "At the same time the consuls send their orders to the allied cities in Italy which they wish to contribute troops, stating the numbers required and the day and place at which the men selected must present themselves. The magistrates, choosing the men and administering the oath in the manner above described, send them off, appointing a commander and a paymaster."[29] Polybius thus catches precisely the fact that allied communities had to organize, pay, and provide officers for the contingents they supplied for Roman service. The same applied to Latin colonies; but no mention of these is made here, although *Latinoi* do appear in the detailed list of Roman and allied forces, which he describes as having been available for service in 225 B.C.[30] Equally, he mentions in passing that in the 150s B.C., the Greek city of Locri in southern Italy had been liable to provide ships for Rome's wars in Spain and Dalmatia.[31]

So there is no doubt that, as was only to be expected, Polybius was well aware of the military structure of Roman Italy in his time. As regards non-Romans, it was not a matter of a confederation, like the Achaean League, but of separate treaties with allied communities on the one hand and of the foundation of "Latin" colonies on the other. That being so, although the system was indeed fundamental to Rome's achievement of a wider domination, it could be regarded as not actually being an aspect of the Roman *politeia*.

It is difficult to feel, however, that it was equally appropriate to ignore either the size of the Roman citizen population (more than three hundred thousand adult males in this period) or their distribution in space. To speak simply of "the people" (*dēmos*), as he does, is to adopt a purely schematic approach while ignoring the form and structure of whatever popular participation there was.

More problematic still, there is no place in his text, as preserved (given that a large portion is missing), where he speaks explicitly of the segmentation of the voters, either as regards the "assembly of the centuries" or that of "tribes." It is possible that he described the different assemblies in the historical survey, now almost entirely missing, with which he introduced his account of the Roman *politeia* as it was in 216 B.C. If so, he perhaps spoke of the obscure reform of the "assembly of centuries," which according to Livy took place after the eventual total of thirty-five tribes had been completed (hence after 241 B.C. but before the Second Punic War, which began in 218).[32] In this new version, the centuries of *equites* (cavalrymen) lost their priority, and the predominance was gained by seventy centuries, two from each of the thirty-five *tribus*, one of *iuniores* ("men of military age"), and one of *seniores*. In Greek terms, the nature of this reform seems (hypothetically) quite intelligible. The cavalry (*hippeis*) had been displaced by the broader mass of infantry (*hoplitai*), in short, the legionary *pedites* on whom success in battle now depended. The principle of social priority (or of a man's "stake in society") was maintained, but it began with what we might call a middle class. One further feature should be noted, if only because it was to find a strange prominence in the work of James Harrington in the seventeenth century (p. 94 below): It was the custom to select by lot one of the thirty-five *centuriae* of *iuniores* (one from each tribe) to vote first and to call this the *tribus praerogativa*, "the prerogative tribe."

All of this finds no explicit reflection in Polybius, any more than does the system of *tribus* and their spatial distribution itself. There is just one passing allusion to "tribal" voting, although it seems, in the light of the reform mentioned above, actually to refer to the "assembly of centuries." This is his allusion to the custom of allowing men on trial for their lives, which should mean before the assembly of centuries meeting as a communal criminal court, to flee and seek asylum "if only even one tribe [= century from one tribe] of those which are determining the verdict still remains without having voted."[33]

Polybius therefore knew, as he could hardly have failed to know, of the system of segmentary voting, and he also must have been familiar with the very different structures of the two forms of assembly. But he chooses, presumably for reasons of clarity and simplicity, in presenting his analysis of the Roman *politeia* to a Greek readership, to speak of the popular element just as the "people" (*dēmos*). This represents a significant limitation, first because of the contrast between the two in social terms (socioeconomic hierarchy and priority in the one, and none in the other), but also because in the period of which Polybius is speaking, the effective functions of the "assembly of centuries" were already quite limited: the election of consuls and praetors (now six in all), perhaps still declarations of war, occasional legislation, and (as above) acting as a court in capital trials. But it was the "assembly of tribes" that normally passed legislation, and it was therefore measures that were due to come before it that were the main subjects of political debate and controversy. Consuls, praetors, or tribunes of the plebs all could summon this assembly and put legislation to it; but, again, it is clear that the role of proposing legislation was progressively falling more and more to the tribunes, whether acting individually, or a few of the ten in concert, or (very occasionally) all together. One relevant factor was a point that, with typical acuity, Polybius does bring out, namely, that within their year of office consuls normally stayed only a short time in Rome before setting out to command armies. The office of tribune by contrast was a wholly "political" or civilian one, and all ten holders spent the whole of their year of office in Rome. That of consul was more military than political, however, and most of the time they were both absent.

These structural limitations in Polybius's deliberately schematic analysis have to be stated in advance. But to express these reservations is not in any way to derogate from his unique achievement in using the frame of reference inherited from earlier Greek philosophical discussions of differently structured *poleis* to produce a penetrating analysis of the Roman *politeia*, one that does not keep merely to broad lines but incorporates many telling and relevant details.

Polybius places his analysis of the Roman *politeia* in *Book VI*, deliberately using the occasion of the major defeat by Hannibal at Cannae to demonstrate how the Roman system had the internal balance and resilience to overcome disaster. Whether he means to imply a contrast, between the *politeia* as it had been at that moment and how it was at the time of writing (the 150s?), has been much debated. A recent article by the greatest modern expert on Polybius, F. W. Walbank, published when its author was a mere eighty-seven, argues convincingly that he does and that he saw both a decline in Roman public morality and signs of steps toward demagoguery as developing over that period.[34]

The structure of Polybius's account, so far as we can reconstruct it, given that it is only partially preserved, is as follows. He begins by discussing what different types of *politeia* had normally been identified: kingship (*basileia*), aristocracy (*aristokratia*), and democracy (*dēmokratia*). The best *politeia*, like that of Lycurgus at Sparta, will be a mixture of all three. But then there were perverted and inferior forms of each of these "pure" types, namely, monarchy (individual rule on the basis of force), oligarchy (where the rulers are not the "best" —*aristoi*), and mob *rule* (*ochlokratia*), where there is no respect for tradition and in which "the whole crowd has the power to do whatever it wishes and proposes" (4.4). He then asserts that there is a natural progression, which runs as follows: monarchy, kingship, tyranny (a new element), aristocracy, oligarchy, democracy, mob rule. He attributes this theory of a natural evolution and transformation of *politeiai* to Plato and also sets out a wider hypothetical conception of how humans will have come together in organized societies in the first place, in a style later followed by Hobbes and Rousseau. He then moves on to a more reasoned exposition of how the sequential pattern of evolution mentioned earlier will have come about, each phase suffering deterioration and giving way to the next. In this version, what democracy finally gives place to is not specifically described as *ochlokratia* but as "force and violence," which finally leads again to monarchy:

> For the people, having grown accustomed to feed at the expense of others and to depend for their livelihood on the property of others, as soon as they find a leader who is enterprising but is excluded from the honors of office by his penury, institute the rule of violence; and now uniting their forces massacre, banish, and plunder, until they degenerate again into perfect savages and find once more a master and monarch.[35]

It is impossible to read his words without being reminded of what was to occur a century later with the rise of Julius Caesar, and then the civil war and the establishment of the monarchy of Augustus. We will return later (p. 181) to the question of whether Polybius really intends these remarks to be predictions about the future of the Roman Republic.

Polybius then describes this evolution, which by its nature comes back to its starting point (monarchy) as a "cycle" (*anakyklōsis*) and does say that it is applicable to the Roman *politeia*; awareness of it will enable the observer to understand the growth by nature (*physis*) of the Roman state to its *akmē* and its future transformation (*metabolē*) for the worse. In view of what he later says about the Roman *politeia*, namely, that it owes its strength to being a mixture of three elements—the monarchic, the aristocratic, and the democratic—the relevance of such a "cycle" is not entirely clear, for the cycle he has just described does not give a place to a mixed constitution of this sort. So it is not self-evident why he should see the cyclical progression as applying to it. Might not a perfectly mixed and balanced constitution actually serve to halt the cycle of change and decline? Apparently not, for he comes at the end (chapter 57) to a categorically pessimistic view of Rome's prospects and descent into *ochlokratia* ("mob rule").

For the moment, Polybius turns to the example of the Spartan constitution, which by the genius of one man had been set up at a single moment as an ideal mixture of kingship, autocracy, and democracy, which had served to preserve freedom (*eleutheria*) for the Spartans "for the longest time of which we know" (10.11)—but not, it seems to be implied, permanently.

The contrast with Rome was that whereas the mythical Lycurgus had allegedly invented the Spartan constitution at a single moment, Rome's had evolved by trial and error:

Lycurgus then, foreseeing, by a process of reasoning, whence and how events naturally happen, constructed his constitution untaught by adversity, but the Romans while they have arrived at the same final result as regards their form of government, have not reached it by any process of reasoning, but by the discipline of many struggles and troubles, and always choosing the best by the light of the experience gained in disaster have thus reached the same result as Lycurgus, that is to say, the best of all existing constitutions.[36]

This view of the Roman constitution was to be borrowed by Cicero in his *On the Republic* (II.27) and is explicitly attributed to Polybius. It will have been at this point, where there is a gap in the text, that Polybius will have traced the evolution of the Roman *politeia* from the foundation through the regal period to the foundation of the Republic, apparently (as Walbank suggests) identifying the period from the mid-fifth century to the Hannibalic War of the late third century as representing its most complete realization: "it was at its finest and most perfect in the Hannibalic period" (11.1).

He then apologizes for omitting many details, stressing the need to keep to essentials, and sets out his basic proposition that even those who knew it best could not assert confidently whether it was aristocratic, democratic, or monarchic. If one looked at the consuls, the Roman *politeuma* seemed monarchical and "royal" (*basilikon*); if at the Senate, aristocratic; and if at the power of "the many" (*hoi polloi*), democratic. He then sets out to describe the functions of the three elements, saying, very significantly, that this is how it had been then (in 216 B.C.) and, but for a few points, still was (12.13).

Polybius's procedure is thus to concentrate on the three key structural elements, first describing the functions of each, and then modifying the picture by showing how each was dependent on the others. As we saw earlier, he does not distinguish the different forms of popular assembly, and he gives no systematic place to any elected magistrates, even the tribunes of the plebs, who come in only when he describes how the power of the Senate is limited by that of the people (16.4–5). Nor is there a place for the other elected magistrates, praetors, aediles, or quaestors (alluded to in passing in 12.8). Yet, if we needed confirmation that he will have been aware of the roles played by these magistrates, we can find him elsewhere describing a praetor presiding in the Senate (XXXIII.1.5), or another making a speech from the rostra inciting the people to war in 167 B.C. and being dragged down by a tribune (XXX.4.6). He also makes no allusion to the distinction between *patricii* and *plebeii*, although he later (X.4.2) records that two of the aedileships were reserved for *patricii*. On the other hand, he says explicitly elsewhere that he had discussed the priesthoods in his treatment of the *politeia* (XXI.13.10–12).[37] Presumably, this must have been in the missing historical survey, and no place is given to them in the schematic analysis.

Although Polybius's account of the three elements is consciously intended as schematic, it is also marked by close empirical observation of relevant features of constitutional practice. So, speaking of the consuls (chapter 12), he begins immediately by describing their political role as being carried out "when being present in Rome before they lead out the armies," and the whole of the second half of the chapter is concerned with their powers as generals in the field. When in Rome they had authority over all magistrates except the tribunes; they presided at the Senate, introduced embassies to it, and carried out its decrees. They also presided at assembly meetings (*ekklēsiai*) and put proposals (*dogmata*) before them (the reference should be to *senatus consulta*, which gained legislative force only when accepted by the people).

An observer, Polybius says, looking at these powers (most conspicuous in the field), might have thought of the *politeuma* as purely *monarchikon* and *basilikon*.

But what then of the Senate (chapter 13)? As we saw earlier, its position in the constitution was anomalous in that it began (it seems) as an advisory body summoned by the consuls, and perhaps earlier the kings; public regulation of its membership had begun only in the fourth century; and it had no power to legislate. But Polybius very effectively catches a range of political, administrative, and financial decisions that it had come de facto to make and that were of central importance. First, in his account, come votes on expenditure, including sums for use by the consuls, and allocation of the sums to be spent each five years by the censors on public works. Then came the conduct of criminal investigations within Italy, or of claims for reparation or protection by communities or individuals in Italy. Then comes the very important role of receiving embassies from communities outside Italy. These were matters that fell to the Senate, and the people had no role. Particularly in the case of embassies, this pattern marked a clear distinction from Greek democracies: in fifth-century Athens, for instance, embassies appeared first before the council (*boulē*) and then before the whole *dēmos*. Polybius shrewdly notes that anyone who was in Rome in the absence of a consul will have been inclined to see the Roman constitution as aristocratic, as would Greek communities and kings whose business was conducted solely with the Senate.

So what, then, of the people, given the extensive powers of Senate and consuls (chapter 14)? Polybius's answer concentrates first on honor (*timē*) and punishment (*timōria*), the exclusive preserve of the people. The people tried offenses leading to a fine (in fact, in the assembly of tribes), and they constituted the only court that tried capital charges (in fact, in the assembly of centuries). As we saw earlier, Polybius chooses not to attempt to differentiate explicitly between the two forms of assembly.

It may seem surprising that Polybius lays the emphasis first on the power of the people meeting (in either form) as a communal criminal court. In fact, it may well be we who underestimate the importance of the power to sit in judgment (*dikazein*), which is very significant, for instance, in Aristotle's *Politics*.[38] At any rate Polybius only then moves to areas that we might naturally see as more important: the power to elect to public offices (*archai*); to pass laws; and to vote on declarations of war, and on alliances, peace terms, and treaties. All that might reasonably lead, Polybius says, to the conclusion that the *politeuma* was really a democratic one.

At this point, Polybius switches his approach and asks how each of the three elements must act interdependently with the other two. Thus, the consul, who seems to have autocratic power in the field, depends on the Senate for supplies and for the soldiers' pay. Moreover, the Senate has the power either to supersede him in his command at the end of his year of office or to leave him in post (as a proconsul). This is, in fact, an extremely important senatorial function, on which Polybius might have laid more stress. For, in this period, the Senate held a strategic debate at the beginning of each year to decide which would be the consular and praetorian provinces for the year and which, if any, of the consuls and praetors of the year just ended should remain in post. By a curious custom, which Polybius does not explore, lots then were drawn for which consuls and which praetors should go to each of the designated *provinciae*.[39] Polybius himself was to record later (XVIII.11–12) how Flamininus, the consul of 198, had gained the chance to stay on in Greece and win his famous victory over Philip V of Macedon only because the Senate had decided that both consuls of 197 were required in Italy.

Furthermore, Polybius says, a general was dependent on the Senate for the votes that would allow him to celebrate a triumph and on the people for ratification of peace terms and treaties. On laying down his office, he also was obliged to give an account to the people (perhaps a reference to trials before the people).

Turning to the Senate (chapter 16), Polybius notes that inquiries into serious offenses could not be instituted by it, except if its decree were confirmed by a popular vote, and that any constitutional measures affecting the Senate could be passed only by the people. Finally, if even one of the tribunes interposed a veto, the Senate could not conclude its business, or even meet at all: "the tribunes are obliged always to do what seems best to the people and above all to aim to meet its wishes" (16.5). This famous formulation of the tribunes' role, probably written a couple of decades before the tribunate of Tiberius Gracchus in 133 B.C., is of crucial importance for Roman political conceptions.

When Polybius turns to the dependence of the people on the other two elements (chapter 17), he begins, in a way that has puzzled specialists, by stressing the Senate's influence in modifying and adjusting contracts for public works in Italy given out by the censors. He then continues, equally surprisingly, by noting that the judges appointed to hear private-law cases were drawn mainly from the Senate; and he finally notes that resistance to the consuls was hampered by awareness that citizens, when serving in the army, would be under their authority.

If, from the perspective of our general knowledge of the Republican system, this last chapter seems less immediately convincing than the rest, it remains the case that Polybius's account combines structural analysis with empirical observation of actual procedures and relationships in a way matched only by Aristotle. He concludes this part by stressing that in crises the three elements would cooperate and that in periods without external pressures, if one tended to predominate, the others would bring it back into line.

After that, there follows a very long section (chapters 19–42) on the military system—very significant in that military service was one of the fundamental aspects of citizenship but not calling for comment here.

After a gap in the text, we find that Polybius turns to comparing the Roman *politeia* with others, primarily taking examples from archaic and classical Greek history, as considered in political writing of the fourth century (thus he does not seek to compare Rome with any contemporary political structures except Carthage). So we find consideration of Thebes and Athens (both ruined by being dominated by the mob), Crete, and Sparta, as regulated by Lycurgus. The Lycurgan constitution, he says, was admirable and effective so long as the Spartans stayed within the bounds of their own territory, but did not enable them, when they attained power abroad, either to retain their social discipline or to observe limits in their dealings with others. The Roman system was superior and more resilient (chapters 43–50).

When he turns to Carthage (chapter 51), the comparison becomes even more pointed and relevant. In principle, the Carthaginian constitution was a mixture of elements similar to that at

Sparta or Rome, with the kings, the council of elders, and the people. By the time of the Hannibalic War, however, this balance had been upset by the growth of the power of the people:

> For by as much as the power and prosperity of Carthage had been earlier than that of Rome, by so much had Carthage already begun to decline; while Rome was exactly at her prime, as far at least as her system of government was concerned. Consequently the multitude at Carthage had already acquired the chief voice in deliberations; while at Rome the senate still retained this; and hence, as in one case the masses deliberated and in the other the most eminent men, the Roman decisions on public affairs were superior, so that although they met with complete disaster, they were finally by the wisdom of their counsels victorious over the Carthaginians in the war.[40]

The remaining chapters, of exceptional interest in themselves, focus on the social institutions of Rome and the way in which these served to foster courage, discipline, commitment, and patriotism. The chapter, that is, chapter 53, on the social role of the funerals of prominent Romans and of the funeral oration, delivered from the rostra in the Forum,[41] that (chapter 56) on Roman propriety in monetary matters, and its further section on the role of religion in including fear and conformity to rules (56.6–15) are particularly significant. We will see later that Rousseau, whose *Social Contract* gives a very prominent place to the Roman Republic as an example of popular sovereignty, ends by giving a very comparable weight to measures designed to produce conformity (p. 119 to follow).

Finally, after another gap in the text, Polybius returns (chapter 57) to his original theme, the liability of constitutions to change and degeneration. He does not explicitly name Rome at this point, but he can hardly *not* be referring to Rome when he explains that when a state has reached a condition of predominance and prosperity, political competition will intensify, and with that the power of the people will increase:

> For now, stirred by fury and swayed by passion in all their counsels, they will no longer consent to obey or even to be the equals of the ruling caste, but will demand the lion's share for themselves. When this happens, the state will change its name to the finest sounding of all, freedom and democracy, but will change its nature to the worst thing of all, mob-rule.[42]

So, despite the fact that he concludes with an episode from the Hannibalic War showing the *akmē* and *dynamis* of the *politeia* "such as it was in those times" (58.1), there is an unmistakable undertone of pessimism about his conception of the evolution of the Roman political system and of Roman values. A similar tone can be found in various other places,[43] perhaps most notably when he records the tribunician legislation of 232 B.C., which authorized the distribution of land in northern Italy to individual citizens: "Gaius Flaminius being the author of this demagoguery and policy, which must be admitted to have been for the Romans, so to speak, the original cause of the transformation of the people for the worse" (II.21.8). Although Polybius has not yet reached the Hannibalic War, which he took to be the period when the three elements were most perfectly in balance, he is surely not thinking only of the consequences in the few years after 232, but he is looking further forward, to his own time, and beyond.

Polybius's conception of the best attainable constitution as being a balance between three elements—monarchical, aristocratic, and popular—was to have a long history, even being seen by some as exemplified by the British system of the seventeenth century, and having a significant influence on the American constitution. It is perhaps only on rereading him in the light of later theorizing that one sees how profoundly wary he was, as James Madison was to be, of the dangers of *ochlokratia*, or mob rule. As we will see when we return finally to the Rome of the late Republic, and ask how it would have been categorized in Aristotelian terms, it will be clear that Polybius's fears were largely justified. In the last decades of the Republic, the crowd (*plēthos* in Greek) could indeed vote whatever it wished, or was persuaded to wish, and *monarchia* followed swiftly.

As for Polybius's analysis, for all its limitations, partly explained by its brevity (for in scale, when dealing with actual institutions, it comes nowhere near the detailed account of the Athenian system provided by the Aristotelian *Athēnaiōn Politeia*), it remains the only serious attempt by any outsider to engage with and understand how the Roman *politeia* worked and how its overall character should be assessed. It would have been invaluable if another Polybius had followed in the age of Cicero, when Rome was of far greater consequence to the whole Greek world. But there was none. There were to be a number of important Greek narrators of Roman Republican history and of Roman biography, but none who rivaled Polybius in intellectual power or moral commitment.

Later Greek Narrators

Already by the later Republic, Roman forces had come to dominate virtually the whole of the Greek-speaking world, and the victory at Actium in 31 B.C., which secured *monarchia* for the future
Augustus, also led directly to the absorption of the last of the
major Hellenistic kingdoms, Egypt. Henceforward, of the Greek-
speaking area essentially created by the conquest of Alexandria
in the later fourth century B.C., only a few surviving Greek cities
in Mesopotamia and Babylonia lay outside Roman control. From
the Black Sea to the middle Euphrates, south to Egypt, and in all
areas further west, all of the Greek world was part of the Roman
Empire, either as provinces ruled by Roman governors or as dependent kingdoms.

Far from leading to any suppression of Greek identity or culture, Roman domination was marked by an elaborate and careful
respect for both. At least in the sense of material prosperity, the
architectural adornment of cities, the celebration of athletic and
cultural festivals and contests, and a conscious attachment to a
wider Greek literary culture and to its continuity with the culture
of the Archaic and Classical periods, Greek civilization flourished.
Whether behind that prosperity lay real nostalgia for the period of
genuine freedom (as opposed to local self-government in hundreds
of cities), for a serious military role for citizen armies, and for
famous wars against each other and above all against Persia is a
hotly debated topic. What is certain is only that the major literary works of the Archaic and Classical periods were still known,
quoted, read, and copied. One such copy, written on papyrus in the
Imperial period, is the Aristotelian *Athēnaiōn Politeia*, which has
been mentioned many times already. We can take it as certain that
at least the broad lines of the Greek political thought of the Classical period, and many of the works of Plato and Aristotle, will
have been familiar in varying degrees to educated Greeks living in
the later Republic or in the Imperial period.

At the same time, there was no room for doubt as to the importance of Rome to the whole Greek world, whether we think of
the progressively greater impact of Republican conquests (or, at
the end of the Republic, of Roman civil wars, many fought in
Greek-speaking areas), or of the all-embracing symbolic presence

(embodied in statues, reliefs and coins) of the emperor, or of the importance of his decisions (often embodied in letters of his written in Greek and publicized in inscriptions put up in the cities). There was thus, it might be thought, ample reason for reflection on Roman history, culture, values and institutions—and not least because, as time went on, more and more upper-class families in the Greek east themselves became Roman citizens. Others entered Roman military service, became Roman civilian or military officials of the second rank (the "equestrian" order), or entered the Senate.

As regards Roman culture and literature, it is clear that a knowledge of Latin never became widespread in the Greek east, and references to Latin literature, even Virgil, are remarkably few. As regards Roman history, as will be seen in a moment, Greek writers of the Imperial period were to make a remarkable contribution; indeed, without them we would hardly have a narrative of, for instance, the last few decades of the Republic. As for that period, we have no surviving writings from any major Greek historian who was present in Rome and could observe it as Polybius had a century earlier. The writers whose works survive were either relatively distant observers of the late-Republican situation or wrote under the Empire, when the wars and social conflicts of the Republic belonged to the past. A number of Greeks, however, did write substantial works on Republican history; therefore, it is worth asking whether in doing so they contributed, even in retrospect, any significant interpretations of the nature and working of its institutions.

In doing so, they still might have continued Polybius's approach of seeing Roman institutions and values as being intelligible in Greek terms, but at the same time as foreign and requiring interpretation and analysis. To some extent we do find this pattern, but largely at a trivial or antiquarian level, as in the *Roman Questions* of Plutarch.[44] Why was the priest, called the *rex sacrorum*, forbidden to hold political office or make a speech to the people? Why did a tribune of the *plebs* not wear a purple-bordered toga like other officeholders? The facts involved, and Plutarch's attempts to explain them, can be of interest, but by their nature these "questions" cannot approach being a serious inquiry about the system as a whole.

Alternatively, as Greeks living in a solidly "Roman" world (and, in several cases as Roman citizens themselves), such writers of narrative histories of the Republic, or of parts of it, might simply have taken the Republican political system for granted as being familiar and not requiring explanation or still less analysis. Rather surprisingly, this is much the more common pattern, especially visible, for instance, in the Republican *Lives* of Plutarch. By and large, these *Lives* are simply biographical narratives, incorporating the history of different periods of the Republic from the beginning (*Publicola* or *Coriolanus*) to the end (*Pompey* or *Caesar*), alluding to institutions and even constitutional innovations, but not explaining or analyzing them, or still less the whole system. On the contrary, Plutarch's narratives either assume indifference on the part of the contemporary Greek reader or, perhaps, possession of an already acquired knowledge of Roman history and institutions.

In short, then, the contribution to reflection on the peculiar system of the Roman Republican city-state, which we might have hoped to gain from Greek writers of the late Republic or the Empire, is often not there. Unlike Polybius, they did not use the inherited criteria of classical Greek political philosophy as an aid to explaining the story that they were telling. This is true, for instance, of the sections on Roman history contained in the universal history (called *Bibliothēkē*, or "library") of Diodorus from Sicily, apparently completed in the 40s B.C.[45] It is also true of the major and rather neglected work by Appian of Alexandria, written in the mid-second century A.D.[46] This work, unlike many narrative histories, at least had an explicit purpose, namely, to explain how—that is, through what campaigns in what areas—Rome had come to rule its present empire. One of the "wars" narrated was the succession of internal conflicts, and actual civil wars, from 133 to 36 B.C., which is how Appian comes to offer one of the two continuous narratives, both Greek, which we have for the last decades of the Republic. With trivial exceptions in the form of passing explanations, he does not dwell on institutions or still less stop to consider the system as a whole.

Two Greek historians of the Imperial period, however, Dionysius of Halicarnassus and Cassius Dio, deserve slightly fuller consideration, although neither is a Polybius, or anything like him.

The first is Dionysius, who came to Rome in 30 B.C. (just at the moment of the conquest of Egypt) and wrote his *History* between then and 7 B.C.[47] This work, which told the history of Rome from its legendary origins to 264 B.C., is noteworthy in various respects. First, it covers the same ground as the first part of the exactly contemporary *History*, written in Latin by Livy, but it does so at *four to five times* the length for each year covered. So the Rome that is being described lies in the remote past, but there is ample scope for comment and explanation by the author or for invented speeches embodying political ideas. Second, he manages both to argue in *Book I* that all the various accounts of Rome's origins lead to the conclusion that in origin the Romans were really Greek, but at the same time to locate himself and his experiences in relation to Rome, in other words to present himself as an informed, but foreign, observer:

> Having thus given the reason for my choice of subject, I wish now to say something concerning the sources I used while preparing for my task. For it is possible that those who have already read Hieronymus, Timaeus, Polybius, or any of the other historians whom I just now mentioned as having slurred over their work, since they will not have found in those authors many things mentioned by me, will suspect me of inventing them and will demand to know how I came by the knowledge of these particulars. Lest anyone, therefore, should entertain such an opinion of me, it is best that I should state in advance what narratives and records I have used as sources. I arrived in Italy at the very time that Augustus Caesar put an end to the civil war, in the middle of the one hundred and eighty-seventh Olympiad; and having from that time to this present day, a period of twenty-two years, lived at Rome, learned the language of the Romans and acquainted myself with their writings, I have devoted myself during all that time to matters bearing upon my subject. Some information I received orally from men of the greatest learning, with whom I associated; and the rest I gathered from histories written by the approved Roman authors—Porcius Cato, Fabius Maximus, Valerius Antias, Licinius Macer, the Aelii, Gellii and Calpurnii, and many others of note; with these works, which are like the Greek annalistic accounts, as a basis, I set about the writing of my history.[48]

Beyond that, Dionysius both moralizes on the values of Roman society, just as Polybius does, and can use the evidence of contemporary observation, in the manner of an anthropologist, to cast light on early institutions. This, for instance, is how he describes the institution by Romulus of the groups called *curiae* and the modest sacrifices that they offered to the gods:

> This institution, it seems to me, Romulus took over from the practice of the Lacedaemonians in the case of their *phiditia* [common meals], which were then the vogue. It would seem that Lycurgus, who had learned the

institution from the Cretans, introduced it at Sparta to the great advantage of his country; for he thereby in time of peace directed the citizens' lives toward frugality and temperance in their daily repasts, and in time of war inspired every man with a sense of shame and concern not to forsake his comrade with whom he had offered libations and sacrifices and shared in common rites. And not alone for his wisdom in these matters does Romulus deserve praise, but also for the frugality of the sacrifices that he appointed for the honoring of the gods, the greatest part of which, if not all, remained to my day, being still performed in the ancient manner. At any rate, I myself have seen in the sacred edifices repasts set before the gods upon ancient wooden tables, in baskets and small earthen plates, consisting of barley bread, cakes and spelt, with the first-offerings of some fruits, and other things of like nature, simple, cheap, and devoid of all vulgar display.[49]

Dionysius thus maintains the posture of the foreign observer while, in a familiar manner, interpreting what he sees in terms of elements in the Greek tradition.

As already mentioned, all of Dionysius's narrative relates to the remote past, at the latest (even in the original complete text) some two-and-a-half centuries before his own time; and, in effect, because the second half of the work survives only in fragments, the full text as preserved covers only up to the mid-fifth century. In the fullness of comment included in the narrative, on the one hand, and in its focus on early evolution on the other, Dionysius' *Roman Antiquities* is thus an extreme case of the general tendency to focus exposition on legendary origins rather than on what could be observed in the present. Nonetheless, it is noticeable that he does often bring his expositions of early institutions into relation with the situation in the present, or recent past.

Because he agrees with Livy that many of the institutions of the Republic began under the kings, we may illustrate this by his account of the constitution allegedly set up by Romulus, when popular voting (already presumed to have existed) took place in the earliest recorded subdivisions of the people, the thirty *curiae*. It is noteworthy that the familiar criterion of balance between monarchy, aristocracy, and democracy is applied and that Dionysius comments, in a way reminiscent of Polybius, on a subsequent shift in favor of the latter:

Having made these regulations, he distinguished the honors and powers which he wished each class to have. For the king he had reserved these prerogatives: in the first place, the supremacy in religious ceremonies and sacrifices and the conduct of everything relating to the worship of the gods;

secondly, the guardianship of the laws and customs of the country and the general oversight of justice in all cases, whether founded on the law of nature or the civil law; he was also to judge in person the greatest crimes, leaving the lesser to the senators, but seeing to it that no error was made in their decisions; he was to summon the senate and call together the popular assembly, to deliver his opinion first and carry out the decision of the majority. These prerogatives he granted to the king and, in addition, the absolute command in war. To the senate he assigned honor and authority as follows: to deliberate and give their votes concerning everything the king should refer to them, the decision of the majority to prevail. This also Romulus took over from the constitution of the Lacedaemonians; for their kings, too, did not have arbitrary power to do everything they wished, but the *gerousia* exercised complete control of public affairs. To the populace he granted these three privileges: to choose magistrates, to ratify laws, and to decide concerning war whenever the king left the decision to them; yet even in these matters their authority was not unrestricted, since the concurrence of the senate was necessary to give effect to their decisions. The people did not give their votes all the at the same time, but were summoned to meet by *curiae*, and whatever was resolved upon by the majority of the *curiae* was reported to the senate. But in our day this practice is reversed, since the senate does not deliberate upon the resolutions passed by the people, but the people have full power over the decrees of the senate; and which of the two customs is the better I leave it open to others to determine.[50]

The established tradition thus saw even the very earliest phase of Rome, under its first king, as being marked by the presence of a complex constitutional order. What matters for our purposes is this perception, and the way in which it is presented in the text, not whether it has any claim to historical truth. Equally, Dionysius, like Cicero and Livy,[51] attributes to the second last of the seven kings, Servius Tullius, the creation of the "assembly of centuries" (*comitia centuriata*), alluded to earlier. In accordance with his general prolixity and fullness of exposition, Dionysius's account is the most expansive of all, both in technical details and in the exposition of the underlying rationale (voting rights for all, but priority for those with the greatest "stake in society"). The quotation that follows omits the elaborate detail, setting out the military role and property qualifications of the successive "classes," and bringing into relation with this the different levels of tax each allegedly paid. Servius Tullius is represented as having sought specifically to correct the egalitarian distribution of voting rights in the *curiae* by giving priority to the rich but maintaining in principle the voting rights of the poor. So (as we saw earlier), in the system now instituted, the eighteen "centuries" of cavalry were recorded to have voted first, followed by the eighty of the first class. If they were unanimous, that already constituted a majority. Dionysius comments as follows:

In establishing this political system, which gave so great an advantage to the rich, Tullius outwitted the people, as I said, without their noticing it and excluded the poor from any part in public affairs. For they all thought that they had an equal share in the government because every man was asked his opinion, each in his own century; but they were deceived in this, that the whole century, whether it consisted of a small or a very large number of citizens, had but one vote; and also in that the centuries which voted first, consisting of men of the highest rating, though they were more in number than all the rest, yet contained fewer citizens; but, above all, in that the poor, who were very numerous, had but one vote and were the last called. When this had been brought about, the rich, though paying out large sums and exposed without intermission to the dangers of war, were less inclined to feel aggrieved now that they had obtained control of the most important matters and had taken the whole power out of the hands of those who were not performing the same services; and the poor, who had but the slightest share in the government, finding themselves exempt both from taxes and from military service, prudently and quietly submitted to this diminution of their power; and the commonwealth itself had the advantage of seeing the same persons who were to deliberate concerning its interests allotted the greatest share of the dangers and ready to do whatever required to be done. This form of government was maintained by the Romans for many generations, but is altered in our times and changed to a more democratic form, some urgent needs having forced the change, which was effected, not by abolishing the centuries, but by no longer observing the strict ancient manner of calling them—a fact which I myself have noted, having often been present at the elections of their magistrates. But this is not the proper occasion to discuss these matters.[52]

It remains uncertain whether Dionysius's reference at the end to a "more democratic" system is (as seems possible) to the new arrangement that came about in the third century, by which the cavalry did not vote first (see p. 27), or whether it is some other change, closer to his own time. To repeat, this and other literary presentations of an archaic system of social priority, which did not as such survive to the historical period, constitute both the fullest descriptions of Roman voting and lie at the origins of long-lasting conceptions about Roman social and political stratification.

Dionysius makes a large number of significant comments on features of the Roman *politeia*, for instance, on their preparedness to extend the citizenship or on the Roman custom of giving the citizenship to freed slaves, with observations on the rationale of this and (as ever) on the corruption of this custom in the present (IV.22–6). Although he nowhere gives a systematic analysis of the whole political structure, he thus shows himself well aware of the importance of the customs that had allowed it to expand in size and numbers.

However, to be consistent, we will focus on what he says about voting and popular rights, coming finally to the Republic proper and to the institution of the "assembly of tribes" (comitia tributa), attributed to the first half of the fifth century. Vague and confused as is the story Dionysius tells, it still may function as a later literary reflection of a development that was progressively to have momentous consequences, namely, the emergence of a voting structure that was independent of traditional restraints, and would be the one in which the plebeians elected their own magistrates (and through which, much later, they could legislate), and that was not structured so as to give priority to the rich.

The story relates to the trial of Marcius Coriolanus in the 490s B.C. Whether it is any more than fiction, and whether it was in fact then that the "assembly of tribes" first met, does not matter for present purposes. What matters is the systematic contrast Dionysius makes between it and the "assembly of centuries," which (as we have seen) was alleged to have existed since the reign of Servius Tullius: the contrast is in structure, in location, in procedure, and in the presence or absence of social differentiation. Dionysius's account runs as follows:

The tribunes then summoned the populace to the tribal assembly, first having roped off portions of the Forum in which the tribes were to take their places separately. And this was the first time the Romans ever met in their tribal assembly to give their votes against a man, the patricians very violently opposing it and demanding that the centuriate assembly should be convened, as was their time-honored custom. For in earlier times, whenever the people were to give their votes upon any point referred to them by the senate, the consuls had summoned the centuriate assembly, after first offering up the sacrifices required by law, some of which are still performed down to our time. The populace was wont to assemble in the field of Mars before the city, drawn up under their centurions and their standards as in war. They did not give their votes all a the same time, but each by their respective centuries, when these were called upon by the consuls.[53]

Dionysius then goes through the whole structure of the assembly of centuries again, concluding with the observation that it would be very surprising if voting even continued long enough to include the poorest centuries. He then continues:

The supporters of Marcius, accordingly, demanded that this assembly based on the census should be called, expecting that he might perhaps be acquitted by the first class with its ninety-eight centuries, or, if not, at least by the second or third class. On the other hand, the tribunes, who also suspected this outcome, thought they ought to call the tribal assembly and to empower it to decide this cause, to the end that neither the poor might be at a disadvantage as compared with the rich nor the light-armed men have a less honorable station that the heavy-armed, nor the mass of plebeians, by being relegated to the last calls, be excluded from equal rights with the others, but that all the citizens might be equal to one another in their votes and equal in honor, and at one call might give their votes by tribes. The claim of the tribunes seemed to be more just than that of the patricians in that they thought the tribunal of the people ought to be a popular, not an oligarchic, tribunal, and that the cognizance of crimes committed against the commonwealth ought to be common to all.[54]

It cannot be stressed too strongly that these fictional narratives, relating to a remote period hundreds of years before the writer's time, still represent the fullest expression available to us of the values attached to the alternative voting systems available in Rome.

A couple of books further on in his immensely detailed narrative, having reached 472 B.C., Dionysius comes to the proposal that (initially) the tribunes, and then also the officials known as aediles, should be elected by the "assembly of tribes." Once again, he emphasizes the long-term significance of this alternative plebeian structure.

In the meantime Publius and the other two tribunes without further delay were again proposing the law which they had been unable to get ratified the year before, with this additional provision that the college of aediles should also be chosen in the same assemblies, and that everything else that was to be done and ratified by the populace should be voted on in like manner by the members of the tribes. This, now, clearly meant the overthrow of the senate and the dominance of the populace.[55]

Dionysius, who is in general not to be regarded as a significant historian, nonetheless is of importance in this respect, that the vast scale of his narrative allows him to feed into it, both in his own person and in comments and explanations given by the actors, a considerable range of the conceptions and values attached by Romans to their own institutions. In the absence, except in the case of Polybius, of either contemporary reflections on

the fundamental character of the Roman *politeia* or of any detailed empirical studies comparable to the *Athēnaiōn Politeia*,
these conventional expositions by Dionysius acquire a value they
would not otherwise have. They do not amount in any way to systematic political thought. But they are examples, placed in the
narrative as the occasions for them arise, of quite detailed explanations of the workings of Republican institutions, and of interpretations and values attached to them. Cumulatively, Dionysius's
long-winded thoughts have a lot to offer students of the Roman
politeia.

We might well have hoped for something at a superior level to
this from the last of the Greek narrative historians to be considered, Cassius Dio.[56] Dio is the prime example of the Greek who
found a place at the heart of the Roman imperial system. Born in
the 160s in Nicaea in Bithynia, he was the son of a Roman senator,
became a senator himself, and was consul twice, on the second
occasion in A.D. 229 along with the Emperor Severus Alexander.
The year 229 was also the terminal date of his major history of
Rome in eighty books, beginning with the arrival of Aeneas in
Italy. His *History* cannot fail to be significant in various ways: as
the only detailed narrative of all of Roman history up to the third
century, as the last full history of Rome to be written, and as being
simultaneously the work of a senatorial insider and ex-consul and
an external observer from a Greek background, writing Roman
history in Greek.

What he has to say about the Roman Republic both loses and
gains in significance from the fact that the whole first third or
so of the work survives only in Byzantine excerpts and epitomes.
Especially with the epitomes, the most important being those of
Xiphilinus in the eleventh century, and of Zonaras in the early
twelfth, the disadvantage is obviously that we cannot be certain
how accurately they have reproduced Dio's words. The gain is one
that deserves some attention, namely, that a narrative discussing
in great detail the history of a republic was being studied and epitomes of it read in the late Byzantine period, many centuries after
the Empire had settled on Constantinople as its capital.

Cassius Dio's *History*, in the original and as surviving in epitomes, has perhaps four main contributions to make to political
thought about the Republic. First, there is his detailed narrative,
which survives in full, of Roman history from the early 60s B.C. to

the establishment of the imperial system by Augustus. Second, there are antiquarian-type explications of Roman political institutions, for instance, his description of the "assembly of centuries" meeting outside the city on the Campus Martius and of the device, using an archaic rule surviving from the early Republic, which the praetor, Metellus Celer, was able to use to cut short the trial of Rabirius before the assembly in 63 B.C.:

> When nothing else would cause them to heed him and they were unconcerned by the fact that the trial had been held in a manner contrary to custom, he ran up to the Janiculum before they took any vote at all, and pulled down the military flag, so that it was no longer lawful for them to reach a decision.
>
> Now this matter of the flag is as follows. In ancient times there were many enemies dwelling near the city, and the Romans, fearing that while they were holding an assembly by centuries foes might occupy the Janiculum and attack the city, decided that not all should vote at once, but that some men under arms should by turns always guard that position. So they guarded it as long as the assembly lasted, but when this was about to be adjourned, the flag was pulled down and the guards departed; for no further business could be transacted when the post was not guarded. This practice was observed only in the case of the centuriate assemblies, for these were held outside the wall and all who bore arms were obliged to attend them. Even to this day it is done as a matter of form.[57]

Precisely the key feature of the Roman political system in the late Republic—and in a formal sense even in Dio's time—was that it preserved the fundamental institution of the sovereign meeting of citizens, but in a context where that in itself could seem an anachronism.

Third, there are explanations and analyses, of the same type as those offered by Dionysius, of the origin and character of republican institutions. One example is his long discussion of the tribunate of the plebs and its evolution:

> The men were called in the tongue of the Latins *tribuni*,—the same name that was given to the commanders of a thousand,—but were styled *dēmarchoi* [leaders of the people] in the Greek language. In order, however, to distinguish between the titles of the tribunes, they added in the one case the phrase "of the soldiers," and in the other the phrase "of the people." Now these tribunes of the people (or *dēmarchoi*) became responsible for great evils that befell Rome. For though they did not immediately secure the title of magistrates, they gained power beyond all the others, defending every one who begged protection and rescuing every one who called upon them not only from private individuals, but from the very magistrates, except the dictators. If any one ever invoked them when

absent, he, too, was released from the person holding him prisoner and was either brought before the populace by them or was set free. And if ever they saw fit that anything should not be done, they prevented it, whether the person acting were a private citizen or a magistrate; and if the populace or the senate was about to do or vote anything and a single tribune opposed it, the action or the vote became null and void. As time went on, they were allowed, or allowed themselves, to summon the senate, to punish anybody who disobeyed them, to practice divination, and to hold court.[58]

A little further on in this long account, Dio describes the evolving relationship of tribunes of the plebs to the Senate:

Now at first they did not enter the senate-house, but sat at the entrance and watched proceedings, and in case anything failed to please them, they would then and there oppose it. Next they were invited inside. Later, however, the ex-tribunes became members of the senate, and finally some of the senators even sought to be tribunes—unless one chanced to be a patrician. Patricians the people would not accept; for after choosing the tribunes to defend them against the patricians, and advancing them to so great power, they feared that a patrician might turn this power to contrary purposes and use it against them. But if a man abjured the rank given him by birth and changed his status to that of a common citizen, they received him gladly.[59]

What we are reading here, however, is not precisely what Dio wrote and what was read by his audience in the third century, but Zonaras's epitome, composed in the first half of the twelfth century, and represented in numerous manuscripts. Even in this period, therefore, an image of a free republic, with open internal conflicts and political strife, could be presented to the minds of the reading public in the Byzantine empire.

Finally, there is Dio's quite clear and categoric assessment of what the change from Republic to Empire meant. First, there are his reflections on the murder of Julius Caesar in 44 B.C. The murderers were mistaken, he says, for *dēmokratia* sounds fine, but *monarchia* is preferable, for it is easier to find one virtuous man than many. Democracies always had been shown to be unstable, and in any case Rome was too large and had a great empire—"for such a city, I say, to practice moderation is impossible, and still more is it impossible for the people, unless moderation prevails, to be harmonious."[60]

The same issue was raised again by the battle of Philippi in 42 B.C., in which the murderers of Caesar were finally defeated: the defeat meant the end of *autonomia* and the democratic element, but it was beneficial for the people all the same.[61] Finally, after recounting the battle of Actium in 31, and the return of the future Augustus to Rome, Dio sums up the history of Rome up to that point: "These then were the things which the Romans both achieved and endured over a period of 725 years, under the kingship (*basileia*) and in the *dēmokratia* and the period of dynasts (*dynasteiai*). But from this moment they began again to be ruled by a monarchy in the full sense."[62]

Greek observers, whether writing as contemporaries or looking back over the centuries, offer between them a fairly consistent set of views: that the Roman *politeia* had its constitutional origins under the kings and evolved step-by-step from that period on; that many of its institutions were complex, peculiar, and required explanation; that its institutions represented (at the best) a balance between different conflicting elements and at the worst outright strife and disorder; that they could be seen as embodying elements of *basileia*, *aristokratia*, and *dēmokratia*; and that there was a danger that the democratic element (*to dēmokratikon*) would get out of hand. All, in short, characterized the Republic as having a very significant democratic element (and Aristotle certainly would have agreed). None, however, showed any tendency to wish that Rome might become more democratic than it was, and Polybius quite clearly felt that steps in that direction already were disturbing the balance, which he saw as the fundamental virtue of the system.

Active political thought about the principles that should govern the structure of self-governing communities ("republics") was to begin again in Italy, just about the time when Zonaras was preparing his epitome of Dio, and was to continue to the present. The Roman Republic might serve, at different moments, as a model to be admired or an example to be avoided; but there were to be very few thinkers who, however deep their commitment to republicanism, equality, or the rule of law, did not share the attitude of Aristotle or Polybius, namely, that too great a preponderance of the democratic element was to be avoided.

3 Looking Back on the Republic

The Empire, the Middle Ages, Machiavelli

Roman Reflections

We have already seen the paradox of Greek writing about the Roman Republic. Aristotle, uniquely equipped for the task, in combining reflections on the nature of city-states with detailed empirical observations, happened not to discuss Rome, although he might have done so. If he had, he would have caught the Roman *res publica* at a vital moment of transformation and expansion. In the event, therefore, of all the numerous Greeks who wrote about Rome—and supply a large proportion of our evidence about it—it was to be Polybius, alone, who set out to analyze how the contemporary Roman state worked.

Following him, Dionysius of Halicarnassus, writing after the Republic had already fallen, made a valiant attempt to fulfill the social anthropologist's role as "participant observer,"[1] to explain the functioning of particular institutions and to make a relation between the story of early Rome and the circumstances of his own time. No other Greek writer would do the same or devote so detailed an exposition to early Roman institutions. That is not to say that very full narratives of the history of the Republic were not produced by Plutarch or by Cassius Dio; but explanation and analysis of the institutions of the Republic were not to be expected in writers living under a long-established imperial monarchy. As regards Rome, Polybius proved to be Aristotle's sole heir. After him, if we look at the age of Cicero and the political struggles of the last few decades of the Republic, there was, so far as we know, no contemporary observer who provided either an empirical analysis of the institutions of the Republic or an assessment of how, as a state, it ought to be characterized. In default of that, and in particular as a means of contributing to the question of whether we should attribute the term *democratic* to Rome, this study will end with a piece of "virtual history": how, applying his own categories, Aristotle might have analyzed the Republic of Cicero's time.

The task can be approached only tentatively, for our greatest handicap is that no observer, and no actual Roman participant, produced any systematic empirical study of the workings of the late-Republican state to rival the Aristotelian *Constitution of the Athenians*. Cicero's *On the Laws*, modeled on Plato's *Laws*, represented not that but observations on the nature of law on the one hand, and his conception of how a reformed *res publica* would work on the other.[2] His *On the Commonwealth*, which in any case survives only in part, comes closer, but it does not address his own time. A dialogue modeled on Plato's *Republic*, it is set in 129 B.C., and (very typically of our evidence) its most systematic treatment of the Roman political system is a historical survey contained in Book II, beginning with the foundation and continuing to the mid-fifth century. Two other features are particularly significant. One is that he borrows the Aristotelian, or Polybian, notion of states as divided into three types, kingship (*regnum*), aristocracy (*civitas optimatium*), and democracy (*civitas popularis*), but without borrowing the Greek terms, finding Latin equivalents instead (I.26.42). As we will see (p. 57), the standard items in Greek political vocabulary were to enter Latin only in the thirteenth century, and even Machiavelli (p. 73) still speaks of aristocrats as *ottimati*. The other feature is Cicero's repeated insistence, probably derived from Polybius, that an appropriate mixture of the three was best.[3] By contrast, his *On Duties*, a work of the first importance for Roman values and Roman public life, is not concerned with the workings of the constitution as such and is in any case already retrospective, written not only after Caesar had seized power and made himself *dictator*, but after his murder in March 44.[4]

The fact that no contemporary Romans were to imitate either Aristotelian political analysis or Aristotelian empirical reporting of how institutions worked was to have consequences for political thought that have lasted until the present day. First, Cicero's idealized visions of an essentially harmonious social and political order under the leadership of the "best" citizens (both those in the Senate and the much wider group outside it) have in an extraordinary way obscured, even from professional historians, the fact that the painful and turbulent reality of his own time was quite different. Second, and perhaps even more important, our understanding of the Roman Republic as a system has to be based, for lack of anything more systematic, on what can be gleaned either from contemporary oratory or from historical narratives. But the most important and detailed of surviving narratives, that of Livy, is the work of an outsider, whose fellow citizens in Patavium were not even Roman citizens when he was born, and who wrote all of his history, *From the Foundation of the City*, after the Republic had fallen. Even if the whole text had survived, therefore—and the books on the last century and more of the Republic are missing—it would still be a literary reconstruction of a history beginning some seven centuries before its author's birth and ending in the radically new circumstances of the sole rule of Augustus.

As subsequent intellectual history was to show, Livy's *History* was to provide abundant material illustrating the working of the *res publica* and for moralizing reflections on political conduct and collective values. It is also true that when it was being written under the rule of Augustus, and indeed long after, the institutions of the Roman *res publica* still existed and in a formal sense still functioned. We have seen earlier (p. 47) the remarkable passage of Cassius Dio's *Roman History*, which indicates that in the first half of the third century A.D. the "assembly of centuries" was still meeting on the Campus Martius.

There was therefore ample scope, in the historical culture of the Imperial period, both for narratives rehearsing the history of the Republic, for reference to episodes from its history or for anti-quarian disquisitions on different aspects of its institutions. One of the most remarkable, and rather neglected, examples of the latter is the work on the institutions of Rome composed in the second century A.D. by one Pomponius, who is otherwise unknown, and bears the Greek title *Enchiridion* ("handbook"). It may be worth quoting a passage from near the beginning of the book:

So it seems necessary to us to expound the origins and development of the law itself. And indeed in the beginning of our *civitas* the *populus* first began to function with no certain *lex* and no certain *ius*, and everything was controlled arbitrarily by the kings. Afterwards it is recorded that when the *civitas* had expanded to a certain extent Romulus himself divided the *populus* into thirty parts, which parts he called *curiae* because he managed the care (*cura*) of the *res publica* through the votes of those parts. And thus even he had taken certain *leges curiatae* to the *populus*; and so did the following kings.[5]

Thus, even in this period, an interest in the foundations of law in popular voting could be expressed. It was also very significant that the legal writers of the Classical period of Roman jurisprudence, from the mid-second to the early part of the third century A.D., expressed a view that properly could be summed up by saying that the Empire was in origin a constitutional monarchy founded on a popular vote. This conception is set out categorically in the *Institutes* of Gaius, also of the mid-second century: "A law (*lex*) is whatever the people (*populus*) orders and lays down . . . A ruling (*constitutio*) of the Emperor is whatever he determines by decree or edict or letter. Nor has it ever been doubted that such a ruling has the force of law, since the Emperor himself receives his *imperium* by a *lex*" (I.1.3–5).

In fact, there is good evidence that the Roman emperors, as the inheritors of the powers of a *res publica* whose institutions still existed, did receive their powers through formal conferment by those institutions;[6] and, as we will see, a very striking piece of documentary evidence for that process was to be discovered in Rome and to play a suitable part in republican ideology in the fourteenth century (pp. 63–64). Nonetheless, there is a clear element of persuasion, or overassertion, in Gaius's formulation, just as there is when the greatest of the Roman jurists, Ulpian, returns to the same point in the early third century, in Book I of his *Institutes*: "Whatever has seemed right to the Princeps (Emperor) has the force of law. This is because by the *lex regia*, which has been carried in respect of his *imperium*, the *populus* transfers to him and confers on him all of its own *imperium* and power (*potestas*)" (quoted in the *Digest* I.4.1 *praef.*). There is a strongly persuasive element in this formulation, for it is certain that whatever *lex* had been passed by the *populus* to confer rights (however defined) on the first emperor, Augustus, nobody would have referred to this as a "royal" law (*lex regia*).

Nonetheless, both passages, written under the established Imperial monarchy, reflect unmistakably the conception that that monarchy had its roots in the popular sovereignty of the Republic, and that the conferment of sovereignty on a succession of individuals involved, or at least had *once* involved, a constitutional act on the part of the *populus.*

These conceptions might have been of no further relevance for intellectual history or political thought but for the continued study (and practical application) of Roman law in the late Empire, when the effective capital had moved to Constantinople, and thereby into a Greek-speaking environment. Latin, however, retained its status as the language of culture in the study of Roman law, in a way that we ought to find more striking and surprising than we do. This led Justinian (A.D. 527–565) to formulate a hugely ambitious plan for a corpus of Roman law in Latin. Leaving aside other aspects of this project, the one that is relevant here, and was to be of immense importance for later European civil law, was the *Digest,* a massive set of extracts from the works of the classical Roman jurists (nearly all of them from the period of Gaius and Ulpian, three or four centuries earlier), taken out of context and arranged under headings. The texts were supposed to have been edited to produce conformity, but for whatever reason it is patent that they were not. What we have, therefore, presented to the world under the authority of the Christian Emperor, is an enormous repertoire of academic legal thinking expressed in the Latin of the pagan jurists of the High Empire. Their thinking in its turn was rooted in the historical fact of the sovereignty of the *populus* in the Republic and in the rules of private law as laid down in the Republic and then expanded and developed under the Empire. The "afterlife" of the sovereignty of the *populus Romanus,* as reflected in writings of the Imperial period, was therefore to be of considerable importance.

The Republic in Medieval Thought

The *Digest,* and more generally the tradition of Roman law as preserved in both the Latin west and the Byzantine east (where, as we have seen, Dio's *Roman History* was still read, to be summarized at great length by Zonaras in the eleventh century), was one of the vehicles, along with the narratives of Livy and Sallust, by which an image of a *res publica,* governed by laws, was to be preserved through the Middle Ages. The political thought of the Middle Ages in the Latin west is a topic of immense complexity and interest, and anyone who ventures on it is fortunate to have invaluable modern guides in the works of Quentin Skinner, Joseph Canning, and Janet Coleman.[7] But for most of the period up to the early Renaissance, it would be fair to say that the main directions of political thought lay in areas other than detailed reflection on the history and institutions of the Republic and on the lessons that might be drawn from them.

The rights of monarchs, and above all, after A.D. 800, those of the emperor, the legal relations of the Church and the clergy to secular power, the ever-contested relations of emperors and popes, and the conflict that arose within the Church over authoritarian rule versus rule by consultation and consent (the "conciliarist controversy"); all this meant that the major issues that confronted political thinkers were shaped, first and fundamentally, by Christianity, and second, by conflicts between secular and ecclesiastical authority. It would therefore be several centuries before the model of the ancient city-state, whether Rome itself or the Greek ones analyzed by Aristotle, could seem of any relevance.

Indirectly, however, the notion of a state as a *res publica*, an impersonal entity logically distinct from the individuals exercising power, was an important legacy of Roman law as early as the Carolingian period,[8] and the rediscovery of the *Digest* in the eleventh century gave further basis for arguments that power should be rooted ultimately in popular consent. At the same time, the notion of an actual republic, in a recognizably "ancient" sense, perhaps owed most to the first Latin translation of Aristotle's *Politics*, made by William of Moerbeke in the mid-thirteenth century. It was here that the word *democratic* made its first appearance in Latin.

It had, however, been earlier than this that "consuls" had made their first reappearance as the elected magistrates of a self-governing city—first at Pisa in 1085, and later at Milan, Genoa, Arezzo, Bologna, Padua, and Siena over the next half-century. The choice of the title cannot but reflect an awareness of at least the outlines of the history of the Roman Republic. The emergence of the self-governing city in Italy in the high Middle Ages was of course, as is well known, to be the context for the reemergence of "republican" theories of freedom from external powers (the Empire or the papacy, and later the kings of France or Spain), of some degree of popular involvement, whether on a relatively broad or relatively narrow basis, of constitutional government and of the exercise of power by officials appointed by due process. In the highly complex and contested history of the Italian city-states,[9] these ideals were rarely in fact achieved and even more rarely maintained on a stable basis. Domination by other cities developing local "empires" of their own, the seizure of power by aristocratic families, papal manipulation, and invasions by foreign armies were important features of the story. Only Venice, with a republican constitution based on a broad hereditary oligarchy, was to maintain its independence, succumbing neither to foreign powers nor to any local duke until 1797—thereby offering food for reflection to all those who asked how a stable republic might function and offer an alternative to monarchy.

As we shall see, it is significant and characteristic that Machiavelli's own reflections on the model of a republic offered by the story of early Rome were themselves written at a moment when Florentine self-government had collapsed and power was once again in the hands of the Medici. In a way that is indeed reminiscent of the history of political thought in the classical Greek world, it was precisely the fact that internal stability on the one hand and external security on the other were both perpetually threatened, which added urgency to political reflection.

In such reflections, what part was played, before Machiavelli, by consideration of the history and institutions of the Roman Republic? The material, in the form of the narratives of Livy and Sallust, was clearly well known, as was Aristotle's *Politics*, once available in Latin translation. Polybius's analysis of the Roman *politeia* in Book VI, on the other hand, seems not to have become known until the early sixteenth century.[10] As always, intellectual history depends on what texts were available to be read, as well as of course on the question of circumstance, that is to say, which were the models that the circumstances of the time made relevant. It is of course useless to speculate, but it does seem likely that if a Latin translation of Book VI of Polybius had been made in, say, the mid-thirteenth century, at the same time as that of Aristotle's *Politics* (see p. 55), the Roman Republic might have played a much more significant part in the political thought of the next few centuries. What is more, because Polybius's analysis was the only such systematic treatment of the political structure of the Republic by a contemporary observer, the logical basis of any later deployment of the lessons to be learned would have been on a quite different basis.

As it is, all that will be attempted here is to look at a few relatively well-known works of the period between the thirteenth century and Machiavelli, taking those that do make some use of the Roman Republic and asking what they made of it. We then will turn to the major figure of Machiavelli, himself, in his *Discorsi* (his *Il Principe*, which, written at the same moment, is much more closely related to the circumstances of the time and makes no significant use of the history of the Republic as a source of reflection).

Two things are immediately striking to someone who (like myself) approaches the political writing of the later Middle Ages for the first time. One is the wide historical culture of the authors of the period, embracing biblical and classical history and a very detailed view of the evolution of the Roman Empire, and to some extent of its Byzantine successor, in particular the history of the "Holy Roman Empire" from its inception at the coronation of Charlemagne in Rome in 800. The other is the absolutely pervasive influence of Aristotle's *Politics* and *Ethics*, from the moment of the first Latin translation of the *Politics* by William of Moerbeke in the 1260s. This introduced into Latin (and hence into modern European languages) a series of key Greek terms reproduced in transliteration: *aristocratia, democratia, oligarchia, politia*. It was certainly the availability of an applicable vocabulary and of the model of a discourse on the nature, advantages, and disadvantages of different sorts of political systems that acted as the key stimulus to political writing, triggered also of course by the conflicting claims of the Church and the Empire, the search for the (always fragile) conditions for independence on the part of the Italian city-states, and by social conflicts within them over the basis of the power of officeholders, or as to what sections of the (adult male) population might have a political voice at all.

In this context, the model, or image, of the Roman Republic, as a self-governing Republic that had thrown off the rule of kings, had a constitution based on annual elected magistrates, achieved military glory, and then fell prey to internal dissensions leading once again to the autocratic rule of the emperors, did play a certain part. The overall narrative history of the Republic was evidently familiar and could function as the source of historical examples relating to the actions of individuals. Moreover, repeated use was made of a sentence from Sallust's *Catiline*, reflecting on the energizing impulse felt in Rome once royal rule had been thrown off: "But it is incredible to recall how, once liberty had been secured, the state waxed strong in so short a time; so great a love of glory had possessed them."[11]

What does not seem, so far as I can discover, to be present is either any detailed discussion of Roman institutions or any systematic analysis of the Republic as a political system using the categories provided by Aristotle (and, of course, applied to Rome by Polybius): kingship and tyranny, aristocracy and oligarchy, democracy or mob rule (*ochlocracy*)—or, still less, ideas derived from these as to the desirability of a mixed constitution, or the sort of balanced and ordered system with reasonably wide political rights that Aristotle had characterized as a *politeia* in a special sense. This absence is perhaps hardly surprising, for Polybius has had few imitators even until today. Nonetheless, a certain consciousness of the Roman Republic as a topic deserving of reflection does appear from the thirteenth century onward.

The first example to be noted comes (or may come) from the greatest of medieval Catholic thinkers, Thomas Aquinas, if indeed it was he who wrote the first part of a treatise *De regimine principum* (conventionally translated as On the government of rulers, although the real meaning is clearly "on government *by* rulers"). If Aquinas was the author, it seems that it must date between the 1260s and Aquinas's death in 1274. At any rate, in the one paragraph that speaks consistently of the Roman Republic, this text has the characteristics mentioned already, of being a moralizing reflection on the story of the Republic rather than an analysis of its institutions—and in deploying the sentence from Sallust mentioned above. It may be worth quoting some of what appears here, keeping examples of the Greek vocabulary now being deployed in Latin:

> Since the best and the worst subsist in monarchy (*monarchia*), that is in the rule of one, the royal dignity is rendered odious to many because of the rule of tyrants (*tyranni*) . . . There is a clear example of this in the Roman Republic. After the people had expelled the kings, whose royal, or rather tyrannical, arrogance they could not bear, they wanted to change the kingdom into an aristocracy (*aristocratia*) and so instituted for themselves consuls and other magistrates. These began to govern and direct them, and, as Sallust reports: "It is incredible to relate how the Roman city grew in a short time once liberty had been obtained."[12]

The author goes on to comment that because the citizens saw this as a regime that was for the common good, they served and contributed willingly, both in the military sphere and in paying for communal expenses. Eventually, because of continuous civil strife, they fell again under the rule of the emperors. Some of these took care of the *res publica* in kingly style, but others acted as *tyranni* and brought it down again.

No more is required for this characterization of the Republic than a knowledge of the outlines of its history and the availability of Greek labels for different types of regimes. Nonetheless, these labels, with their positive or negative connotations, now could be applied to any known historical regime (the case that immediately follows is that of the Israelite monarchy), but also of course to the present day.

Considerably more extensive reflection on the Roman Republic is to be found in the rest of the Latin text *De regimine principum* (On the government of princes), written at the very beginning of the fourteenth century, whose author was Ptolemy (or Bartholomew) of Lucca (c. 1236–1327), and which draws on a strikingly wide range of historical examples in considering different political systems in a manner not unworthy of Aristotle. Above all, Ptolemy was the first medieval thinker we know who was systematically opposed to monarchy and who praised republicanism as a system that could, under appropriate circumstances, be stable and effective. Moreover, in this context, he speaks positively of the Roman Republic, returning several times to what was indeed a very striking contemporary observer's view of the Republic, contained in the first book of Maccabees, probably written at the end of the second century B.C., and looking back to the first Jewish contacts with Rome in 161 B.C.[13] In this as in other contexts, Ptolemy both draws on a wide range of historical material and specifically underlines its relevance to the circumstances of his own time. His principal theme is to borrow from Aristotle the notion of a *politia*, in which power is exercised under constitutional and legal restraints. One example of this and of his use of Maccabees will suffice:

So it is written in the First Book of Maccabees that the Romans made a senate-house, and that 320 men took counsel there daily, debating on behalf of the multitude, in order that they should do those things that were worthy. For these reasons it can be accepted that in the Roman system after the expulsion of the kings there was a "political govern-ment" (*dominium politicum*), until the usurpation of the empire, which took place when Julius Caesar, after the defeat of his enemies and the deaths of Pompey and his sons, and the subjugation of the world, took to himself an individual dominion and *monarchia*, and converted the *politia* into a despotic or tyrannical pre-eminence (*despoticum principatum, sive tyrannicum*) . . .

It should be noted here that although (at Rome) one man was in charge each year, as is written in the aforesaid Book of Maccabees [Ptolemy copies the mistake in the original], as happens in the cities of Italy even now (he means the office called potestà), the system however depended on a number of people, and could therefore be called not "royal" but "politi-cal." This was also the case with the judges of the Israelite people, since nonetheless they ruled the people not in royal but in "political" style (*non regaliter, sed politice*). We should take into account also that (today) in all regions, whether in Germania or in Scythia or in Gallia, cities live politi-cally (*politice*), but limited by the power of a king, or Emperor, to whom they are bound under certain laws.[14]

Elsewhere (II.9.6), Ptolemy rehearses the same story as Aquinas about the period of constitutional government that the Romans had enjoyed between the expulsion of the kings and the rise of the Imperial regime. Of much more significance, however, is the passage in which, and at first following Aristotle's *Politics*, he moves from the political system of the "Chalcedonii" (in fact, the Carthaginians) to the similar type of *politia*, which was character-istic today of the *civitates* of Italy, and especially Tuscany, and then to Rome.[15]

What he says of Rome involves his asserting that in the course of time the Republic acquired a "democratic" element—so far as I know the first time, since Polybius, and later Cassius Dio (p. 49), that anyone had used this word of Rome. Ptolemy's observations do not, of course, approach the level of detail of those in Polybius, which themselves in fact only occupy a few pages (p. 36). But they did represent the first attempt for centuries to analyze the balance of power in Rome in terms of the character of the various offices:

This procedure was also observed in the City [Rome] for the whole period over which the consulate endured. First *consules* were elected, two in number, and afterwards a *dictator* and *magister equitum*, as the histories relate, to whom the whole civil government pertained; and thus it was ruled by an aristocratic predominance (*principatus aristocraticus*). After-wards *tribuni plebis* were instituted for the benefit of the *plebs* and *popu-lus*, without whom the *consules* and the other aforementioned magistrates could not conduct the government; and thus there was added a democratic predominance (*democraticus principatus*).[16]

As a sort of philosophical history, or historically based comparative study of institutions, Ptolemy's work is of a remarkably high quality, significant in many ways other than its essentially favorable view of the Republic and of republics. This favorable view is not unequivocal. As J. M. Blythe shows, Ptolemy admits that not all societies are fit for a "political" regime, and for those that are not, a benevolent monarchy, or "royal" regime (*regale regimen*, II.9), is necessary. He also accepts the predominance of the Papacy, in a way that distinguishes him from his great successor, Marsilius of Padua. Nonetheless, the "ancient Romans" occupy a special place in his picture of the world, one that anticipates features of the image of them in Machiavelli. In a state of nature (*status integer humanae naturae*), there would not be a royal regime but a "political" one, in which influence would depend on personal qualities: "Therefore, political government was better for wise and virtuous persons, such as the ancient Romans, since it imitated this state of nature."[17]

In fame and importance in the history of political thought, Ptolemy was indeed to be, by far, overshadowed by his younger contemporary, Marsilius (Marsiglio) of Padua (c. 1275–1342), whose *Defensor Pacis* (Defender of the peace), completed in 1324, represented both a prodigious display of learning and argument and the first substantial argument directed against the power of the Papacy and the Church and in favor of the predominance of the secular authorities, the Emperor (Ludwig of Bavaria) above all.[18] But from the perspective of the subsequent role played in political thought by considerations drawn from the history of the Republic, this truly major work shows precisely how, in the absence of any treatment by Aristotle and his school, and with Polybius's analysis still remaining unknown, the Republic and its institutions occupied no significant place. The first book of the *Defensor* rests throughout on Aristotle, the second on texts relating to the history of the Church, which are used to demonstrate two major propositions: the dependence of the Church on the secular power, beginning with the Roman Empire; and the necessity of consensus, as expressed in the major church councils, for the formulation of doctrine and ecclesiastical discipline. Even when Marsilius turns to the constitutional bases of secular legislation and of the exercise of authority by magistrates, he does not bring in the Republic as providing examples—except for a passing allusion to Cicero's *prudentia* in having the Catilinarian conspirators executed (I.14. 3).

In other words, Marsilius's great work, directed to a major contemporary ideological battle, in which the author himself was to participate in person, was written from a considerable knowledge of biblical, late Roman, and medieval history and culture: but, as with other political writers of the period, the classical work that was truly influential was Aristotle's *Politics*. It was only in his later summary of his argument, the *Defensor Minor* (Lesser defender) of 1339 to 1342,[19] that Marsilius was to turn, briefly, to Republican history to provide evidence of the ultimate foundations of imperial rule in popular, or communal, assent (*Def. Min.* 12.1–3). On the rather compressed and schematized view presented in this work, power had been voluntarily transferred by the peoples of the provinces to the Roman people (and here Marsilius, once again, uses the favorable picture of Rome given in *First Maccabees* 8), and the Roman people then had transferred the right to legislate to the emperors.

A rather more detailed, but still very schematic, view of the Republic informs the treatise *De regimine civitatis* (On the government of a city) written in the same period by Bartolus of Sassoferrato.[20] Here the categories of government deployed are drawn quite explicitly, once again, from Aristotle, who is named at the beginning. But the topic of the first book is the various types of government found in Rome after the expulsion of the kings, whether a moderate popular regime aiming at the common good, to be labeled *politia* or *politicum*, or one where the common people sought their own advantage, a *democratia*; similarly for a senatorial regime, whether an *aristocratia* (like the regime of the notables—*regimen maiorentium*—at Venice) or an *oligarchia*; or if individual rule (*per unum*) whether a benevolent kingship, *regnum* (a word applicable even if the holder of power were a duke, marquis or count—Bartolus has slipped here, as he does often, into the contemporary world), or simply by tyrannies (*tyrannides*).

The conjunction of Aristotelian terminology with the model of the Republic and with concern for the contemporary world is, of course, important, if only because the two different aspects of the legacy of the classical world gave a sense of perspective on contemporary issues and a means of categorizing current forms of rule. But there is no detailed treatment of the Republic or its institutions, or even anecdotes from its history; and in the second book, the "Roman" element that plays an important part is constant recourse to the *Digest*, accompanied by repeated examples drawn not from Roman history but from the Bible. Nonetheless, in a certain sense, Bartolus could be seen as "anticipating" the application of Greek categories to the Republic by Polybius, whose text was still unknown and would not become known again until the early sixteenth century.

In the first part of the fourteenth century, therefore, there is a vision of Rome, in the period of several centuries between the expulsion of the kings and the reassertion of monarchic rule by Julius Caesar and then Augustus, as a state that had both achieved greatness and had possessed republican institutions, within which aristocratic or oligarchic elements on the one hand and democratic ones on the other might predominate. This vision also played a significant part in the assertion of republican values (persisting even when more and more cities fell under the rule of *signori* or under the control of emperor or pope), and in the maintenance of the fundamental proposition that all rule, even in monarchic systems, should be rooted in popular assent.

In a formal sense, this view of Rome, when retrojected also to the Imperial period, was not, in historical fact, wholly misleading. For the public ideology of the early Empire, which was still reflected, as we have seen (p. 53), in later juristic writings, had indeed been that sovereignty resided in the *populus Romanus* and that power had been conferred on the Emperor by a *lex*. It is worth noting in passing, therefore, that a genuine Roman document, recently unearthed in Rome, was put to use by a champion of republicanism who rose to brief prominence in the middle of the fourteenth century. The person who attempted to reestablish a self-governing republic at Rome in 1347 was Cola (Nicola) di Rienzi; and the document whose significance he expounded to the people was the Latin inscription engraved on a bronze tablet, found (it is not known where) in 1344, placed by Cola in St. John Lateran, and now in the Capitoline Museum. This is the so-called Lex de Imperio Vespasiani, which is in fact the record of the specific and general powers conferred on Vespasian after his successful coup d'état in A.D. 69.[21] That the text appeared so opportunely seems to be simply coincidence. But it both was confirmation that in a formal sense the early Imperial regime had been a constitutional monarchy, resting on the conferment of powers by Senate and people, and it was justifiably interpreted and publicly expounded as embodying this message.

Cola di Rienzi's movement was very short-lived, and it does not seem that the deployment of the image of republican Rome, either in theoretical writings on political systems or as providing a basis for current republican movements, played any significant part for another century and a half. When the image of Rome does reemerge, it is above all as an element in the troubled and conflict-ridden history of republican values in Florence.

Florence and Machiavelli

As will be obvious, a treatment of the topic that is the purpose of this book, namely, the various uses made of the image of the Republic in later political writings, cannot do justice to the immense literature deriving from Florence in the fifteenth and sixteenth centuries, to its complex history, to the thought of major figures like Leonardo Bruni, Poliziano, or Savonarola, or to the range of interpretations to be found in modern literature.[22] What follows therefore is no more than a sketch, followed by an examination of the treatment of Rome, first by Mario Salamonio in his *De Principatu* of 1512–14, and then in the *Discorsi* of the major figure in Renaissance political thought, Niccolò Machiavelli.

Both works expressed, but in very different ways, republican ideals. But, in a way which by now will not be surprising, both were written after the fall of a republican regime and the relapse of Florence into individual rule.

Florence had come under the rule of the Medici much earlier, in 1434, and their rule had lasted until 1494, when Piero di Medici fell, overthrown by the forces of Charles VIII of France. What then replaced Medicean rule was a broad-based republican system with a great council (*consiglio maggiore*), or assembly of propertied citizens, of some three thousand persons, a council of eighty, and a magistracy of ten men. To an ancient historian, such a constitution bears a quite close resemblance to what Athenians in 411 B.C.

had seen as an oligarchy, with a citizen base of five thousand men, qualified by property and the capacity to provide their own armor. In the contemporary context, however, it was a broad-based constitution, satisfying the requirement that sovereignty should rest, if not on the body of all adult males, at any rate on a large, not a small, group. It was within this system that the monk Savonarola preached and rose to a brief predominance, only to fall in 1498, and it was after this that Machiavelli himself was appointed to a chancery post, in which he was to conduct a number of important diplomatic missions. Then in 1512 Spanish forces allied with those of Pope John II forced the Florentines to surrender. The Medici were restored, the republic was dissolved, and Machiavelli was later condemned and imprisoned, only to be released in 1513 when Cardinal Giovanni di Medici became pope. It was thus in the early years of restored Medicean rule that both Machiavelli's most influential works and the much less well-known *De principatu* of Mario Salamonio were written. Although the Medici were to be driven out again in 1527, their definitive recapture of power came soon, in 1530. The year 1512 was the effective end of the Florentine republic.

It is easy to imagine that the disaster of 1512 might have stimulated thought about the viability of republics in the context of the great-power rivalries that dominated early sixteenth-century Italy and how that in its turn might have prompted reflection on classical Rome and on the characteristics of the Republic. If Machiavelli's *Discorsi* is by far the best-known and most significant product of this moment, Salamonio's *De principatu* takes a very different and very interesting approach and is considered first.[23]

Salamonio is distinctive in that, in stressing the principle of popular sovereignty and deriving expressions of that principle from Roman evidence, he uses a wider range of original material than any of his predecessors. Given that one of his key propositions is that popular sovereignty underlay not only the Republic itself but the Empire, he brings together evidence from both periods and makes significant use of juristic writings of the Imperial period. His *Book II* begins (p. 11) by citing the passage of Ulpian, mentioned earlier (p. 53), in which he asserts that by a *lex regia* the *populus Romanus* had transferred its powers to the emperor (*Digest*

I.4.1). Later, in Book VI (p. 65), he quotes *in extenso* a passage of Pomponius in which he also offers the (quite unhistorical) reflection that the *populus*, given the difficulty of having so many people meet in assembly, had transferred the care of the *res publica* to the Senate while later practical necessity had led to the power being concentrated in the hands of the one man (*Digest* I.1.5). This notion of course served to maintain the fundamental proposition that imperial rule was delegated to the emperor by the assent of the people. This is an example of what must certainly be a very rare phenomenon in intellectual history, namely, use being made later of Pomponius's curious and neglected second-century *Handbook* on the history of Roman institutions.

Salamonio, however, knows how to put to use other items of evidence that did not form part of any conventional repertoire. Thus, he quotes Cicero's speech *In Defence of Cluentius* (53.146), where he expounds the principle that *lex* (law) is the foundation of liberty and equity and the spirit of the Roman condition: "So in short we are all the slaves of the laws, in order that we may be free." It is not easy, however, for the citizen of a modern democracy, in which the voice of the citizen can be heard, if at all, only at the moment of periodic elections, to appreciate the force of the term *lex* or *leges* in Roman discourse; for in that context a *lex* was a statute on which, by definition, every citizen had had in principle the right to vote. Salamonio, like other Florentines, could look back to a restricted democracy, or broad oligarchy, but not to a universal right to vote directly on legislation possessed by all adult male citizens. Certainly he was aware of the Roman precedent, for, in discussing the limits of the control exercised by emperors over elections, he explains that "gatherings of the people for the purpose of electing magistrates and passing laws were called *comitia*," and then he goes into a quite detailed antiquarian account of the different forms of *comitia*, directed primarily (given the context) to their role in elections (Book II, p. 20). Antiquarian learning, put to active interpretative use, is indeed one of his intellectual characteristics. So, for instance, in Book VI (pp. 68–69) he can quote in Latin translation the final paragraph of Strabo's *Geography*, written in Greek in the early Empire, for the view that the emperors exercised the responsibility only for those provinces where there were military challenges. He goes on to express the proposition that the Populus Romanus had established the Emperors not as its masters but its protectors (*defensores*). In Book VI (p. 69), he also cites as evidence the inscription from the arch of Septimius Severus, "which still stands complete at the foot of the Capitol" (as it still does now). The words quoted are "on account of the propagation of the imperium of the Populus Romanus" (*ob imperium populi Romani propagatum*), and the inscription was and is testimony to the proposition that in the early third century A.D. (when the Empire in fact reached its greatest ever extent) formal sovereignty still lay in theory with the Populus Romanus.[24]

Finally, when he comes to the brief seventh and last book of his dialogue, Salamonio discusses the principle that what the Roman Emperors enjoyed was not a blanket exemption from, or superiority to, the laws but specific rights and exemptions conferred by legal process. To this purpose (p. 73), he quotes the entire text of the "Lex de Imperio Vespasiani" (p. 63), from the bronze tablet, which, as he says, "still hangs in the Lateran Basilica."

Enough has been said to illustrate the way in which Salamonio is able to deploy a considerable variety of textual material, juristic literary and documentary, to support an argument concerning the question of in what sense the Roman emperor had been "freed from the laws" (*legibus solutus*), and hence whether he was to be understood as a leader (*Princeps*) or a tyrant (*tyrannus*). The dialogue begins with a quotation from Aristotle's *Politics*, as was only to be expected, and his use of juristic writings is not unique, although it is strikingly apposite and focused. But, while he writes in a very different style, his range of learning, his power of argument, and his engagement with the Roman past make him worthy of comparison with his much more famous contemporary.

Niccolò Machiavelli wrote his two major works against the immensely rich and well-documented intellectual background of Italian humanism and as a reaction to the complex history of both the Florentine republic, culminating in the return to power by the Medici in 1512, and the Italian city-states, riven by internal and external conflicts and buffeted by the forces of the major powers, above all the Papacy and the Spanish and French monarchies. Moreover, as a central figure in European thought, he is the subject of an immense modern bibliography, which only a lifetime of study would enable one to absorb properly.[25] Furthermore, neither the *Discorsi* nor the *Principe*, both written in the years while he was in private life after the return of the Medici, was actually published during his lifetime. So any attempt to assess their apparently conflicting ideals, or any ulterior motives he may have had in writing them, must be a matter of speculation.

The few pages that follow can claim to make only a very specific and limited contribution to the study of Machiavelli's thought, as reflecting the reaction of a specialist in the ancient world to the representation of the Roman Republic that Machiavelli offers in the *Discorsi*. His other major work, the *Principe*, will not come into the picture in this context because it makes no significant use of the Republic as a model, or as a source of lessons to be followed or avoided.

What follows therefore is an ancient historian's reading of the *Discorsi sopra la Prima Deca di Tito Livio* (Discourses on the first ten books of Livy).[26] The work is divided into three books, and references to it are given by book, chapter, and paragraph (e.g., II.8.1). How does Machiavelli approach the Republic, and what does he make of it?

The first essential, as the preface makes clear, is that Machiavelli is looking to the Republic in search of cures for the evils of the present: Physicians base their treatments on Ancient remedies, but those who run modern states, whether republics or kingdoms, do not have recourse to the examples of the ancients. His plan is therefore to write on all those books of Livy that had not fallen victim to the ravages of time. This is a curious claim, of great significance because it is not, strictly speaking, true: Machiavelli deliberately chose to concentrate on books I–X, although much more of Livy was available and had not been lost. For while it is true that the first ten books survive intact, and while Books XI–XX were (and still are) missing, the great bulk of Livy's massive *History* that survives, nearly all of which was available in the early sixteenth century, is represented by Books XXI–XLV, covering the Hannibalic War and the classical Republic of 202–167. Given that Livy was writing in the last three decades of the first century B.C., there are of course many problems about the sources of his detailed and systematic year-by-year account of how the middle Republic functioned and how it fared in its wars. But he could depend at least in part on contemporary sources, above all Polybius, who, as we saw earlier, was in Rome from 167 to 150 B.C. If many controversies surround his history of the Hannibalic War and his explanations of events,[27] it would be hypercritical not to accept that his record of the second-century Republic is both broadly historical, gives a systematic account year by year of the workings of the state, and concerns itself with a period of unchallenged dominance and of relative internal peace.

As we will see later in chapter 7, the fact that no such systematic year-by-year narrative (neither that which Livy actually wrote nor any other) survives for the last century or so of the Republic has consequences that affect intellectual history and political thought to the present day. It is easy to see why the confusing range of contemporary speeches and letters and of later narratives that provide our evidence for that period could not have offered a convenient field for reflection on the present. But the puzzling and highly consequential fact remains that Machiavelli could have chosen to use as his material almost the whole of what we have of Livy's record of the second-century Republic (in fact, all except Books XLI–XLV, which were not yet in circulation)—but in fact he did not. What he did was to take the legendary history of the kings and the semilegendary narrative of the early Republic, covering the years 509 to 292 B.C. This was indeed the period to which the historical Republic owed the origins of its institutions; but how far, if at all, we can regard the narrative account of any one year, the roles given to individuals, or the context or meaning given to the various stages by which the elements of the constitution were established as being anything more than literary constructs is a matter still of acute controversy.[28] It was even argued recently that the prominent figure of Camillus, who allegedly saved Rome from the Gauls, is itself a patriotic literary construct.[29] Camillus appears repeatedly in the pages of the *Discorsi*.

In fact, it is best to accept that such problems were not an issue for Machiavelli. For him, the text will have gained in deployability and force precisely from its having been a familiar series of moralizing, rhetorical, and exemplary narratives that could be used to all the greater effect as a foil for the present. Morever, there was a certain necessary appropriateness in choosing the early history of Rome, when it had been, as Florence was, one Italian city-state among others, not yet ruling any overseas territories. Nonetheless, when we read Machiavelli's reflections, it is essential to recall that the text to which they relate is itself a patriotic learned fiction, written more than two and a half centuries after the latest of the events to which it refers.

That said, Machiavelli's reflections can be of considerable force and interest, above all in the way Roman past and Italian present are brought into constant dialogue with each other. The conjunction of past and present can be expressed, for instance, in the use of language and terminology. So, when he comes to the Gallic invasion of the early fourth century B.C., he speaks of Rome as having been occupied by the "Franciosi" who had taken "la Lombardia" from the "Toscani" and had settled there (II.8.1). In a more profound sense, he also reflects on the social structures that make a true republic possible or impossible. One fatal obstruction, he says, is the presence of noblemen (*gentiluomini*) who have private revenues, followers, and castles (*castella*). Their presence in the kingdom of Naples, and in Rome, the Romagna and Lombardy, made a republic, or any political life (*alcuno vivere politico*), impossible (I.55.4). The Venetian republic might be seen as an exception—but not in reality—because there the nobility had rank and political power, but their wealth came from trade, and they had neither castles nor dependents (I.55.6). Machiavelli might have commented, although he does not, on the absence of "barons" in this sense both from the story of early Rome and from the societies with which Rome came into conflict. He does stress elsewhere (II.2) that the story records no kings, other than those of Rome itself, and Porsenna in Tuscany (Clusium in fact). It was this, the love of freedom on the part of all the other peoples of Italy, that made Roman conquest so hard. It was only the even greater *virtú* of the Romans that made the conquest possible; here, almost inevitably, he paraphrases the much-quoted line from Sallust's *Catiline* (7), which we have encountered before (p. 58): it is marvelous to consider what *grandezza* Rome arrived at after freeing itself from its kings. That accords with his fundamental thesis, which is a moral or social one, that it is only in the context of the freedom of a republic that the citizens can attain the *virtú* necessary for greatness. Speaking elsewhere of the use of castles, by cities not by individual noblemen, he comments that the use of them for defense, or for holding down subjects (as by Francesco Sforza in Milan and in many other current examples), is a delusion, for what counts is the quality of the army (II.24).

What Machiavelli sought to hold up as a model drawn from the history of the early Republic was the image of a city-state that induced and then maintained the right level of *virtú* among its (male) citizens. In that sense, the lesson to be drawn is a moral or social one and does not relate in any detailed way to the working of institutions. It is striking, for instance, that he nowhere has any detailed discussion, or even substantial reference, to the complex systems under which Romans voted on legislation or in elections. Nor indeed does he stress the underlying principle that each man did have a vote, even if its effect was structured through voting units. Of course, he refers repeatedly to the main political institutions of Rome, discussing in broad terms in I.2–3 the overthrow of the kings and the prominence of the consuls and the Senate, bringing about the need for the creation of *tribuni* to protect the *plebs* and to create a balance between the different elements. He continues the discussion by observing that public conflict was necessary and that the price of keeping power in the hands of an aristocracy, as in Sparta or Venice, would have been a limitation of citizen military manpower:

If someone wished, therefore, to order a republic anew, he would have to examine whether he wished it to expand like Rome in dominion and in power or truly to remain within narrow limits. In the first case it is necessary to order it like Rome and make a place for tumults and universal dissensions, as best one can; for without a great number of men, and well armed, a republic can never grow, or, if it grows, maintain itself. In the second case, you can order it like Sparta and like Venice, but because expansion is poison for such republics, he who orders them should, in all the modes he can, prohibit them from acquiring, because such acquisitions, founded on a weak republic, are its ruin altogether. (I.6.4)

In Rome, therefore, it was the *plebs* who acted as the watchdog of liberty (*guardia alla libertà*). Internal conflict had to be tolerated as the price of popular participation and commitment; and the people must have the right to hear accusations against prominent people as a means of venting suspicion and resentment (I.7).

To Machiavelli, therefore, the fundamental reason why it was necessary to accept a degree of popular power is that this is the necessary condition for the creation of a citizen army, and one that is trained and informed. The opposite was shown in the recent collapse of the forces of Venice in the face of those of France, where a single partial defeat had caused them to surrender territory to both the pope and the king of Spain (III.31.3). The Romans offered a better example:

Although it was said another time that the foundation of all states is a good military, and that where this does not exist there can be neither good laws nor any other good thing, it does not appear to me superfluous to repeat it. For at every point in reading this history one sees this necessity appear; and one sees that the military cannot be good unless it is trained, and that it cannot be trained unless it is composed of your subjects. For one does not always remain at war, nor can one remain at it; so one must be able to train in time of peace, and with others than subjects one cannot do this training out of regard for the expense . . . Thus, if a city is armed and ordered as was Rome, and every day it falls to its citizens, both in particular and in public, to make experiment both of their virtue and of the power of fortune, it will always happen that they are of the same spirit in every condition of time and will maintain their same dignity. But if they are unarmed and rely only on the thrust of fortune and not on their own virtue, they vary with its varying and they will always give an example of themselves such as the Venetians gave. (III.31.4)

Machiavelli's fundamental message is thus not unlike that of Polybius: that the political and the military orders go together and that what really counts as evidence of the strength and coherence of a *politeia* in its capacity for resilience in a moment of crisis, in particular, for this to be achieved, the best formula is a mixed constitution that gives appropriate rights to all the elements within it. Machiavelli might even have read, and it seems that he must at least have heard of, Polybius's Book VI. For, as Arnaldo Momigliano showed in a typically learned essay,[30] manuscripts of it were available in Italy, although the first printed edition of this book did not appear until 1549. As Momigliano notes, Polybius' view of the Roman constitution was referred to in Bernardo Rucellai's *Liber de urbe Roma*, written before 1505. Machiavelli himself, however, could not read Greek, and no Latin translation had yet been published. We cannot exclude the possibility, indeed probability, of verbal reports of its contents having reached him or of his having had access to an unpublished Latin translation. So it remains tantalizingly uncertain whether Machiavelli's discussion of Rome was informed by Polybius's analysis or not. What is certain is that, in the *Discorsi*, he never refers to him by name.

He does, however, produce his own analysis of the different types of constitution in a way that might echo Polybius—but equally could reflect the medieval applications of Aristotle's characterizations of different types of state that depended on the availability of a Latin translation of the *Politics* and were themselves written in Latin (pp. 58–63). To my knowledge, Machiavelli's version was the first to be written in Italian.

Machiavelli begins with an exposition of the various possible types of state (where *stato* means something closer to "type of state" than just to "state":

Wishing thus to discourse of what were the orders (*ordini*) of the city of Rome and what accidents led to its perfection. I say that some who have written on republics say that in them is one of three states—called by them principality (*principato*), aristocrats (*ottimati*) and popular (*popolare*)—and that those who order a city should turn to one of these according as it appears to them more to the purpose. Some others, wiser according to the opinion of many, have the opinion that there are six types of government, of which three are the worst . . . For the principality easily becomes tyrannical (*tirannico*); the aristocrats with ease become a state of the few; the popular is without difficulty converted into the licentious. (I.2.2)

Machiavelli then turns (I.2.3–4) to an exposition, surely borrowed directly or indirectly from Polybius, of the sequence by which each type of constitution tends to degenerate into its worse form and then to the next type, explicitly using the concept of a cycle (*cerchio*). In this section, he is talking in the abstract and then comes (like Polybius again) to the case of Sparta. When he comes to Rome (I.2.7), his analysis is also cast in very Polybian terms. Useful laws had been passed by the kings, and after their expulsion, a "kingly" element remained in the form of the consuls, functioning alongside the Senate, thus producing a mixture of two elements, *principato* and *ottimati*. Then, when there was a popular reaction to the excesses of the aristocrats, tribunes of the plebs were appointed, producing a mixed constitution in which all three elements had their part:

Fortune was so favorable to it that although it passed from the government of kings and of aristocrats to that of the people, by the same degrees and for the same causes that have been discoursed of above, nonetheless it never took away all authority from kingly qualities so as to give it to the people. But, remaining mixed, it made a perfect republic, to which perfection it came through the disunion of the plebs and the Senate, as will be demonstrated at length in the next two chapters.

The following chapters represent Machiavelli's most concentrated thoughts on the significance of the model presented by the Roman Republic. For he argues, against an opinion that often was expressed in the ancient world itself, that the "tumults" that marked the early history of the Republic were not a sign of weakness but ultimately of strength. For, first, until the time of the Gracchi, the actual level of violence was very low; and second, the acquisition of rights by the people, whose aim was not to oppress but to avoid being oppressed themselves, meant that they had a means of expressing discontent, and hence a safety valve. Machiavelli, in fact, admits that ultimately the conventional account was correct, namely, that in the end, in the time of Marius and after, the popular element sought too much power, and the Republic was destroyed. Throughout, he sets the case of Rome against the traditional one of Sparta on the one hand and against the contemporary example of Venice on the other. Both had achieved greater stability than Rome, but at a cost. In each of these cases, stability was gained at the cost of expansion and the chance of greatness:

Considering thus all these things, one sees that it was necessary for the legislators of Rome to do one of two things if they wished Rome to stay quiet like the above-mentioned republics: either not employ the plebs in war, as did the Venetians, or not open the way to foreigners, as did the Spartans. They did both, which gave the plebs strength and increase and infinite opportunities for tumult. But if the Roman state had come to be quieter, this inconvenience would have followed: that it would also have been weaker because it cut off the way by which it could come to the greatness it achieved, so that if Rome wished to remove the causes of tumults, it removed too the causes of expansion. (I.6.3)

It is very relevant to Machiavelli's thought that he thinks above all of a "republic" that will engage the energies of its citizens, be active and aggressive, and above all employ its own citizens, not mercenaries, in its army. That was, as is obvious, the primary lesson to be learned from the history of the Roman Republic. But there was also a consequential need for a system of public accusation of those thought to have served the state ill, one that must involve not a small court of judges but the people as a whole. Again, the examples are ones from the legendary narrative of early Rome, Coriolanus, Camillus, and Manlius Capitolinus (I.6–8).

That was implicitly a reference to a very distinctive feature of the Roman Republic, namely, that the two very differently structured forms of popular assembly, the "assembly of centuries" (*comitia centuriata*) and "assembly of tribes" (*comitia tributa*), both briefly discussed already (pp. 18–20) also could function as mass-participation popular courts that could give criminal penalties. Machiavelli does not spell this out in any detail (less so even than Polybius in his brief pages on the working of the Republican system), and more generally it is noticeable that although he attaches the greatest importance to the broad principle that, as a condition of willing commitment to military service, the people should, as in Rome, have an established constitutional role, he never gives any detailed attention either to the principle of the majority vote or to the peculiar and distinctive structures within which Romans voted. The *Discorsi* can in no way be seen as a detailed study of Republican institutions. The purpose is rather the drawing of moral and social lessons as to what the conditions were that enabled Rome to draw on its "human resources" and thus achieve greatness (see III.31.4, quoted on p. 72).

Nonetheless, Machiavelli does see in the way in which the Republic had worked two features to which even Polybius had not (at least in the surviving part of the text) drawn attention. One was the scale of Roman manpower, achieved by absorbing whole populations into its citizenship (II.3); he might have discussed, but does not, the extremely important principle that Rome also contributed to this end by giving citizenship to freed slaves and their descendants. The other, which is discussed in chapter 4 (II.4), is the means Rome employed in relations with its allies in Italy. Machiavelli brings in for comparison a range of other ancient peoples—the Etruscans, Achaeans, Aetolians, Sparta, and Athens—and one contemporary example, the Swiss confederation. In effect, he sets up three models: the federation of equal cities, well designed for durability but not for expansion; treating other people not as partners but as subjects, as had Athens and Sparta, which leads rapidly to disaster; and the means practiced by Rome. For Rome both saw to the increase of its own population and treated its allies in Italy as partners—but "reserved to itself the seat of empire and the title of command." This method had been adopted by Rome alone.

Machiavelli again goes into no detail here and does not refer at this point, although he does in passing elsewhere, to Roman colonization,[31] which also had a marked effect on the structure of republican Italy. Only in one place, where he is discussing the capacity of different states to resist invasion, does he sum up the different elements that contributed to Roman forces. The lesson is drawn in relation to Hannibal's invasion of Italy and to Roman resistance: "All this arose from having the heart well armed and taking less account of the extremities. For the foundation of its state was the people of Rome, the other partner towns in Italy, and their colonies, from which they drew so many soldiers that with them they were able to combat and hold the world" (II.30.4).

The Roman political and military system in Italy, which corresponded neither to a confederation nor (at this moment) to a unified national state (compare pp. 162–63 to follow), but was the essential precondition for the impact of the Republic on the history of the world, would indeed deserve attention from students of comparative institutions. As so often, Machiavelli does see the essentials but is not concerned to explore the details.

It will be evident by now how distinctive a choice of subject matter Machiavelli made, namely, a patriotic narrative covering the semihistorical and semilegendary history of the early Republic, as well as how focused and limited his essential object was, namely, to read off from that narrative lessons concerning the necessary preconditions for the achievement of political and military vitality by the Italian city-states of his own day, Florence itself above all. It will not be necessary to explore all the details of his use of this material, which frequently focused on the fortunes of the major protagonists, such as Camillus or Coriolanus, as represented in dramatic episodes. So it remains only to stress that, whereas Machiavelli sees the laws that gave freedom to the plebs as essential to such stability as the Republic achieved, he sees the ultimate cause of its dissolution as having been what he calls generically "the agrarian law" (*la legge agraria*), by which he means any law for the distribution to individuals of land in the possession of the state; for well-ordered republics must keep the public treasury rich and their citizens poor (I.37.1). The effects took a long time to make themselves felt because the earliest agrarian law to which he implicitly alludes belonged, according to Livy's narrative, to 486 B.C. But Machiavelli sees this issue as the one that led to the Gracchi, then Marius, and in the end to Caesar (I.37). Later Machiavelli returns to this cause and adds another one, namely, the prolongation of military commands after the end of an individual's completion of a year of elective office, which as he notes first happened with Publilius Philo (in 326 B.C.). The lesson that Machiavelli draws from the further extension of this practice is perceptive, if by now entirely conventional:

> Although started by the Senate for public utility, that thing was what in time made Rome servile. For the farther the Romans went abroad with arms, the more such extension appeared necessary to them and the more they used it. That thing produced two inconveniences: one, that a lesser number of men were practiced in commands, and because of this they came to restrict reputation to a few; the other, that when a citizen remained commander of an army for a very long time, he would win it over to himself and make it partisan to him, for the army would in time forget the Senate and recognize that head. Because of this, Sulla and Marius could find soldiers who would follow them against the public good; because of this, Caesar could seize the fatherland. For if the Romans had never prolonged magistracies and commands, if they would not have come so soon to so much power, and if their acquisitions had been later, they would have come later still to servitude. (III.24)

Here, as in many places, Machiavelli steps outside the bounds of his central subject matter and draws general historical and moralizing historical conclusions that relate to the whole history of the Republic; but that, it should be stressed, is the nature of his thought and the character of his contribution. It is only in a very general way that he is interested in actual institutions. So, although he knows it had been the Senate that was recorded as having given an extension of his command to Publilius Philo in 326 B.C., he does not note that by Caesar's time it had been the people, exercising their sovereign rights, who had overridden this by now customary function of the Senate and had taken it into their own hands to vote on long-term commands.

Enormously important as Machiavelli's *Discorsi* were later to become, and fascinating as are his reflections on past and present on every page, the very special character and the limits of the enterprise have to be borne in mind. His material was a literary narrative dealing with a remote and semihistorical past; and his object was to evoke from it the model of a republic with an active citizenry, who would also bear arms. He was not in intention a student of institutions, and he hardly concerned himself with how in practice the voting rights of the Roman citizen were exercised. The early sixteenth century could be seen as the last moment in the history of Europe when there both were city-states that could aspire to military independence and to constitutional self-government in a style analogous to that of Republican Rome and also left a legacy of theoretical discussions of the issues involved that themselves were to be influential in the very different circumstances of the established monarchic nation-state of the seventeenth century and after. But before we look at this much-altered world, it is worth mentioning one implicit response to the ideas in Machiavelli's *Discorsi*, namely, the *Dialogue on the Government of Florence*, written by Machiavelli's famous contemporary, Francesco Guicciardini, a few years later, in 1521 to 1524.[32] Most of this very interesting exchange, whose dramatic date is 1494, just after the fall of the Medici, is closely tied to Florentine history and institutions. One substantial section of Book II takes issue with Machiavelli's proposition that the "tumults" that marked the early history of the Republic had been beneficial. Support for this view is put in the mouth of Guicciardini's father, who then is answered by Bernardo del Nero, who discourses in some detail, on early Roman history, the distinction between patricians and plebeians and the fact that a plebeian reaction and demand for power had been provoked in the early Republic by patrician excesses. On this view, it was only the excellence of the army, as already instituted by the kings, that saved the city. What the plebeian reaction led to was the excessive power of the tribunes, not merely their negative rights but their positive power to initiate legislation. Indeed, this was a crucial feature of the Roman system, both as regards the right of initiative by the tribunes and in the sovereign power of the people to vote on laws. Guicciardini, in the mouth of Bernardo del Nero, expounds this important aspect of the Roman constitution much more clearly than Machiavelli ever does:

For the authority they enjoyed singly and jointly to bring laws before the people was pernicious, in view of the fact that the people aren't sufficiently able, and cities are ruined by taking important decisions to them before they have been digested in a maturer place. The same is true of their powers concerning the public assemblies, from which I would absolutely want to exclude the people—if not from those held by the magistrates, or by their order, to persuade them of something already decided on by the senate. If you read Livy and the other writers, you will know how often the city was upset by the assemblies of the tribunes and the laws taken by them before the people—during the last years of the Gracchi, the dominance of Marius, the tyranny of Sulla and the excessive power of Pompey: all these evils were introduced through the instrument of this magistracy. And although the consuls had the same right to call assemblies and propose laws, they rarely used them, for as members of the senate it seems less fitting to them to do so than the tribunes, who were paid for this; and when they did so, the plebs did not trust them like the tribunes, who were their officers and were entitled to look after the interests of the plebs.[33]

Guicciardini's *Dialogue* cannot be claimed to have exercised any wider influence, since it was first published only in the nineteenth century, but it may serve as an indication of the attitudes that were to prevail in the following centuries. Insofar as anyone recognized that the Republic had indeed been a direct democracy, in which most legislation was proposed by tribunes, and the people meeting in assembly were sovereign, they took this as a dangerous model to be avoided. Even Machiavelli, whose emphasis on citizen participation and service was indeed to be very influential, had not in fact placed much emphasis on the popular voting of laws.

4   Three Views from Seventeenth-Century England

Introduction

Machiavelli and his contemporary Guicciardini might be seen as the last major contributors to debates on republicanism who were writing in the context of what in their lifetime still had been, at least at a certain period (A.D. 1494–1512), an independent self-governing city-state, not dominated by any single ruler or single dynasty. In that sense, they could feel a direct connection with the early Roman Republic and the lessons that might be drawn from its history, in a way that would never be possible again. It is true that there did remain on the European scene one example of a independent republic, governed by a broad oligarchy, but still a republic, namely, Venice, which kept its independence and its constitution until the arrival of Napoleon's forces in 1797. So far as I can discover, Venice, although often referred to—in positive or negative terms—by writers from outside, produced no examples of political writing of its own that have entered the mainstream of political thought.[1]

The conventional story of the history of republican thought—which by definition is what matters—sees instead a progression from Machiavelli to the literature of seventeenth-century England, in two very different forms. The one, represented above all by Hobbes's *Leviathan*, takes for granted the existence of the nation-state, or territorial state with a sovereign, and asks what are the bases of the relation between the private individual and the state. The other, which is much more relevant to the themes discussed in this book and the use made of the image of the Roman Republic in political thought, arises out of the English Revolution and the setting up of the Commonwealth, advocates a republic marked by citizen rights and citizen participation, and asks (at least in the case of James Harrington's truly remarkable work, *The Commonwealth of Oceana*) what institutional structures would be necessary for such a republic to work.[2] In a very striking way, Harrington's *Oceana* represents the only example of a systematic attempt to imagine how the institutions of the Roman Republic could be transformed (sometimes out of all recognition) to function as those of a republic that was also an extensive territorial state: namely, England itself, "Oceana," with "Marpesia" (Scotland) and "Panopea" (Ireland) functioning, as ever, as awkward and anomalous attachments.

James Harrington is in many ways the most original and surprising of all the political thinkers (not many indeed, in any case) who have devoted serious thought to which aspects of the Roman Republic were worthy of imitation or development. So, particularly given that this book derives from lectures given in Jerusalem (the capital of an independent republic whose citizen army would surely have earned Machiavelli's approval), it may be worth noting that Harrington was the first to suggest one of the major themes of Zionism, that Jews might return to being farmers. It is true that he does so in not wholly sympathetic terms, and that the particular suggestion he makes is of an acutely unfortunate character, namely, the use of Jews as colonists in Ireland. Nonetheless, his observations on this point will serve to give a foretaste of the remarkable originality of his mind. He is speaking of "Panopea, the soft mother of a slothful and pusillanimous people." Because the country was no use for providing soldiers, it should be organized so as to provide a revenue for Oceana:

Which in my opinion (if it had been thought upon in time) might have been best done by planting it with Jews, allowing them their own rites and laws, for that would have brought them suddenly from all parts of the world, and in sufficient numbers; and though the Jews be now altogether for merchandise, yet in the land of Canaan (since their exile from whence they have not been landlords) they were altogether for agriculture; and there is no cause why a man should doubt but, having a fruitful country and good ports too, they would be good at both. Panopea well peopled would be worth a matter of four millions dry rents, that is besides the advantage of the agriculture and trade, which in a nation of that industry comes at least unto as much more.[3]

To turn from Machiavelli to English political thought, and essentially to works published in the decade after the execution of Charles I in 1649, is of course to follow the track laid down in the major modern work that dominates the study of this period, J. G. A. Pococke's *The Machiavellian Movement: Florentine Political Thought and the Atlantic Republican Tradition*. As the title implies, it follows the evolution of republican ideas from Machiavelli to the American Revolution. The other major corpus of work essential to the period is a series of studies of republicanism by Quentin Skinner.[4] The discussion that follows, focused as always on the specific question of the use made of the image of the Roman Republic in the works of the writers concerned, takes these profoundly illuminating major modern works for granted.

So far as the greatest and most original contribution to political thought from seventeenth-century England is concerned, Hobbes's *Leviathan* of 1651, we need not delay long.[5] For the fundamental argument of the work, namely, the necessity of a state with a recognized sovereign for the control of the "state of nature," and hence for the liberty and security of the subject, inevitably turns the model provided by the Republic into a negative one. Hobbes is of course familiar with the by now conventional Aristotelian division of "commonwealths" into monarchy, aristocracy, and democracy, while asserting the superiority of monarchy (II.19). He is also fully aware of the theory that had laid down that England had exhibited a mixed constitution in which sovereign power had been—and had properly been—divided between King, Lords, and Commons (the division that in the next century Montesquieu was to admire, p. 109 to follow). But he saw this division as precisely the factor which had led to civil war (II.18.6).

In Hobbes's view, therefore, no weight was to be given to positive political rights or to the idea that "tumults" might actually be necessary for these rights to be established and protected. Hence he is able, in magnificently scornful style, to dismiss the claim that ancient Greece and Rome could offer valid models of liberty. His thought here closely anticipates that of the famous lecture by Benjamin Constant comparing the "liberty of the ancients" to that of the moderns (p. 132 to follow). Hobbes writes:

The liberty, whereof there is so frequent, and honourable mention, in the histories, and philosophy of the ancient Greeks, and Romans, and in the writings, and discourse of those that from them have received all their learning in the politics, is not the liberty of particular men; but the liberty of the commonwealth: which is the same with that, which every man then should have, if there were no civil laws, nor commonwealth at all.

And the effects of it also be the same. For as amongst masterless men, there is perpetual war, of every man against his neighbor; no inheritance, to transmit to the son, nor to expect from the father; no propriety of goods, or lands; no security; but a full and absolute liberty in every particular man: so in states, and commonwealths not dependent on one another, every commonwealth, (not every man) has an absolute liberty, to do what it shall judge (that is to say, what that man, or assembly that representeth it, shall judge) most conducing to their benefit. But withal, they live in the condition of a perpetual war, and upon the confines of battle, with their frontiers armed, and cannons planted against their neighbors round about. The Athenians, and Romans were free; that is, free commonwealths: not that any particular men had the liberty to resist their own representative; but that their representative had the liberty to resist, or invade other people. There is written on the turrets of the city of Lucca in great characters at this day, the word LIBERTAS; yet no man can thence infer, that a particular man has more liberty, or immunity from the service of the commonwealth there, than in Constantinople. Whether a commonwealth be monarchical, or popular, the freedom is still the same. (II.21.8)

In the next paragraph, Hobbes sets out to argue that ancient political thought, both Greek and Roman, had been taken wrongly as a model for the present, both because it originated in a different context, namely "popular states," and because it encouraged conflict and challenge to authority:

In these western parts of the world, we are made to receive our opinions concerning the institution, and rights of commonwealths, from Aristotle, Cicero, and other men, Greeks and Romans, that living under popular states, derived those rights, not from the principles of nature, but transcribed them into their books, out of the practice of their own commonwealths, which were popular . . . And as Aristotle; so Cicero, and other writers have grounded their civil doctrine, on the opinions of the Romans, who were taught to hate monarchy, at first, by them that having deposed their sovereign, shared amongst them the sovereignty of Rome; and afterwards by their successors. And by reading of these Greek, and Latin authors, men from their childhood have gotten a habit (under a false show of liberty,) of favouring tumults, and of licentious controlling the actions of their sovereigns; and again of controlling those controllers; with the effusion of so much blood; as I think I may truly say, there was never any thing so dearly bought, as these western parts have bought the learning of the Greek and Latin tongues. (II.21.9)

Hobbes returns later to the divisions caused in Rome by the idea of the sharing of sovereignty between Senate and people (II.29.4) and to the damaging character of classical notions about the acceptability of killing tyrants (II.29.14). But by the nature of the "commonwealth" that he envisages, and by the tenor of his overall argument, he never has occasion to explore either the institutions or the history of the Republic in any detail. To Hobbes, the place that the history of Greece and Rome (in which he himself was steeped) occupied in the consciousness of educated men could lead only to profoundly damaging lessons for the present. By contrast, in the following years, three other men drew quite different lessons for the present from the model provided by the Roman Republic.

Marchamont Nedham

In the year or two after publication of the *Leviathan*, a completely different lesson was to be drawn from the history of the Republic in the articles published by Marchamont Nedham in *Mercurius Politicus* and later (in 1656) collected and republished in book form in his splendid exposition of republican values, *The Excellency of a Free State*. It must remain a mystery to any nonspecialist why this classic defense of the necessity of positive political rights can be read now only in the edition published in London in 1767.[6] Reference will be to the page numbers of this edition.

Highly readable and evocative as the work is, we need not dwell on it at great length. For although its author's conception of the Republic is fundamental to the work throughout, its character as a collection of previously published articles shows through in the high level of repetition. He also treats hardly any of the institutions of the Republic in any detail; furthermore, in a way that is typical, he tends to take his examples either from the legendary history of the early Republic of the fifth century B.C. or from the fortunes of the familiar protagonists of the struggles of the last century, Sulla, Pompey, and Caesar. As is so often the case, the (more or less) fully historical Republic of the first half of the second century B.C., at the height of its (relative) internal concord and external prestige, plays very little part.

Nonetheless, Nedham's work must represent the most emphatic statement of the proposition that both sovereignty and effective power must reside in the people and that the best model for that state of affairs was the Roman Republic. Nedham is well aware of his predecessors, quoting (p. xxv) both the familiar passage of Sallust (*Catiline* 7) on the greatness the Roman people attained after expulsion of the kings and Guicciardini on the effect of a "free state" both on attention to the common good and on personal virtue. Machiavelli too is quoted: "It was a noble saying (although Machiavel's) 'Not he that placeth a virtuous government in his own hands, or family; but he that establisheth a free and lasting form, for the people's constant security, is most to be commended'" (p. xxiv). Contemporary parallels are also brought in: Venice might be a "free state," but the people were in fact little better than slaves (p. xvi); Florence, even when it seemed most free, "could never quite shake off the interest of monarchy"; when freedom is gained, people become magnanimous and courageous—witness the Swiss and the Dutch and even (briefly) "our own nation" (p. 28); the legislative and executive function must be separated—but "only Genoa remains as a free posture, by keeping the power of legislation only in their supreme assemblies, and leaving the execution of law in a titular duke and a council" (pp. 151–52). This lesson had been ignored by the late king of England (Charles I) who should have played the role of an officer in trust to see to the execution of the laws:

But by aiming at the same ends which Lewis (Louis XI of France) attained, and straining, by the ruin of parliaments, to reduce the legislative power, as well as the executive into his own hands, he, instead of an absolute tyranny, which might have followed his project, brought a swift destruction upon himself and his family. (p. 153)

Nedham's work is thus essentially controversial political journalism, aimed at present circumstances, and drawing in contemporary and historical examples. Nonetheless, it is striking how fundamental to his thought the Roman Republic is, as the model of a "free state," in which the people exercised not merely a formal sovereignty, but a specific set of constitutional rights:

The best way to determine this (the means of preserving liberty), is by observation out of Roman stories; whereby it plainly appears, that the people never had any real liberty, till they were possessed of the power of calling and dissolving the supreme assemblies, changing governments, enacting and repealing laws, together with a power of chusing and deputing whom they pleased to this work, as often as they should judge expedient, for their own well-being, and the good of the public. (pp. xiv–v)

Nedham exaggerates the people's power at certain points here, as (for instance) the right to summon assemblies had always lain with elected officeholders. His observations are indeed cast in general terms and represent lessons drawn from the narrative history of the Republic rather than from any precise knowledge of constitutional details. So he returns repeatedly to the story of the Decemviri, who had attempted in the mid-fifth century to concentrate power in their own hands (e.g., pp. xix, 101, 161), or he uses the story of Coriolanus to show that civil strife had been avoided only because the tribunes could promise the people that a popular trial would be held (pp. 74–5). As he later expresses it, in more general terms, "it is the secret of Liberty, that all magistrates, and public officers, be kept in an accountable state, liable to render an account of their behaviour and actions; and also, that the people have freedom to accuse whom they please" (pp. 132–33). It was also a fundamental principle, which he reinforces with a succession of Roman examples, not to permit the continuation of office by individuals or within families (pp. 107–11).

It is not necessary to explore in more detail the principles that Nedham sets out, which begin from the proposition that sovereignty must reside in the people, who are the best defenders of their own liberty (p. 2). He also returns several times to the familiar theme of Machiavelli, that freedom is necessary for a state to achieve greatness (e.g., p. 15) and that it must train its own citizens in military skills (pp. 114–16).

Although Nedham quite clearly intended his ideas to be directly relevant to the choices facing England during the Commonwealth and then Cromwell's Protectorate, he does not treat the institutions of the Roman Republic in any precise way, and a fortiori does not draw any deductions from them as to constitutional structures that might be adopted in the present. His work remains an impressive statement of general principles, fleshed out and informed by his historical reading.

Harrington's Commonwealth

The case is very different with James Harrington's The Commonwealth of Oceana of 1656, also published, like the book version of Nedham's work, under the Protectorate. As noted (p. 81), this work seems to be unique among all reflections on the Roman Republic in taking it not merely as offering general principles (of a mixed constitution or as representing popular sovereignty or the virtues of a citizen army) but as having embodied institutions that could be used for the construction of a new constitutional order in the present.

Like Nedham, Harrington, about whom not much is known of his life story,[7] wrote on the basis of wide reading: in the Bible, in classical history and thought, and in Italian republican thought, for example quoting (p. 8) Gianotti's *Libro della repubblica de' Veniziani*, published in 1540.[8] He also quotes Francis Bacon (pp. 3–4) and repeatedly refers to Machiavelli, quoting the *Discorsi* in translation (e.g., p. 15), and reacting also to Hobbes' *Leviathan*, and not least to Hobbes's remarks (p. 83 above) to the effect that the freedom enjoyed by a citizen of Lucca was no different from that enjoyed in Constantinople. Harrington's comment summarizes some of the fundamentals of his notion of a participatory property-owning democracy with a constitutional framework:

For to say that a Lucchese hath no more liberty or immunity from the laws of Lucca than a Turk hath from those of Constantinople, and to say that a Lucchese hath no more liberty or immunity by the laws of Lucca than a Turk hath by those of Constantinople, are pretty different speeches. The first may be said of all governments alike, the second scarce of any two; much less of these, seeing it is known that whereas the greatest bashaw is a tenant, as well of his head as of his estate, at the will of his lord, the meanest Lucchese that hath land is a freeholder of both, and not to be controlled but by the law; and that framed by every private man unto no other end (or they may thank themselves) than to protect the liberty of every private man, which by that means comes to be the liberty of the commonwealth. (p. 20)

As for ancient evidence on which to draw, Harrington inevitably uses Aristotle and Livy, as well as the Bible (Old Testament), but specifically quotes also Polybius on the working of the Roman levy (p. 208), as well as Cicero's *De Republica* (p. 14) and his speech *In Defence of Flaccus* (p. 149) for the view that Greek cities were damaged by the uncontrolled nature of their popular assemblies. But Harrington immediately comments that Cicero should have made an exception of Sparta and that contemporary Venice was another counterexample, namely, a constitutional republic where the "great council" met to vote but did not debate. As we will see, Harrington's very detailed plan for a constitution for "Oceana" is in essence that of representative democracy, with rights, but limited positive participation, for its citizens.

As indicated earlier, the geographic context of Harrington's proposed commonwealth is Great Britain, with the essential role being played by England ("Oceana"), with Ireland, as we have seen (p. 81), settled by Jews engaging in both agriculture and trade and producing a large revenue, and with "Marpesia" (Scotland) providing a supply of soldiers. This commonwealth, first brought together by "Morpheus the Marpesian" (James I), but then riven by civil war, could become a "commonwealth for increase," compared with the static condition of Venice (a "commonwealth for preservation") if certain principles of government were followed (pp. 5–7).

Not every detail of Harrington's elaborate system (which in its more detailed sections does become somewhat tedious) need be followed here. But we do need both to look at its basic principles and at the way in which he, more than any other political writer before or since, *uses* what he understands to be the institutions of the Roman Republic and deploys them in designing a commonwealth on a geographic scale much larger than that of an ancient city-state. This transition is not so difficult for Harrington as it might seem. First, his commonwealth is to rest on a citizenry of landowners, and very early in the work (p. 5) he quotes Aristotle (*Pol.* VI.4) in Latin for the proposition that a democratic commonwealth of farmers is best (*agricolarum democratia respublica optima*). Equally, he says, Rome always valued those who belonged to the "rustic" tribes more highly. Moreover, he is aware that the spread of Roman colonization throughout Italy was "the best way of propagating herself and naturalizing the country" (p. 16). By implication, although he does not refer to the steps by which in the late Republic the whole of Italy had gained the Roman citizenship (p. 151 to follow), he is aware that the citizenry of the Roman "commonwealth" itself had been spread widely over the country. He also returns to Roman colonization in Italy later (pp. 221–24) in following up and commenting on Machiavelli's remarks in *Discorsi* II.4 (p. 75 preceding) on the three methods by which a commonwealth may come to control others: by straight domination, by equal leagues, and (as with Rome) by unequal leagues, or in other words by the combination, within republican Italy, of colonization and settlement, leaving non-Roman communities to be self-governing but under an obligation to supply troops. Unlike Machiavelli, he discusses, also, grants of citizenship without the vote and the form of half-citizenship known as "Latin rights" (p. 223).

Harrington was thus correct in assuming that Republican Italy was not in fact a wholly inappropriate and remote model for a prospective commonwealth of Oceana. Several principles are to underlie his commonwealth. First, it is to be marked by a broad distribution of property, so that the few may not dominate the many. Harrington is of course familiar with Machiavelli's deployment of the Aristotelian categories of monarchy, aristocracy, and democracy and their respective corrupted forms, and he takes a balance between the few and the many as being the essential condition for a commonwealth (a conception rather close to Aristotle's notion of a *politeia*, in the special sense of a balanced constitution in which no one element predominates). The distribution of property is the key: "And if the whole people be landlords, or hold the lands so divided among them, that no one man, or number of men, within the compass of the few or aristocracy, overbalance them, the empire (without the interposition of force) is a commonwealth" (p. 12). Second, it is to be "the empire of laws not of men," in short, the conception that Aristotle and Livy had represented, which the medieval kingdoms had obliterated, which Machiavelli had "gone about to retrieve," and which Hobbes in the *Leviathan* had sought to subvert (pp. 8, 9).

Third, in contradiction to Hobbes, the commonwealth is to be conceived of as resting on an agreement in which sovereignty resides with the assembly of the people and in which any council or individual officeholder, if granted power by the people, will not become sovereign but will exercise power conditionally. This principle can be shown to have been at work in early Roman history; otherwise, once the Decemviri had gained power, the people could not legally have deposed them (p. 14).

When he comes in more detail to the constitutional structure of the proposed commonwealth, Harrington both draws constantly on Roman vocabulary and applies what he takes to be the fundamental principles of the Roman Republic. These principles are that there should be a council of wise men to deliberate on affairs of state, but *not* to legislate; for, as in Rome, the role of the council, or senate, was to offer advice, but it is the people who legislate:

Wherefore the office of the senate is not to be commanders but counselors of the people; and that which is proper unto counselors is first to debate the business whereupon they are to give advice, and afterward to give advice in the business whereupon they have debated; whence the decrees of the senate are never laws, nor so called, but *senatusconsulta*, and these, being maturely framed, it is their duty *ferre ad populum*, to propose in the case unto the people. Wherefore the senate is no more than the debate of the commonwealth. (p. 23)

Whether Harrington's expression "the *debate* (meaning the deliberative body) of the commonwealth" would have seemed puzzling to his contemporaries, I do not know; but he has grasped the essential truth about the Republican Senate, that it was not a legislative body. Who then should legislate? Here he brings into play his unique procedure of actively *using* the model presented by Rome, but being prepared to readjust it to the circumstances of Oceana. So the power to choose or decide must rest with a body that embodies the whole commonwealth. Given that now we are speaking of the whole nation, the principle of representation must come in, in a way in which in Rome it did not:

Nor is there any remedy but to have another council to choose. The wisdom of the few may be the light of mankind, but the interest of the few is not the profit of mankind, nor of a commonwealth; wherefore, seeing we have granted interest to be reason, they must not choose, lest it put out their light; but as the council dividing consisteth of the wisdom of the commonwealth, so the assembly or council choosing should consist of the interest of the commonwealth. As the wisdom of the commonwealth is in the aristocracy, so the interest of the commonwealth is in the whole body of the people, and whereas this, in case the commonwealth consist of an whole nation, is too unwieldy a body to be assembled, this council is to consist of such a representative as may be equal, and so constituted as can never contract any other interest than that of the whole people; the manner whereof, being such as is best shown by exemplification, I remit unto the model. (p. 24)

As Harrington indicates, the composition of this representative body is to be considered later, and we will look at it subsequently, for the moment, he turns to laying down the third element, namely that there should be an executive, but one operating within the constraints of law: "as the hand of the magistrate is the executive power of the law, so the head of the magistrate is answerable into the people that his execution be according to the law" (p. 25).

Having laid down the basic principles, he turns to some historical examples, beginning with the "commonwealth of Israel" as visible in the Old Testament. Rome does not figure here except in a brief paragraph which, as so often, shows how clearly he has perceived how the Republican system worked and how prepared he is to distance himself from it: "Rome consisted of the senate proposing, the *concio* or people resolving and too often debating, which caused her storms; as also of the consuls, censors, aediles, tribunes, praetors, quaestors, and other magistrates executing" (p. 29). In other words, he has seen that at Rome, although the formal assemblies (*comitia*) simply voted yes or no, without debate, on propositions put to them, the people could and did meet in *contiones* ("gatherings"), at which there was actual debate, or at least speeches expressing contrary points of view. That aspect of Roman public life Harrington proposes firmly to reject, and in that sense his commonwealth might be seen as less democratic in intended character than the Roman Republic itself.

At the conclusion of this section, Harrington comes back to giving another version of the three principles of an "equal commonwealth" (pp. 33–4): first, one that by an appropriate distribution of landed property prevents one man or a few from dominating the rest; second, rotation of office; and third, free and secret voting. Here Harrington appositely quotes Cicero in his speech *In Defence of Plancius* (p. 16), when the necessities of the case he was arguing caused him to utter an uncharacteristically democratic sentiment: "the (secret) voting tablet is welcome to the people, in that it reveals their faces but conceals their intentions, and gives them the freedom to do what they wish." As we will see later (p. 164), the passing of a series of ballot laws in the 130s B.C. had in fact represented between them an important moment in the securing of popular rights. Cicero had not always expressed himself so favorably when speaking of this great change.

In the second section of his work, Harrington begins with a discussion of the factors that led to the establishment of the imperial system at Rome, and then he goes on to medieval monarchy and to the history and government of England as a kingdom. From there, he leads on (p. 67) to the declaration of Cromwell as Lord Protector (with observations on the remark of Machiavelli in *Discorsi* I.2, that a single legislator may be needed to set a republic on the right basis), and from there, to his imaginary commonwealth of Oceana, presented as if it were the work of a council of legislators set up by Cromwell.

The "model" of the commonwealth begins with a survey of

three comparable historical (or to be more precise mythical) examples: the organization of the people of Israel by Moses; that of Sparta by Lycurgus, as represented in Plutarch's *Life*; and the structuring of the early Roman community, "or those parts of it which are comprised in the first and second books of Livy" (pp. 72–3). These books cover the regal period and the early decades of the Republic, down to 468 B.C. That Harrington should have chosen as the historical models for his commonwealth political structures that in all three cases owe their existence to literary representations written centuries later is a perfect example of the power of texts in the history of political thought.

Of the three models, however, it is the Roman one that receives detailed attention in the three pages that follow (pp. 73–5). First, he looks at the original division of the Roman citizens into *curiae* ("parishes") and notes that the "assembly of *curiae*" (*comitia curiata*) formally appointed the kings, validated laws, and had capital jurisdiction. After that, he recalls the subsequent effective replacement of the *comitia curiata* by the "assembly of centuries" (*comitia centuriata*), structured on a voting sequence dependent on wealth (pp. 19–20 preceding), and then creation of the "assembly of tribes" (*comitia tributa*), "being a council where the people in exigencies made laws without the senate, which laws were called *plebiscita*." Harrington was a republican, but not by any means a democrat, and he takes this institution as a sign of anarchy. The section concludes with brief remarks on voting procedures, in which he amalgamates the earlier period of open voting with the later one of a secret vote by wooden voting tablet, a major democratizing step in the 130s (see p. 164 to follow). In any case, what is important is Harrington's focus on the divisions of the citizenry and on their capacity to vote. He then adds two further principles, both derived from the tradition about Rome: that the army of the commonwealth should be made up of citizens and that they should be divided into horse and foot by wealth.

Harrington then launches into a long, detailed account of how deputies from each parish should be elected, and from them, by a meeting of deputies from one hundred parishes, an additional set of deputies for hundreds would be elected, twenty "hundreds" making a *tribe*. Oceana thus would be divided into ten thousand parishes, one thousand "hundreds," and fifty "tribes." The details of all this are not drawn from Roman practice and need not be followed here, except to note that within it civil and military functions are to be performed in parallel, and that it amounts to a three-tiered system of representative government.

In this system, each tribe has a council that Harrington, very oddly, called a *phylarch* or *prerogative troop* (oddly, because *phylarchos* in Greek is a term for an individual official, whereas *praerogativa* is used in Latin for the century chosen by lot to vote first in the Roman "assembly of centuries"—so both terms are wrenched out of context). At any rate, this body is to act as the representative council of the tribe.

Each tribe then produces by election two "knights" who are to serve for three years, each in the Senate of Oceana, and seven deputies who are to do the same in what the author calls the "prerogative tribe or equal representative of the people," in other words a *parliament*.

The two fundamental principles are then repeated (p. 100): rules controlling the distribution of landed property and limiting extremes of inequality; and use of the ballot. The entire system is to be based on election by secret ballot, producing tiers of representation from parish to "hundred" to tribe to Senate and "prerogative tribe"—"commonly called the people" (p. 118). There is no place in it for a hereditary nobility. Instead, the division between Senate and *people*, or *prerogative tribe*, is functional. The Senate is to debate and may pass decrees if they fall within the existing law; otherwise, they require the assent of the representatives of the people. It may be worth quoting the section of the imaginary law code in which this is laid down, both to catch the flavor of Harrington's stilted prose, whose exact meaning is often far from easy to follow, and to see the way in which he has transferred elements of Roman terminology into the very different context of his imaginary commonwealth:

> This in case the debate conclude not in a decree; but if a decree be passed, it is either in matter of state, or government according to law enacted already, and then it is good without going any farther; or it is in matter of law to be enacted, repealed or amended, and then the decree of the senate, especially if it be for a war, or for levy of men or money, is invalid without the result of the commonwealth, which is in the prerogative tribe, or representative of the people. (p. 135)

In imagining this system, he is in fact mirroring a fundamental aspect of the Roman system whereby the Senate could debate and pass decrees, but only the people could legislate. The difference here is that *the people* are a preselected representative body; but in the Roman Republic, any citizen had in principle the right to come to vote.

Harrington later reflects at length on the history of the early Roman Republic and on the conflict between patricians and plebeians, comparing Rome with Venice, paraphrasing (p. 155) a section of Machiavelli's *Discorsi* I.6. Then he comes back to emphasizing the necessity of popular rights on the one hand, but the need for these to be mediated through a representative system on the other. This was especially necessary when the commonwealth was an extensive national state:

> Wherefore, go which way you will, it should seem that, without a representative of the people, your commonwealth consisting of an whole nation can never avoid falling either into oligarchy or confusion. This was seen by the Romans, whose rustic tribes, extending themselves from the river Arno unto the Vulturnus, that is from Fesulae or Florence unto Capua, invented a way of representative by lots; the tribe upon which the first fell being the prerogative, and some two or three more that had the rest, the *iure vocatae*. These gave the suffrage of the commonwealth *binis comitiis*; the prerogative at the first assembly, and the *iure vocatae* at a second. (pp. 164–65)

Harrington's remarks are typical of his combination of exceptional perception in essentials with occasional confusion over details. It was indeed precisely the spread of its citizens over a large part of central Italy that gave Rome, with the institutions of a nuclear city-state, so distinctive a character as a republic. But the idea that they solved the problem by selecting a tribe by lot *in advance* to come to vote first, and in some way represent the whole citizen body, is a complete confusion. In fact, the lot was drawn on the day of voting and related to the "assembly of centuries." The "prerogative tribe" in the Roman system was the century of *iuniores* (men of fighting age) from one of the thirty-five tribes, selected by lot to vote first.[9] The origins and purpose of this process are obscure; but certainly this process was not a means of dealing with the problems of the geographic extension of the citizenry. Nonetheless, as we saw earlier (p. 88), Harrington's awareness of this aspect of the Roman Republic is so crucial to his confidence that its essential features could be re-deployed for a large-scale commonwealth in the present. The Roman *tribus* had been divisions of the citizens both by locality and by voting units.

It is not necessary in this context to explore further the many passing observations on the lessons to be drawn from Roman history that Harrington makes or to discuss the long passage (pp. 206–13) in which he lays down in detail, quoting Polybius at length, that the essential basis of the commonwealth must lie in the crucial feature of the Roman Republic, namely, military service by its citizens. But, to catch once again the tone of Harrington's prose, to see a further example of the way in which Roman terminology is re-deployed, and above all to understand the central role of representative government in his system, it is worth quoting the twenty-third clause of his imaginary constitution. The passage relates to the role of the proposed representative legislative assembly, or "prerogative tribe," in his system:

The twenty-third order: showing the power, function, and manner of proceeding of the prerogative tribe.

The power or function of the prerogative is of two parts: the one of result, in which it is the legislative power, the other of judicature, in which regard it is the highest court and the last appeal in this commonwealth.

For the former part, the people by this constitution being not obliged by any law that is not of their own making or confirmation by the result of the prerogative, their equal representative, it shall not be lawful for the senate to require obedience from the people, nor for the people to give due obedience unto the senate, in or by any law that hath not been promulgated or printed and published for the space of six weeks and afterwards proposed by the authority of the senate unto the prerogative tribe, and resolved by the major vote of the same in the affirmative. Nor shall the senate have any power to levy war, men or money, otherwise than by the consent of the people so given, or by a law so enacted, except in cases of exigence, in which it is agreed that the power, both of the senate and the people, shall be in the dictator, so qualified and for such a term of time as is according unto that constitution already prescribed. While a law is in promulgation the censors shall animadvert upon the senate, and the tribunes upon the people, that there be no laying of heads together, conventicles or canvassing to carry on or oppose anything, but that all may be done in a free and open way. (pp. 166–67)

The Commonwealth of Oceana, although it was known and commented on, had no immediate effect, and the Restoration of Charles II was to follow only four years after its publication. Monarchy and a hereditary aristocracy were to remain central to the British social and political system for the next three centuries, and are so still. Nonetheless, his work is of the greatest importance: in general terms as showing that it was possible to rethink the entire institutions of an extensive nation-state along republican lines, and to write a detailed constitution for it; and in relation to the Roman Republic as being by far the most detailed—if sometimes erratic—use of its institutions (far more detailed than by Machiavelli) to construct a feasible model for the present.

Milton's *Commonwealth*

One final proposal for a republican system in England may be briefly considered here, *The Readie and Easie Way to Establish a Free Commonwealth*, which John Milton published in two successive editions in the early part of 1660, in the face of growing expectations that Parliament would restore Charles II to the throne.[10] Milton had argued in a succession of works, of which the *Areopagitica* of 1644 is by far the most famous, for the freedom of speech and for the principle that all political power derives from the sovereign people. In his *Defence of the People of England*, originally published in Latin in 1651 to argue that it had been within the people's constitutional power to execute Charles I, he had for instance quoted Cicero's *In Defence of Plancius* (4.11) on the sovereignty of the Roman People, and he had commented that this had applied in "democratic" conditions, since the Lex Regia, by which power had been transferred to the Emperors (p. 53 preceding) had not yet been passed.[11] Sallust's much-quoted remark about the success of Rome after the expulsion of the kings comes in again, though with no mention of the source: "Did you not remember that the Romans had a most flourishing and glorious commonwealth after they had banished their kings?"[12]

Nonetheless, Milton had never previously argued for the establishment of a republic, or commonwealth, a case that was now put, as we have seen, in his *Readie and Easie Way*.[13] As always in medieval and early modern political thought, the proposal is set against a background of historical parallels culled from literature and (as so often) from the contemporary example of Venice. Milton's scheme is decidedly not for a popular democracy, but for a representative system based on the election of knights and burgesses to Parliament, to which sovereignty is "not transferred, but delegated only." Parliament is to be designated as a "grand council" and should be permanent, not subject to the summoning of successive Parliaments. It should also elect a "council of state" for urgent or confidential matters. Furthermore, the membership of this body, which he now turns to calling a "senate," should preferably be lifelong, except in case of criminal conviction. Milton does, however, contemplate the idea, but as a second best, that one third should retire in rotation (thus, of course, foreshadowing the system of the United States Senate).

That lifelong membership was preferable was suggested by parallel cases:

> Therefor among the *Jews*, the supreme councel of seaventie, call'd the *Sanhedrim*, founded by *Moses*, in *Athens*, that of *Areopagus*, in *Sparta*, that of the Ancients, in *Rome*, the Senat, consisted of members chosen for term of life; and by that means remaind as it were still the same to generations. In *Venice* they change indeed ofter then every year som particular councels of State, as that of six, or such other; but true Senat, which upholds and sustains the government, is the whole aristocracie immovable.[14]

Milton's preference is unambiguously for a system in which the sovereign power of the people is indeed acknowledged, but where its actual effect is essentially limited to the election of representatives with lifelong tenure. And he explicitly argues against following models expressing a balance of power, as in Athens, Sparta, or Rome and, indeed, without naming the author, argues against Harrington's proposal for a "prerogative tribe," whose assent would be required for the passing of legislation.

> It will be objected, that in those places where they had perpetual Senats, they had also popular remedies against thir growing too imperious; as in *Athens*, besides *Aeropagus*, another Senat of four or five hundred; in *Sparta*, the *Ephori*; in *Rome*, the Tribunes of the people. But the event tels us, that these remedies either little availd the people, or brought them to such a licentious and unbridl'd democratie, as in fine ruind themselves with thir own excessive power. So that the main reason urg'd why popular assemblies are to be trusted with the peoples libertie, rather then a Senat of principal men, because great men will be still endeavoring to inlarge thir power, but the common sort will be contented to maintain thir own libertie, is by experience found false; none being more immoderat and ambitious to amplifie thir power, then such popularities; which was seen in the people of *Rome*; who at first contended to have thir Tribunes, at length contended with the Senat that one Consul, then both; soon after, that the Censors and Praeters also should be created Plebeian, and the whole empire put into their hands; adoring lastly those, who most were advers to the Senat, till *Marius* by fulfilling thir inordinat desires, quite lost them all the power for which they had so long bin striving, and

left them under the tyrannie of *Sylla*: the ballance therefor must be exactly so set, as to preserve and keep up due authoritie on either side, as well in the Senat as in the people. And this annual rotation of a Senat to consist of three hundred, as is lately propounded, requires also another popular assembly upward of a thousand, with an answerable rotation. Which besides that it will be liable to all those inconveniencies found in the foresaid remedies, cannot but be troublesom and chargeable, both in thir motion and thir session, to the whole land; unweildie with thir own bulk, unable in so great a number to mature thir consultations as they ought, if any be allotted them, and that they meet not from so many parts remote to sit a whole year lieger in one place, only now and then to hold up a forrest of fingers, or to convey each man his bean or ballot into the box, without reason shewn or common deliberation; incontinent of secrets, if any be imparted to them, emulous and always jarring with the other Senat.[15]

It is interesting that Milton should have seen the Roman Republic as having developed into "a licentious and unbridled democracy," and that the whole tenor of his proposal is to aim for stability and for the delegation of power by the many to the well-qualified few. Nonetheless, he goes on to propose that there should be local assemblies in the chief town of each county.[16] When he returns to this proposal later, however, it too takes on a rather aristocratic coloring. For it is in the first instance the nobility and gentry from each region who should maintain residences in each main city, make laws, and exercise jurisdiction. They may, however, summon more general assemblies, empowered to express assent or dissent as regards laws (those affecting public liberty) made by the grand "council"; but the majority opinion of the counties shall prevail.[17]

Milton thus touches, if briefly, on arguments that were to be fundamental to the debate on the constitution of the United States and are very relevant to those (such as there are) on the European Union. He himself, however, is concerned to imagine a unitary sovereign commonwealth, which would allow for local representatives but not be victim to the divisions that marked the Dutch United Provinces:

In which happy firmness as in the particular above mentiond, we shall also far exceed the United Provinces, by having, not as they (to the retarding and distracting oft times of thir counsels or urgentest occasions), many Sovranties united in one Commonwealth, but many Commonwealths under one united and entrusted Sovrantie.[18]

In speaking of "many Commonwealths" as constituent elements of a sovereign state, Milton was expressing the view that a federal structure was necessary for political liberty.[19]

To Milton, therefore, the Roman Republic was, if anything, an example to be avoided, as giving too much uncontrolled power to the people. Harrington thus seems to be alone in having sought systematically to translate the positive features of the Roman system into the context of contemporary England. It would be more than a century before the construction of republican systems within extensive nation-states again became a live issue. In the interval, monarchies, whether tempered by representative institutions or not, held sway everywhere; but the models provided by Greek or Roman Antiquity were still present to the minds of all educated persons.

5 From Restoration to Revolution

England, France, and America

England

The period that culminates in the American and French Revolutions and in the creation of the constitution of the United States can properly be treated as a unity. From one point of view, the legacy of Machiavelli and of English republicanism was still active, even though in the century after the Restoration of Charles II, there was no real danger to monarchy. The British system of monarchy, Lords, and Commons might even be regarded as the perfect exemplar of a Polybian mixed constitution, but an actual republic was never in prospect there (and still is not). On the other hand, in all three countries, there is abundant evidence of political thought and debate, with influences readily crossing political boundaries. To say that the treatment here cannot even scratch the surface of a vast political literature of speeches, pamphlets, journalism and (above all in France) major works of political theory, or of subsequent discussions of them, is merely to state the obvious. Furthermore, it is also a statement of the obvious that in all three countries classical learning provided the foundations of education and that Roman history, stories drawn from it, and—but (as always) to a much lesser degree—the details of Roman institutions were familiar to all educated persons.[1]

The examples provided by Greece and Rome, whether monarchies or confederations or city-states or republics, would be bound to inform all political thinking, whether as models to be followed or as lessons to be avoided. On the other hand, taken individually, all three areas were characterized by considerable geographic extent and by large populations, and nowhere did anyone make any systematic attempt to imagine, as Harrington had, what a "Roman" republic, spread across an entire country, would be like, or still less to put such an idea into practice. As so often, it is J. G. A. Pocock who best sums up Harrington's imaginary republic: "Oceana is a dispersed *polis*, or rather a dispersed *comitia centuriata*, in which the county assemblies are at once assemblies of the electorate and musters of the militia."[2]

If no such conceptions were resurrected and put into practice in detail (and if Venice continued to provide the only familiar example of a stable constitutional republic with relatively wide, but still restricted, political rights), the central moral ideas of Machiavelli and Harrington continued to be influential: that is, the principle of political rights and political participation enjoyed by educated, adult male property-owners, often labeled *civic humanism*; and the counterpart of that, namely, that it should be these same citizens who should bear arms, and by doing so, both exhibit civic virtue and responsibility, and prevent the dangers of a standing professional army.

It was not until the last few decades of the eighteenth century that men found themselves in France unexpectedly constructing an actual republic out of the ruins of monarchy, or in America casting off the British monarchy and constructing a sovereign republican federal state out of thirteen existing states. Until those two historic moments arrived, "republican" thinking in relation to monarchy could take (to oversimplify drastically) one of two forms. First, it could be, and was, argued that even a monarchy, provided it functioned within a constitutional framework and was subject to the checks and balance provided by representative institutions, could be understood as a type of "republic." Second, there could be a vigorous stream of principled criticism of monarchic power, and of the influence of the court and its hangers-on, and warnings of the danger of a standing army under royal control. It was of course this stream in English eighteenth-century thought that Bernard Bailyn, in a classic study, showed to be so influential in the origins of the American Revolution.[3]

However, not even the beginnings of an attempt to characterize the complexities of eighteenth-century political thought can be made here. Rather, all that can be attempted is to look at the relatively few occasions when the Roman Republic and its institutions were the subject of sustained attention, as opposed to providing (like classical Greece and ancient Israel) a common stock of familiar narratives and examples, positive or negative. The two major figures in this respect are inevitably the two great French political thinkers of the century, Montesquieu in *L'esprit des lois* of 1748 and Rousseau in *Le contrat social* of 1762. But before we turn to them, a number of much less well-known English writers deserve some attention. As always, the purpose is the limited one of picking out from the vast mass of political literature cases in which particularly systematic attention is paid to Rome, or where the Roman example is put to particularly significant use.

Thus, before we turn to the two major French thinkers, it may first be worth illustrating from within contemporary literature the sorts of significance that Rome might have in contemporary political thought in England. By far the most systematic treatment of the Roman Republic known from this period is the truly remarkable pamphlet by Walter Moyle (1672–1721), written in about 1699 and published posthumously in the first volume of his collected *Works* in 1726 under the title "An Essay upon the Constitution of the Roman Government." Very significantly, it was republished in 1796, with a preface and notes by John Thelwall, and an expanded title, *Democracy Vindicated: an Essay on the Constitution and Government of the Roman State.*[4] The new title clearly goes beyond the intentions of the original work, which only rarely uses the word *democracy*. It does, however, do so once when speaking of the cycle of constitutions under which Rome went from monarchy to aristocracy to democracy and then "relapsed into a monarchy" (p. 231). Again, a few pages later (p. 233), Moyle writes: "I have often wondered that the Romans, instead of setting a democracy after the expulsion of their kings, should make choice of an aristocracy." Moyle thus clearly does see the middle and later Republic as a democracy, but he does not use the word as a slogan. Moreover, as we will see at the end, he laments the absence of entrenched clauses in the Roman constitution as a check on the will of a current majority. Nonetheless, he was explicitly writing in the tradition of Machiavelli and Harrington, to both of whom he refers by name, and was using the case of the Roman Republic as an example of the principles that could and should inform a commonwealth or republic.

Moyle's procedure, nonetheless, is quite different from Harrington's. He makes no explicit allusion to current circumstances, even (like Harrington) by the use of pseudonyms, and makes no actual proposals for the government of England or of Britain. Instead, the work is a remarkably acute and pointed analysis of the constitutional principles that had come step by step to inform the Roman Republic and that accounted for its military success, its avoidance for a long time of significant political violence, and its preservation of the freedom of the people. He takes the complete form of the Republic as having been achieved by the Licinian Law of 387 B.C., which opened the consulship to plebeians (thus in essence settling the "struggle of the orders") and placed a limit on property of five hundred acres (the limit in fact applied only to the amount of *public* land that an individual could exploit, and may in any case be anachronistic). At any rate, to Moyle, it was this that "established the great balance of the commonwealth" (p. 231). The reference to this date will immediately reveal that Moyle, like Machiavelli, is taking as the source of his conception of the Republic the literary image of the early Republic presented by Livy. At certain points, particularly in the second part of the work where he is talking about the "decision" of the Republic, he refers to episodes and figures from the late Republic—Marius, Pompey, Caesar, Cicero. But, in essence, the work is yet another tribute to the power of Livy's semihistorical, or semifictional, image of the Rome of centuries before his own lifetime.

Allowing for the fact that its basis, or source, is a standard literary narrative, Moyle's analysis is both remarkably penetrating and clearly directed to delivering a message for the present. One example is his exposition of the fact that in Rome the "clergy" were not a separate order, but that "priesthoods" were offices held by lay people; moreover, the practice of religion was subject to the authority of the Senate and People; public revenues devoted to the cults of the gods did not provide an income for the priests themselves as individuals. In short, he summarizes what is essentially the most influential modern view of Roman religion, namely, that it was "embedded" in the framework of the secular state.[5] But here Moyle, for once, draws an explicit message for the present:

As the religion of the Romans was a part of their policy, so their clergy likewise was a part of their laity, and interwoven into the general interest of the state: not a separate independent body from the rest of the community, nor any considerable balance of the civil government; but settled upon such an institution, as they could have neither interest nor power to act against the public good. A constitution which the modern policy has overlooked out of ignorance or neglected out of design; as appears from the unlimited power of the modern priesthood, who have usurped a supremacy, or at least an independency on the civil power over half of Europe, and (where their jurisdiction is more restrained) by virtue of their great possessions and endowments, look the civil government in the face, and have raised such convulsions in the later ages, as were unknown to the ancient world (pp. 215–16).

A similar, if less deliberate and explicit, topical relevance is clearly intended also later (pp. 242–43), where Moyle argues against those who defended monarchy as productive of "quiet and tranquility." The story of the Roman kings, Moyle argues, also exhibited sedition; and, in any case, under kingly government there can be no sufficient security for the liberties of the people "for want of a due balance to keep the constitution steady."

Moyle's work, therefore, is to be seen as a republican tract. But it is also a very penetrating analysis of the developing nature of the Roman republican system, as narrated by Livy. There is no need to discuss all the different aspects of his treatment, but it will be worth quoting one long, and quite strikingly "modern" passage, analyzing the key steps that led to the establishment of popular government at Rome. In any modern reconstruction of the evolution of early Rome, almost all the details mentioned would be open to debate, and it would be possible to regard the entire story as essentially unhistorical. Granted that Moyle takes his source, Livy, as being historical, the acuity of his summary is impressive:

The first blow given to the aristocracy, was the rescission of the debts to the commons, which weakened the interest of the nobility, by taking off the great dependence of the inferior rank of the people upon them. The second was the erection of the tribunes and other plebeian magistrates, for the security and protection of the commons, with a sacred authority and negative vote upon all the proceedings of the senate. The institution of this magistracy of the people, besides all the other advantages derived from it to the commons, united the whole body of the people under the general conduct of leaders and demagogues of their own order, made their counsels steady, and their resolutions unanimous; and took off that impression of single fear, which the commons had of the patricians, from the ignorance of union; was a certain refuge to appeal to, for the redress of all their grievances; and taught them to make regular advances and approaches to the destruction of the aristocracy.

The third was the power of proposing and debating laws, which the commons assumed by virtue of their new magistrates, whom they advanced at last to a power of enacting laws, with the authority of the senate. The fourth was the usurping a right to try the nobility for crimes committed against the state; which was a security wisely provided for by the people, to soften the absolute power of the dictator, who by this law was accountable to the people, after the resignation of his office, for severities exercised against them in the time of his jurisdiction. This likewise confirmed the old law of appeals to the people from the magistrates, which had been dextrously destroyed by the nobility by introducing the dictatorial power. The fifth was regaining an equality of suffrages in the elections of their own magistrates, and in the enacting of their laws; a right which they formerly enjoyed in the *Comitia Curiata*, but which they lost in the *Comitia Centuriata*, introduced by Servius Tullius, and recovered again in the trial of Coriolanus by the *Comitia Tributa*. The sixth was the obtaining a standing body of laws, collected from the wise institutions of the Grecian commonwealths. This system of laws prescribed the bounds of right and wrong, and regulated the proceedings of their courts of judicature; whereas formerly all controversies between man and man were decided by the arbitrary will of the consul, without any known forms or established methods of judging.

Seventhly, the excluding the diviners from interposing their authority and jurisdiction in the debates and resolutions of any popular assemblies: for whereas by their ancient constitution, no election of any magistrate, nor any public determination was valid, till ratified by their approbation, under this pretence they opposed all the just rights and pretensions of the people. To destroy therefore the negative vote of the diviners, the tribunes contrived an expedient to institute a new form of assembling, which they called the *Comitia Tributa*, wherein the augurs were not allowed to consult the gods; and by consequence the people were left absolute masters of their own proceedings and resolutions. Eighthly, the Agrarian Law; which though the people never perfectly obtained, yet they got large shares of the conquered lands into their possession, either by allotments to the citizens at home, or by planting colonies in the enemies' territories abroad; which confirmed and kept up the popular balance against the encroachments of the nobility. Ninthly, the mighty growth and increase of the numbers of the people, occasioned by laws prohibiting the barbarous practice of exposing their children; by manumitting their slaves, and enrolling them in the list of their free citizens: by the institution of such laws as compelled every Roman citizen to marry at such a determinate age, under severe penalties: And lastly, by the promiscuous naturalization of all foreigners. (pp. 236–37)

It remains only to stress that, as mentioned earlier, Moyle's message is not advocacy of a purely democratic system, but of a republic or commonwealth in which there is no king or clergy, and in which the liberties of the subject are protected by constitutional checks and balances. Hence, when he comes to considering the decline of the Republic and its relapse into monarchy, he lays the greatest stress, first, on the failure to observe the existing laws, and second on the absence of entrenched clauses. The people could vote whatever they wanted:

And although there was an outward appearance of liberty in the maxim on which this proceeding was founded, to wit, that the last resolution of the people was the undoubted law of the commonwealth; yet nothing can be more certain, than that no constitution can submit, where the whole frame of the laws may be shaken or suspended by the sudden temporary counsels of a multitude, and where the laws are governed by the people, instead of the people being governed by the laws. (p. 255)

Moyle thus anticipated profound concerns on the part of James Madison, about preventing too free an operation of the popular will. Moreover, as we will see (p. 175), the absence of entrenched clauses would have seemed relevant also to Aristotle if he had had the opportunity to analyze the later Roman Republic.

Compared with Moyle's significant and systematic work, a couple of allusions to the Republic elsewhere in English literature of the eighteenth century may be noted merely for illustration. Both of these are owed to Philip Ayres's excellent book on the role of Rome in eighteenth-century English culture. The first comes from Joseph Addison, writing in the *Spectator* in 1712:

I could never read a Passage in *Polybius*, and another in *Cicero*, to this purpose, without a secret Pleasure in applying it to the *English* Constitution, which it suits much better than the *Roman*. Both these great Authors give the Pre-eminence to a mixt Government, consisting of three Branches, the Regal, the Noble, and the Popular. They had doubtless in their Thoughts the Constitution of the *Roman* Common-wealth, in which the Consul represented the King, the Senate the Nobles, and the Tribunes the People. This Division of the three Powers in the *Roman* Constitution, was by no means so distinct and natural, as it is in the *English* form of Government. Among several Objections that might be made to it, I think the chief are those that affect the Consular Power, which had only the Ornaments without the Force of the Regal Authority. Their Number had not a casting Voice in it; for which reason, if one did not chance to be employed Abroad, while the other sat at Home, the Publick Business was sometimes at a stand, while the Consuls pulled two different ways in it. Besides, I do not find that the Consuls ever had a Negative Voice in the passing of a Law, or Decree of Senate, so that indeed they were rather the chief Body of the Nobility, or the first Ministers of State, than a distinct Branch of the Sovereignty, in which none can be looked upon as a part, who are not a part of the Legislature. Had the Consuls been invested with the Regal Authority to as great a Degree as our Monarchs, there would never have been any Occasions for a Dictatorship, which had in it the Power of all the three Orders, and ended in the Subversion of the whole Constitution.[6]

It is striking how clear the impact of Polybius's analysis is, and equally striking that Addison sees the main defect in the Roman system, as opposed to the contemporary English constitutional monarchy, as having been the division of power between the consuls (which Polybius had not stressed) and their limited constitutional rights.

The same sense of satisfaction with the British constitutional order is felt, but with a different emphasis, in Sir William Blackstone's remarks on voting rights in Rome and in England. It may be noted that he is one of the few commentators of any period to underline the difference between the "assembly of centuries" and the "assembly of tribes" and to recognize explicitly that in the latter all (that is, all adult males) could vote, with no property qualifications. As is clear, however, he regards this as a disadvantage and as a factor that had led to too much "levelling":

This constitution of suffrages [based on a moderate property qualification] is framed upon a wiser principle, with us, than either of the methods of voting, by centuries or by tribes, among the Romans. In the method by centuries, instituted by Servius Tullius, it was principally property, and not numbers, that turned the scale: in the method by tribes, gradually introduced by the tribunes of the people, numbers only were regarded, and property entirely overlooked. Hence the laws passed by the former method had usually too great a tendency to aggrandize the patricians or rich nobles; and those by the latter had too much of a levelling principle. Our constitution steers between the two extremes.[7]

Blackstone's comment might be taken as typical of one stream of political thought in Britain in the eighteenth century, namely, a complacent view of the British constitution, which was regarded as exemplifying a satisfactory balance between what in effect were Polybius' components of a state, monarchy, aristocracy, and democracy, in the form of elected representatives. That view clearly coexisted with a vigorous tradition of criticism of the actual exercise of monarchic, or court, power, with a more explicitly republican, or democratic, tradition on the part of commonwealth men,[8] among whom John Thelwall was a conspicuously outspoken example.[9] But the opportunity actually to construct a republic, and to debate on what principle, or following which historical models, it should be designed, never arose. Nor did eighteenth-century

Britain produce any individual political thinker, in the narrow sense, whose works might have entered the canon of major texts. To say that, of course, is not to deny the importance of the "political" writers in a wider sense who represented the Scottish Enlightenment, David Hume, Adam Ferguson, or, of course, Adam Smith. Nonetheless, if we are looking for thinkers of this period who put their conceptions of the Roman Republic to constructive use, it is to the two major French writers, Montesquieu and Rousseau, that we need to turn.

France

Both Montesquieu and Rousseau, like all educated people of the time, were steeped in knowledge of the ancient world, which provided for them, as for their predecessors, a major source of historical examples. Montesquieu in particular, fourteen years before the publication of his *L'esprit des lois* in 1748, had published his extended essay "Considérations sur la grandeur et la décadence des Romains" of 1734. His major work, *The Spirit of the Laws*, is perhaps at least as much an extraordinary feat of historical and legal scholarship as it is of political analysis.[10] A vast range of material is incorporated, not always in an order, or following any logic, which is immediately transparent to the reader. Indeed, the second half of the work in particular could fairly be described in large part as a succession of jottings or observations on historical examples of laws and how they operated. A large part relates to the Roman Empire, to the medieval monarchies, especially in France itself, and to the recent or contemporary French monarchy. The Roman republic nonetheless plays a significant part, based as always on Livy, on occasion on Polybius, and rather more frequently on Dionysius of Halicarnassus, whose very full and rhetorical explications of early Roman institutions and their meaning we have encountered earlier (pp. 39–46). Cicero is also quoted quite frequently; but it should be stressed that in Montesquieu, as in all his predecessors, the "Rome" that presented itself to his mind when thinking of historical examples was fundamentally that of the monarchy and early republic as portrayed in the earlier books of Livy. He does draw examples from his reading of Livy on the middle republic; but it is not that republic (or still less that in which Cicero lived) that provides his material.

In this vast assemblage of material, it is possible to discern two related leading themes: first, that any government, including a monarchy, requires a legal or constitutional framework that embodies a system of checks and balances; and second, as the title of the work is clearly intended to indicate, that everything also depends on the "spirit" or principles of the laws that are operative in any one society and that function to inform or determine how the "constitution" actually works.

If there is one chapter that summarizes the essence of the work (a bold claim), it might be identified as XI.6, headed "On the constitution of England,"[11] but (rather typically) saying very little directly about England; instead, it raises some general principles and illustrates them from a variety of historical contexts. The general principle invoked is that of the separation of powers: legislative power; "executive" power over the things depending on the right of nations (foreign affairs and war); and "executive" power over the things depending on civil right (essentially jurisdiction). Freedom can be lost within any type of state, republic, or monarchy if these powers are confused. It is significant here that Montesquieu is categorically opposed to direct democracy, in which people vote on laws, as opposed to a representative system:

A great vice in most ancient republics was that the people had the right to make resolutions for action, resolutions which required some execution, which altogether exceeds the people's capacity. The people should not enter the government except to choose their representatives; this is quite within their reach. For if there are few people who know the precise degree of a man's ability, yet every one is able to know, in general, if the one he chooses sees more clearly than most of the others.

Nor should the representative body be chosen in order to make some resolution for action, a thing it would not do well, but in order to make laws or in order to see if those they have made have been well executed; these are things it can do very well and that only it can do very well.

In a state there are always some people who are distinguished by birth, wealth, or honors; but if they mixed among the people and if they had only one voice like the others, the common liberty would be their enslavement and they would have no interest in defending it, because most of the resolutions would be against them. Therefore, the part they have in the state should be in proportion to the other advantages they have in the state, which will happen if they form a body that has the right to check the enterprises of the people, as the people have the right to check theirs.

Thus, legislative power will be entrusted both to the body of the nobles and to the body that will be chosen to represent the people, each of which will have assemblies and deliberations apart and have separate views and interests.[12]

For Montesquieu, therefore, the role of the assemblies in Rome would have been doubly objectionable. For they could and did vote on measures that would constitute legislation in the normal sense, but also (in just the same form) on practical steps, such as declarations of war or (later) the granting of long-term commands to individuals. In Montesquieu's preferred system, legislation would be moved "upwards" to the elected representatives, and practical decisions would be reserved for the executive. Not only that, but the legislative function would be divided between a chamber of representatives and one in which the aristocracy alone would sit, presumably an implicit reference to the British system. There is, of course, no explicit reference to Rome here; rather, Rome is considered, quite reasonably, among the wider class of "ancient republics."

Montesquieu is more open to accepting the merits of another power that the Roman people, meeting in assembly, had possessed, namely, that of judging individuals—cases of high treason as Montesquieu expresses it (VI.5), though in fact the range of cases was much wider. Here, as he does only rarely, he quotes Machiavelli by name, for the view that it had been the lack of this popular power that had led to the fall of the Florentine republic (*Discorsi* I.7). Montesquieu is hesitant about this on the grounds of the obtrusion of politics on the verdicts of such popular courts.[13] Given his general principles, it could not be expected that Montesquieu would in reality approve of popular possession of the right to try criminal cases; and, in fact, in his main discussion of Rome in Book XI, he takes the view that the Senate had not had, or not had for long, an adequate share in the right to pass criminal judgments and that when their share was lost, liberty was lost with it: "When the Gracchi deprived the senators of the power of judging, the senate could no longer stand up to the people. Therefore, they ran counter to the liberty of the citizens, but the latter was lost along with the former" (XI.18). Viewed historically, Montesquieu is abbreviating drastically but is still making a significant point; and he is also, if briefly, bringing into the discussion events from the historical Republic of the second and first centuries.

He does so also earlier, in Book II, when he discusses the divisions of the Roman population and the organizational structures within which they voted. He notes the elaborate description by

Livy and Dionysius of Halicarnassus of the class-based structure of the "assembly of centuries," following the "spirit of aristocracy" applied by Servius Tullius—but, as is so common, he does not note the absence of this principle in the "assembly of tribes." More strikingly, he moves to the later republic in discussing Cicero's view of the laws of the 130s B.C., which had introduced the secret ballot. As always, Montesquieu's ideal is a mixed constitution with a constitutional framework, but decidedly not a pure democracy:

The law that determines the way ballots are cast is another fundamental law in democracy. Whether the votes should be public or secret is a great question. Cicero writes that the laws that made them secret in the late period of the Roman republic were one of the major causes of its fall. Given that this practice varies in different republics, here, I believe, is what must be thought about it.

When the people cast votes, their votes should no doubt be public; and this should be regarded as a fundamental law of democracy. The lesser people must be enlightened by the principal people and subdued by the gravity of certain eminent men. Thus in the Roman republic all was destroyed by making the votes secret; it was no longer possible to enlighten a populace on its way to ruin. But votes cannot be too secret in an aristocracy when the body of nobles casts the votes, or in a democracy when the senate does so, for here the only issue is to guard against intrigues.[14]

Montesquieu's main discussion of the Roman republic comes in a succession of chapters (chapters 12–18) in Book XI, entitled "On the Laws that Form Political Liberty in Its Relation with the Constitution." Very broadly, these chapters follow the constitutional development of Rome from the monarchy (chapter 12) to the earliest republic after the expulsion of the kings (chapter 13), to subsequent changes (chapter 14), to the loss of liberty under the Decemviri of the mid-fifth century (chapter 15), to the assumption of legislative power by the plebeian assembly, in the form of the "assembly of tribes," achieved by the Hortensian Law of 287 B.C. (chapter 16).

By this point, reached in a chapter, which is entitled "On Legislative Power in the Roman Republic," the underlying narrative sequence is already becoming less significant, as it is also in the two following chapters: chapter 17, entitled "On Executive Power in the Same Republic," and chapter 18, "On the Power of Judging in the Roman Government." Even so, it is chapter 17 that for the first time brings in the name of Polybius and in essence offers a partial version of Polybius' analysis of how the Roman *politeia* had worked at the end of the third century. Furthermore, it is in chapter 18, as we have seen, that Montesquieu, in a survey of judicial practice covering the monarchic period and the whole course of the Republic, comes down to the Gracchan laws of the 120s A.D., and then in fact goes on to the excessive power wielded by the "knights," or equestrian order, in the late Republic (the connection is that it was this order which under Gaius Gracchus's legislation replaced senators as jurors in the criminal courts).

As regards the focus of attention, it is therefore clear that the subject of analysis is (once again) the familiar narrative of the early Republic, reinforced this time by points drawn from Polybius and by salient episodes from the late Republic. As for the type of analysis offered, it is centered round the Aristotelian, or Polybian, categories of monarchy, aristocracy, and democracy, but in the sense that what was significant was not the formal description of the constitution but the "spirit" in which it operated, and the presence or absence of effective checks and balances as between the different elements. Thus, Montesquieu can argue that under Romulus and his successor as kings, "The constitution was monarchical, aristocratic and popular" (XI.12); Servius Tullius, on the other hand, had increased the popular element while Tarquin attempted to unite the three powers in himself. For the Republic proper, in the chapters mentioned, Montesquieu follows the changing balance of executive, legislative, and judicial power, constantly emphasizing that excess in any direction could lead to the loss of liberty. Thus, for instance, the creation of the assembly of tribes, and its eventual acquisition of electoral and legislative power is an important theme of chapters 14 and 16, in which Montesquieu comments, "It was a frenzy of liberty. The people, in order establish democracy, ran counter to the very principles of democracy." He goes on to propose, rather unconvincingly, that what acted as a restraint was the power of the censors on the one hand, and the right of the senate to appoint a dictator on the other (XI.16).

We need not pursue the details further, because what matters is that Montesquieu takes seriously both the institutions of (predominantly) the early Republic, as he finds them in the canonical narratives, and the real conflicts of interest and of constitutional power, which that narrative contained. Above all, he takes the democratic or popular element seriously, and precisely for that reason, he argues consistently, in a spirit by no means far from that of Aristotle himself, that a state must have institutions that place effective limits on popular power, as on that of the various elements of the constitution, as well as balancing the executive, legislative, and judicial functions. In consequence, his name was to recur frequently in the debates on the constitution of the United States.

Very different principles inform the other great expression of French political thought of the eighteenth century, Jean-Jacques Rousseau's *Le contrat social*, published in 1762. An incomparably greater writer, in his capacity for marshaling clear, coherent, and original arguments, Rousseau both explicitly starts from a more democratic standpoint and centers his whole thought on the condition of the individual at various stages of human social evolution—and therefore, as we will see, deploys his conception of Roman republican institutions in a very different way.

The fact that Rousseau, although he wrote in French, was not a subject of the French monarchy, but by origin a citizen of the self-governing republic of Geneva, is surely of fundamental importance to his outlook, duly stressed by himself in the preface to his *Social Contract*. So also, as he recalls, were his observations of the working of collective self-government, with direct voting by the members, in the cantons of Switzerland.[15]

The fundamental principle Rousseau advocated was that freedom could only be attained under the rule of law, more particularly of a set of laws that derived from the sovereignty of the people and had been voted on by them. It is thus that he arrives at his famous and controversial concept of the General Will, to whose effects as expressed in law each individual, by virtue of being a member of the political community in question, must subscribe. This concept of the General Will, however, applies only to legislation. As regards the actual conduct of government, his system allows for a government, or "prince." His preference in fact is for an elective aristocracy, provided these elections are themselves regulated by laws (III.5). In this section, he speaks both of "magistrates" and of "venerable senators," apparently, though not explicitly, meaning to distinguish between elected senators meeting in assembly and elected holders of office. His concept of a political community, or nation, also allows for, and perhaps even requires, an initial "lawgiver" who brings the community into existence as a political community. In the chapter of the *Social Contract* in which this idea is expressed (II.7), he speaks of Lycurgus and other Greek lawgivers, of Calvin and the Republic of Geneva, and of the institution of Jewish and Islamic law (without naming either Moses or Mahomet). Rome comes in here in a somewhat ambiguous way. On the one hand, the Decemvirs, appointed to produce a code of laws for Rome in the mid-fifth century, had actually given rise to a tyranny; on the other hand, they were recorded (by Livy) as proclaiming formally that their laws were only proposals, subject to acceptance or rejection by the people. Here, too, he gives hints of the conception of "civil religion" as a necessary force in creating allegiance to the nation and its laws, which he develops, in a way that has been perturbing to many readers, in his last chapter (IV.8).

It will be evident already, first, that his examples will be drawn from much the same stock of canonical material common to all educated men as we have found with all the political thinkers considered so far, and with the same complete disregard of the question of whether the material was genuinely historical, semihistorical, or mythical. Second, it will be evident that the story of the Roman Republic, as narrated by Livy, will have been particularly well suited to provide material for Rousseau, for it is the story of a political community formed by a succession of "lawgivers," beginning with Romulus, in which at all stages a law (*lex*) was by definition—and could not be other than—something voted on by the people. This is not to say that Rousseau necessarily saw republican Rome as a democracy or, if he did, that he approved. On the contrary, he takes *democracy* as denoting a community where everything is determined by direct voting, a condition that cannot be achieved even in a very small community and, in any case, would be subject to constant instability: "If there were a people of Gods they would govern themselves democratically. So perfect a Government is not suited to men" (III.4).

A few chapters later (III.10–14), he first devotes detailed attention to Rome. Here he begins with the abuse of government and its tendency to degenerate, and he enunciates the principle that the natural progression in forms of government is by contraction, from democracy to aristocracy to kingship. Then, in a long footnote, he seeks to demonstrate that the history of the Roman Republic conformed to this principle, rather than contradicting it:

Romulus's initial establishment was a mixed Government which promptly degenerated into Despotism. Owing to some particular causes, the State perished before its time, just as a newborn child sometimes dies before reaching manhood. The expulsion of the Tarquins was the genuine period of the Republic's birth. But it did not assume a stable form from the first, because the failure to abolish the patriciate left the work only half done. For since in this way the hereditary Aristocracy, which is the worst of legitimate administrations, remained in conflict with the Democracy, the form of the Government, forever uncertain and unstable was, as Machiavelli has proved, not settled until the establishment of the Tribunes; only then was there a true Government and a genuine Democracy. Indeed, the people was then not only Sovereign, but also magistrate and judge, the Senate was no more than a subordinate tribunal to temper or to concentrate the Government, and even the Consuls, although Patricians, although the first Magistrates, although absolute Generals in war, were, in Rome, no more than the presidents of the people.

From that time on the Government was also seen to follow its natural inclination and to tend strongly toward Aristocracy. With the Patriciate abolishing itself as if on its own, the Aristocracy no longer resided in the body of Patricians as it does in Venice and in Genoa, but in the body of the Senate which was composed of both Patricians and Plebeians, and even in the body of the Tribunes once they began to usurp active power: for words do not change things, and when the people has chiefs who govern on its behalf then, regardless of the name these chiefs bear, it is still an Aristocracy.

From the abuse of the Aristocracy arose the civil wars and the Triumvirate. Sulla, Julius Caesar, Augustus became genuine Monarchs in fact, and finally under the Despotism of Tiberius the State was dissolved. Roman history thus does not belie my principle; it confirms it.[16]

The point that in the established Republic the people went beyond the role of voting on laws as the sovereign body in the state to function also as a sort of executive, reappears a couple of chapters later. He uses the example of Rome, with its four hundred thousand citizens, to show that even a large political community could function on a democratic basis (momentarily ignoring his earlier proposition that this idea was unrealistic and his principle that the sovereign people should confine themselves to legislation):

What difficulty might one not imagine about frequently assembling the immense people of this capital and its environs? Yet few weeks went by when the Roman people was not assembled, and even several times. It exercised not only the right of sovereignty, but a part of those of Government as well. It dealt with some business, tried some cases, and on the public square this entire people was nearly as often magistrate as it was Citizen. (III.12)

In fact, we find two chapters later that he has derived from Roman practice a different principle, namely, that when the sovereign people are assembled, the executive power is suspended:

The instant the People is legitimately assembled as a Sovereign body, all jurisdiction of the Government ceases, the executive power is suspended, and the person of the last Citizen is as sacred and inviolable as that of the first Magistrate, because where the Represented is, there no longer is a Representative. Most of the commotions that arose in the comitia in Rome came from ignorance or neglect of this rule. On those occasions the Consuls were nothing but the Presidents of the People, the Tribunes were mere Speakers, the Senate was nothing at all. (III.14)

From these, Rousseau passes to the famous chapter (III.15) in which he contrasts the modern state, in which the individual's concern is solely with his own economic interests, with the ancient one, in which public business was everyone's concern, and the citizens did not allow the deceptive principle of representation to deprive them of their freedom (thus expressing in two pages the essence of Benjamin Constant's well-known essay, p. 132 to follow). In the course of this (III.15.5), he expresses his trenchant view of the much vaunted freedom of the English:

Sovereignty cannot be represented for the same reason that it cannot be alienated; it consists essentially in the general will, and the will does not admit of being represented: either it is the same or it is different; there is no middle ground. The deputies of the people therefore are not and cannot be its representatives, they are merely its agents; they cannot conclude anything definitively. Any law which the People has not ratified in person is null; it is not a law. The English people thinks it is free; it is greatly mistaken, it is free only during the election of Members of Parliament; as soon as they are elected, it is enslaved, it is nothing. The use it makes of its freedom during the brief moments it has it fully warrants its losing it.[17]

So far as Rousseau's view of the Roman Republic is concerned, all this is preliminary to the very detailed treatment in Book IV, the last book of the *Social Contract*, and therefore, but for the controversial final chapter on "Civil Religion" (IV.8), the culmination of the whole work. Because, within the history of Western thought, the *Social Contract* is the primary expression of the notion of popular sovereignty, the place that the Roman Republic occupies in the work is highly significant.

Rousseau arrives at this quite substantial section (IV.4–7) in an apparently haphazard way, discussing the necessary unity of the general will (IV.1), various conditions relating to voting (IV.2), and the possible means, including voting, by which holders of office may be appointed (IV.3). It is only at the end of this section that he attaches some systematic importance to popular voting in Rome:

> It remains for me to speak about the way votes should be cast and collected in the assembly of the people; but perhaps the historical sketch of Roman administration in this matter will explain more concretely all the maxims which I might establish. It is not unworthy of a judicious reader to consider in some detail how public and particular business was conducted in a Council of two hundred thousand men. (IV.3.10)

What is important in this context is Rousseau's perception that Rome did indeed offer an important example of a system in which popular sovereignty operated through voting. It will not be necessary, therefore, to touch on all the details of Rousseau's description of the successive systems of group voting that evolved at Rome, according to the established story, which he is well aware was, at least in the early stages, fictitious. But he is sensitive to quite important features of the system: the greater prestige attached to the thirty-one "rustic" tribes, as apposed to the four "urban" ones; the fact that freed slaves, although they became citizens, generally were confined to the urban tribes and could not hold office; the fact that (although probably for rather different reasons than he supposes) the notion of a "tribe" lost its coherence as an organization of those living in a particular locality "so that the idea of the word *Tribe* thus shifted from the residential to the personal, or rather it became almost a chimera" (IV.4.11).

He also, in the course of a complex discussion of the forms of assembly, by *curiae* (in the earliest period), by "centuries," and by "tribes," makes the essential point: "No law was sanctioned, no magistrate elected except in the Comitia, and since there was not a single Citizen was not enrolled in a Curia, a Century or a Tribe, it follows that no citizen was excluded from the right to vote, and that the Roman people was genuinely Sovereign both by right and in fact" (IV.4.21). It should be recalled that when Rousseau was writing there was no significant political community in the world where all adult male citizens had the right to vote without any property qualification. A little later, he reiterates the point about the effective sovereignty of the Comitia:

> The Laws and the election of the chiefs were not the only matters submitted to the judgement of the Comitia: The Roman people having usurped the most important functions of Government, the fate of Europe

may be said to have been determined in its assemblies. This variety of objects gave rise to the various forms which these assemblies assumed according to the matters they had to decide. (IV.4.24)

Leaving aside his discussion of the way in which the "assembly of centuries" favored aristocracy—although with some counter-vailing factors—while the "assembly of tribes" was in principle a sectional element, representing only the plebeians, we may look at what he says about how votes were recorded and counted: first by being given orally, and written down, and the totals for each voting unit, of whatever type, then added together; later (as we have seen above, p. 91) by secret ballot, which Rousseau sees as characteristic of a period (the 130s B.C.) when corruption had set in. For that very reason, however, the change was necessary (IV.4.35)—and was so even though Cicero expressed disapproval:

I know that Cicero condemns this change and holds it partly responsible for the ruin of the Republic. But although I am sensible of the weight Cicero's authority should carry in this, I cannot share his opinion. I think, on the contrary, that the loss of the State was hastened because not enough such changes were made. Just as the regimen of healthy people is not suited to the sick, one must not try to govern a corrupt people by the same Laws as those that suit a good people. Nothing proves these maxims bet-ter than the long life of the Republic of Venice, which still retains a simu-lacrum of existence, solely because its laws are suited only to wicked men.

Hence tablets were distributed to the Citizens allowing everyone to vote without anyone else's knowing his opinion. New procedures were also established for collecting these tablets, tallying votes, comparing num-bers, etc. None of this prevented the integrity of the officers in charge of these functions from frequently coming under suspicion. In the end, to prevent intrigue and the buying and selling of votes, Edicts were issued, the large number of which proves their uselessness.

Toward the final times [of the Republic], they were often compelled to resort to extraordinary expedients in order to make up for the inadequacy of the laws. Sometimes prodigies were alleged; but this means, which could impose on the people, could not impose on those who governed it; some-times an assembly was convened all of a sudden before the candidates had time to engage in their intrigues; sometimes when the people was found to have been won over and ready to make a bad choice, an entire session was taken up with talk: but finally ambition eluded everything; and what is incredible is that thanks to its ancient regulations this immense people, in the midst of so many abuses, did not cease to elect Magistrates, pass laws, try cases, dispatch private and public business almost as readily as the Senate itself might have done. (IV.4.36)

Rousseau thus manages to combine a sense of the way in which the fundamental popular institutions of the Republic continued to operate right down to the end with a strongly moralizing tone, borrowed from Roman writers themselves, about the rising tide of corruption. These sections in fact represent his main treatment of the Republic as an example of popular sovereignty. For the three remaining chapters, although they bear the names of Roman offices and take Rome as their standing point, deal with types of public office and their potential uses: the tribunate (IV.5), the dictatorship (IV.6), and the censorship (IV.7). He sees the tribunate as a type of office whose nature is to be a an intermediary between populace and senate, potentially capable of leaning in either direction (a view that in fact does not do justice to the positive role of the Roman tribunes in proposing legislation, and thus in giving expression to the popular sovereignty that marked the system). As the remaining two sections show, Rousseau's conviction of the desirability, and the possibility, of an active popular sovereignty depends heavily on a precondition, namely, the achievement and maintenance of an appropriate level of popular morality and popular commitment to the accepted values of society. Hence the next chapter (IV.6) is devoted to the dictatorship and embodies strong claims that it would have been better if the dictatorship had been brought into effect in the late Republic, for instance, at the time of Catiline's conspiracy in 63 B.C. Perhaps even more strikingly, he devotes the next section (IV.7) to the censorship, whose role (not just in Rome) should be to preserve public morals—but not either to establish them in the first place or to restore them after they have collapsed. In all three of these chapters, in fact, Rousseau is plucking an institution out of its Roman context and asking what steadying function each—tribunate, (temporary) dictatorship, and censorship—could play in any state. The significance of these Roman models, especially the censorship in IV.7, is revealed when we see that it is exactly from there that he passes on to his (otherwise) unexpected final chapter (IV.8), which discusses the necessity of "civil religion" to hold a society together. Rousseau thus goes far further than any other thinker of his time in asserting the validity and viability of the idea of a genuine popular sovereignty—but on the strict condition of there being a collective code of morality and beliefs that was effectively maintained.

There is no reason to think that Rousseau could have foreseen that three decades later a French republic would actually come into existence. So, in writing the *Social Contract*, he was not (even on a theoretical basis, as with Harrington's *Oceana*) designing a constitution for an actual political community (although he was to do so for both Poland and Corsica), still less one that currently occupied the extensive territory of a monarchy. He was, however, categorically attempting to reintroduce the conception, which had to varying degrees been actualized in the self-governing city states of the ancient world, of a citizenry that not only was in principle sovereign but that actually met to pass legislation. Commitment to the idea of popular sovereignty in this sense is very rare, and by no means just for reasons of practicality, in other words the difficulty of assembling the citizens, or a fair proportion of them, even in a small city-state. Aversion to the idea that ordinary people might have the decisive voice in the fundamental rules of their own society is deep rooted. So the fact that Rousseau both expressed a commitment to this idea, and looked on the Roman Republic as the primary historical example of it, is noteworthy, even if the idea was not in reality to have a future either in political thought or in the practice of Western countries. The future was indeed to lie with extensive republics but not with popular democracies.

America: The Debate on the Constitution

It hardly needs to be demonstrated here that those who drew up the Constitution of the United States in 1787–88 and secured its ratification, in a context of vigorous and explicit debate, in each of the thirteen states, did so in the light of a broad shared education and in full consciousness of the historic step they were taking. In that broad education, as Carl Richard demonstrated with great force and clarity,[18] the learning of Latin and Greek and the reading of the main works of classical literature played a central role. Richard argued further that it was precisely the presence of classical exemplars of resistance to tyranny that provided the moral justification and sense of righteous purpose that were necessary if they were to embolden themselves for the two drastic steps of throwing off allegiance to the British Crown in the Declaration of Independence and then setting up a federal republic with a new constitution. Classical learning was of course not the only area of historical knowledge that could be brought to bear, as is shown nowhere better than in the massive survey of contemporary and historical "republics" of various sorts, whether democratic like the cantons of Switzerland or aristocratic like Geneva or Venice, contained in John Adams' *Defence of the Constitutions of Government* of 1787.[19] That work illustrates also how they deliberated with explicit reference to political thinkers and historians from Plato onward, including Polybius, Dionysius of Halicarnassus, Machiavelli, Harrington, Milton, and above all Montesquieu. It is surely striking that in all the exceptionally powerful literature produced on either the "federalist" or the "anti-federalist" side, there appears to be only one single reference to Rousseau, "a republican by birth and education, one of the most exalted geniuses and one of the greatest writers of his age," who is quoted as urging that the people should "examine and determine" every public act themselves.[20] Montesquieu, by contrast, is the single most influential point of reference in these debates. Along with that (and in coherence with Montesquieu's admiration for the checks and balances in the British constitution) went a general respect for the role of representation in Britain and for the tripartite system of elected Parliament, House of Lords, and monarchy, which was to be reproduced in the structure of House of Representatives, Senate and president.

As is well known, the debates on ratification of the Constitution produced, on both sides, not merely a vast outpouring of speeches, articles, letters, and books but contributions to political thought at an intellectual and literary level that surely has never been equaled in the course of resolving an immensely difficult set of practical, theoretical, and moral issues.[21] In particular, the eighty-five *Federalist Papers*, written by James Madison, Alexander Hamilton, and John Jay, taken together represent one of the great classics of political thought.[22] But the anti-federalist arguments, essentially defending the autonomy of the individual states in the face of the proposed creation of an integral federal government, are often also exceptionally fine expressions of political principle and are equally informed by a profound historical awareness.[23] The arguments provided by Roman history naturally would play a significant part, and before we come to the role played by Rome in the *Federalist Papers*, it may be relevant to give a couple of examples from the literature of their opponents. The first comes from the "Essays of an Old Whig," published in the *Independent Gazette* in Philadelphia in 1787–78. The essay in question (IV) argues the impossibility of there being a republic which was both unitary and covered so vast an area:

It is beyond a doubt that the new federal constitution, if adopted, will in a great measure destroy, if it do not totally annihilate, the separate governments of the several states. We shall, in effect, become one great Republic. Every measure of any importance will be Continental. What will be the consequence of this? One thing is evident—that no Republic, of so great a magnitude, ever did, or even can exist. But a few years elapsed, from the time in which ancient Rome extended her dominions beyond the bounds of Italy, until the downfall of her Republic; and all political writers agree, that a Republican government can exist only in a narrow territory; but a confederacy of different Republics has, in many instances, existed and flourished for a long time together. The celebrated *Helvetian* league . . . is one, among many examples on this head . . . A confederacy of Republics must be the establishment in America, or we must cease altogether to retain the Republican form of government. From the moment we become one great Republic, either in form or substance, the period is very shortly removed, when we shall sink first into monarchy, and then into despotism.[24]

The influence of Aristotelian, or more immediately Polybian, ideas about the cycle of constitutions is clear, as is the oft-repeated lesson provided by the replacement of the Roman Republic by monarchic rule.

A different view of the defects of the Roman system is provided by the extremely impressive "Letters from the Federal Farmer," published as pamphlets in the same period.[25] In one extensive paragraph from Letter VIII, the author argues that what Rome lacked was an appropriate system of representation. They did have the power to oppose laws but not in an effective way: "The people were too numerous to assemble, and do anything properly themselves; the voice of a few, the dupes of artifice, was called the voice of the people." The ten tribunes were no substitute for the proper level of representation shown in the British House of Commons, for they were mere individuals who belonged to the same class as the other Senators. Liberty might have been achieved if the people of Italy had elected, annually or biennially, four or five hundred well-informed men from among themselves to form "an honest, respectable assembly." The author takes this principle as being effective, in the American case, "in the forms of a federal republic, where we can divide and place it in several state or district legislatures." It would be these bodies that would resist oppression from the center. He gives Connecticut as an example of a small republic where there could be, and was, genuine representation. It is quite correct that in Roman Italy, an area of comparable size, no attempt ever was made to construct a representative system. The parallel is important, for what is concerned is neither a nuclear city-state with a restricted territory nor a vast territory like the United States. It is a vast tribute to the remarkable intellectual powers, and capacity for compromise, of the framers of the Constitution that the Federal Farmer's predictions have not been fulfilled. As for Rome, the weaknesses to which he points were very real, and we will return to them later, in chapter 7.

The Farmer does not, however, advance any very extensive arguments against the idea that representation could be effective at the federal level, and just this point is taken up from a federalist point of view by John Stevens, under the pseudonym "Americanus" in New York in 1787.[26] He starts from Montesquieu's proposition that it was a requirement for a real democracy that the people should assemble to pass laws, and consequently that such a republic could have only a small territory. Both in Greece and Rome, he says, this had been achieved, but at the cost of demanding too much from the citizens. The solution was representation, both at the state and at federal levels, and these representatives would serve as a far more effective check on the executive than the ten tribunes in Rome, who had been intended "to be the guardians of the people's right, and to defend their privileges against the power of the Senate and the Consuls."[27]

Perhaps the most remarkable of all discussions of the Roman Republic and its relevance to the proposed Constitution of the United States, however, is the *Examination into the Leading Principles of the Federal Constitution*, published by Noah Webster in October 1787, under the pseudonym "A Citizen of America."[28] It is striking, first, for its very explicit awareness that a great turning point in history had been reached. Indeed it had, and many of the participants were clearly aware of it. But few expressed that awareness in such sonorous rhetoric as in Webster's second paragraph:

This western world now beholds an aera important beyond conception, and which posterity will number with the age of Czar of Muscovy, and with the promulgation of the Jewish laws at Mount Sinai. The names of those men who have digested a system of constitutions for the American empire, will be enrolled with those of Zamolxis and Odin, and celebrated by posterity with the honors which less enlightened nations have paid to the fabled demi-gods of antiquity.

Second, he defends with unusual explicitness both the principle of representation (as opposed to the direct voting, which was "practised in the free states of antiquity; and was the cause of innumerable evils") and the desirability of dividing the legislature into two bodies, with the one designed, through greater prestige and experience, to act as a check on the other. He is aware that some took the view that the proposal for a Senate derived from imitation of the constitutions of European states, with monarch, nobility, and people, but he argues that the reason for it is functional, not based on social privilege. All the same, he makes an explicit comparison between the proposed American Constitution "and the two *best constitutions* that ever existed in Europe, the *Roman* and the *British*." This quite widespread view of the British Constitution may seem surprising to anyone who experiences its gross defects now; but the three-way comparison is in any case striking and important, in offering also detailed reflections on the Roman Republic and its workings. The tone is markedly conservative and in no way marked by populist tendencies. Thus, he says, whereas the British king is hereditary, the Roman kings (and subsequently the consuls) were elective, as would be the President—not by "the body of the people in their public assemblies," but by electors chosen by the state legislatures. On the other hand, an annual term of office was too short—the President would serve for four years, and be re-eligible, but would not be able to canvass for reasons of distance.

As regards the powers of the President, Webster again shows a markedly nondemocratic tendency, supporting the effects of the Constitution in limiting the sphere of direct election:

The powers vested in the president resemble the powers of the supreme magistrates in Rome. They are not so extensive as those of the British king; but in one instance, the president, with concurrence of the senate, has powers exceeding those of the Roman consuls; I mean in the appointment of judges and other subordinate executive officers. The praetors or judges in Rome were chosen annually by the people. This was a defect in the Roman government. One half the evils in a state arise from a lax execution of the laws; and it is impossible that an executive officer can act with rigor and impartiality, when his office depends on the popular voice.

An annual popular election of executive officers is the sure source of a negligent, partial and corrupt administration. The independence of judges in England has produced a course of the most just, impartial and energetic judicial decisions, for many centuries, that can be exhibited in any nation on earth.[29]

When he comes to the proposed U.S. Senate, he is again able to claim that the system would be an improvement on both the British House of Lords and the Roman Senate. The members of the House of Lords owed their seats either to ecclesiastical office (as bishops), to heredity, or to a grant from the king. Hence it was "wholly independent of the people." The Roman Senate was elective, but the places were then held for life. At this point, the author writes a long and well-informed footnote on the complex and difficult evidence as to how, in the early Republic, senators had been appointed (see p. 22 above). He is broadly correct to say that in the middle Republic membership depended, if indirectly, on election, because the censors controlled enrollment, and normally included all those elected to public office. In the late Republic, membership came to depend directly on election to the quaestorship.[30]

Webster can again claim that the American system would be better: election of Senators by the state legislatures (as remained the case until 1913), with a term of six years. He then defends the historic compromise by which each state, irrespective of size, would have two senators. Unlike Roman senators, however, the American senators would have to stand for reelection every six years and could be impeached. They thus retained their (indirect) connection to the electorate and were also subject to no property qualification (as there seems always to have been for public office at Rome). He then turns to the House of Representatives:

The house of representatives is formed on very equitable principles; and is calculated to guard the privileges of the people. The English house of commons is chosen by a small part of the people of England, and continues for seven years. The Romans never discovered the secret of representation— the whole body of citizens assembled for the purposes of legislation—a circumstance that exposed their government to frequent convulsions, and to capricious measures. The federal house of representatives is chosen by the people qualified to vote for state-representatives, and continues two years.[31]

Again, a footnote discusses whether there should be a property qualification for voting (as in all of the thirteen states there was), without noting that in Rome there was no such rule; all men of free birth (and freed slaves) could vote. Webster looks instead at the destabilizing effects of the extension of the Roman franchise to all of Italy in the first century B.C.: "Representation would have, in some measure, prevented these consequences; but the admission of every man to a suffrage will ever open the door to corruption."

As in the *Federalist Papers* (discussion to follow), one of the major themes of Noah Webster's argument is that the proposed Constitution would obviate the dangers of popular turbulence, of corruption, or of undue influence by individuals. The latter point comes up again when he considers the tribunes' power of veto:

The method of passing laws in Congress is much preferable to that of ancient Rome or of modern Britain. Not to mention other defects in Rome, it lay in the power of a single tribune to obstruct the passing of a law. As the tribunes were popular magistrates, the right was often exercised in favor of liberty; but it was also abused, and the best regulations were prevented, to gratify the spleen, the ambition, or the resentment of an individual.

The king of Great-Britain has the same power, but seldom exercises it. It is however a dangerous power—it is absurd and hazardous to lodge in *one man* the right of controlling the will of a state.[32]

It seems indeed as though Webster was unaware of, or certainly did not take account of, the fact that any one of the ten tribunes also had been able to exercise a positive, not merely negative, power in putting forward legislation to the "assembly of tribes." The effectiveness of this right, by contrast with the power of veto, of course depended on the acceptance of the proposed legislation by the people. Nonetheless, the reality had been that the Roman system had given even greater power, unchecked by the Senate or any other body, to the tribunes than he apparently supposed.

From this point on, Webster launches into a powerful and interesting defense of the centralizing powers embodied in the Constitution, returning to Rome only to dismiss the idea of there being any danger that the use made of religion by the Roman Senate could be replicated in America.[33] Later, however, he comes to a survey of the way in which, step by step, the Roman people had thrown off the domination of the patrician aristocracy, for instance in the election of tribunes, the enactment of laws without senatorial approval, the acquisition of a written code of laws (the so-called Twelve Tables), and the recognition of the "assembly of tribes" as a body to which the hindrances represented by augury (the observation of unfavorable signs, leading to the abandonment of the proceedings) did not apply. Finally, he mentions the Licinian Law of 367 B.C., by which individual property was reportedly limited to five hundred acres. In fact, we can be certain that the law, if historical at all, applied only to the occupation of public land.

Three features of this account are important. First is the emphasis on property and the idea that it was the fact that early Roman society was composed of property-owning citizens that had meant that aristocratic domination could not last. Second is the fact that this idea is explicitly attributed to Moyle's *Essay on the Roman Government* (p. 102 preceding), an indication, to which I have not encountered any parallel, that this significant work was in circulation and was known in America. Third, as ever, the history of the Roman Republic to which he appeals so effectively is the (at best) semihistorical story of early Rome, down to the fourth century B.C., as told by Livy. As we have seen, however, there is a certain ambivalence in Webster's attitude about the story of the struggle for popular rights in that he regards some of its effects as excessive and undesirable.

Finally, and in a striking way, Webster takes issue with the main conclusion, which Montesquieu, following Machiavelli, had drawn from his knowledge of the history of the ancient republics:

A general and tolerably equal distribution of landed property is the whole basis of national freedom: The system of the great Montesquieu will ever be erroneous, till the words *property or lands in fee simple* are substituted for *virtue*, throughout his *Spirit of Laws*.[34]

What Webster meant here is essentially the theme dwelt on, if in different spirit, in Paul Rahe's major work *Republics Ancient and Modern*,[35] namely, the predominance of militarism in their conception of citizenship. The point is spelled out in a footnote:

Montesquieu supposed *virtue* to be the principle of a republic. He derived his notions of this form of government, from the astonishing firmness, courage and patriotism which distinguished the republics of Greece and Rome. But this *virtue* consisted in pride, contempt of strangers and a martial enthusiasm which sometimes displayed itself in defence of their country. These principles are never permanent—they decay with refinement, intercourse with other nations and increase of wealth. No wonder then that these republics declined, for they were not founded on fixed principles and hence authors imagine that republics cannot be durable.

Both as an exposition of the principles of the Constitution and (even more) as an exploration of how it compared with the Roman Republic and with contemporary Britain, Noah Webster's essay would well deserve a place in the canon of Western political thought along with the *Federalist Papers* themselves.

In the *Federalist Papers*, the Roman Republic plays a significant part in providing comparative material, but nowhere as systematic a one as in Webster's *Examination*. As in his essay, their central thrust is to argue the merits, and argue away the perceived dangers, of a Constitution that would essentially locate sovereignty at the center, in the Presidency, Supreme Court, Senate and House of Representatives, with the abandonment of the confederation as a structure of sovereign states and with recognition of the notion of a direct authority of the United States government in relation to individual citizens. In the *Papers*, there is much explicit debate with Montesquieu (for instance in no. IX, by Alexander Hamilton) and repeated references to leagues or confederations known (often from very slight evidence) from the ancient world: the Amphictyonic Council centered at Delphi; the Achaean League, whose merits had been expounded by Polybius; and the Lycian league as described by Strabo; but the Roman Republic enters the argument only at a quite limited number of specific points.

One quite striking example comes in *Paper* XXXIV, again by Alexander Hamilton, in the argument that historical evidence showed that there could be two coequal authorities within the same state (the point at issue is the parallel revenue-raising powers of the Union and the separate states). Interestingly, his argument vividly illustrates the assumption that his readership was familiar with the history of the Republic while exhibiting a not entirely secure grasp on the facts in question:

It is well known that in the Roman republic the legislative authority in the last resort resided for ages in two different political bodies—not as branches of the same legislature, but as distinct and independent legislatures, in each of which an opposite interest prevailed: in one, the patrician; in the other, the plebeian. Many arguments might have been adduced to prove the unfitness of two such seemingly contradictory authorities, each having power to *annul* or *repeal* the acts of the other. But a man would have been regarded as frantic who should have attempted at Rome to disprove their existence. It will readily be understood that I allude to the COMITIA CENTURIATA and COMITIA TRIBUTA. The former, in which the people voted by centuries, was so arranged as to give a superiority to the patrician interest; in the latter, in which numbers prevailed, the plebeian interest had an entire predominancy. And yet these two legislatures coexisted for ages, and the Roman republic attained to the pinnacle of human greatness.[36]

In fact, the "assembly of centuries" had given an explicit weighting to wealth, but not to patrician status as such; and the two forms of assembly could annul or repeal each other's acts only in the sense that any subsequent *lex* could render obsolete any provision in an earlier law. The notion of a *lex* devoted to the annulment of an earlier named law does not seem to hold.

Nevertheless, in one sense, Hamilton was right that there were two parallel assemblies, very differently structured, both of which could pass legislation. It remains a not very apposite case for Hamilton's argument, which concerns the concurrence of federal and state powers.

Hamilton was also the author of *Paper* LXX, arguing against the idea "that a vigorous executive is inconsistent with the genius of republican government."[37] The counterargument was, of course, for the necessity of a single president: "Energy in the executive is a leading character in the definition of good government." Hence everyone who had any acquaintance with Roman history knew that it had often been necessary to appoint a dictator to deal with particular crises. At any rate, a single executive was desirable, and there were many examples of disputes between the two consuls at Rome or between the "military tribunes" who had replaced them for a period in the later fifth and early fourth century (again, we are in the world of Livy's narrative of early Rome). Later, the consuls had drawn lots, so that one stayed at Rome and the other went to the provinces (in fact, until the first century B.C. all consuls had commands outside Rome). Hamilton's grasp on republican institutions was somewhat weak, but the significance of his references, which do not in any case play a central part in *Federalist* LXX, is in reality just to illustrate once again the role of Livy's narrative as a point of reference, and source of examples, in public debate.

With *Federalist* LXIII by James Madison, entitled "A Further View of the Constitution of the Senate in Regard to the Duration of Appointment of its Members," we reach a different level of reflection on the lessons to be drawn from the history of the ancient world.[38] The argument starts from the proposition that the public interest required a deliberative body that should be not too numerous, and whose members should have a relatively long tenure, to impress foreign nations and act as a check on hasty decisions: "It adds no small weight to these considerations to recollect that history informs us of no long-lived republic which had not a senate. Sparta, Rome, and Carthage are, in fact, the only states to whom that character can be applied." But could these be appropriate models if they did not embody the principle of representation? Madison sets out to argue that the representation was not in fact wholly unknown to the Ancient republics. There was what he calls the "assembly" (the *boulē*, or council) at Athens of four hundred and then six hundred members (in fact, in the Classical period, five hundred), whereas at Sparta there were the (five) annually elected *ephors*, and at Rome the (ten) annually elected tribunes. Both these latter, however, were officeholders, and to say that they in some sense "represented" the people (as they did) was to use the word in a different sense from *representation* in a deliberative or legislative body.

These examples bring him to a categorical statement of the fundamental principle that, in his view, would distinguish federal American government from that of the ancient republics, namely, the total absence of direct democracy:

From these facts, to which many others might be added, it is clear that the principle of representation was neither unknown to the ancients nor wholly overlooked in their political constitutions. The true distinction between these and the American governments lies *in the total exclusion of the people in their collective capacity*, from any share in the *latter*, and not in the *total exclusion of the representatives of the people* from the administration of the *former*. The distinction, however, thus qualified, must be admitted to leave a most advantageous superiority in favor of the United States. But to insure to this advantage its full effect, we must be careful not to separate it from the other advantage, of an extensive territory. For it cannot be believed that any form of representative government could have succeeded within the narrow limits occupied by the democracies of Greece.[39]

As is clear, his focus is not solely on Rome, and he also does not take into account the period in the later Republic when direct democracy had functioned, however erratically, in the context of a citizenship that extended over the whole of Italy south of the Po River (an area comparable in size to several of the thirteen States taken individually, if not of course to the whole territory of the United States even as it was then). As always, "the Roman Republic" in the minds of educated men of later ages was the early Republic.

Might not a Senate whose members would be elected for six years by the legislatures of each state be able to transform itself into a "tyrannical aristocracy"? Madison argues that this was both unlikely in itself and contradicted by historical experience, which showed that in the end the representatives of the people always gained the upper hand over "aristocratic" bodies. This was true, so he argues, even of Britain when the "Senate" (the House of Lords) was hereditary, and the "House of Representatives" (the House of Commons) was elected for seven years by a very limited electorate. To support his case, Madison goes back to the (not entirely appropriate) example of the ephors at Sparta and the tribunes at Rome:

As far as antiquity can instruct us on this subject, its examples support the reasoning which we have employed. In Sparta, the Ephori, the annual representatives of the people, were found an overmatch for the senate for life, continually gained on its authority and finally drew all power into their own hands. The Tribunes of Rome who were the representatives of the people prevailed, it is well known, in almost every contest with the senate for life, and in the end gained the most complete triumph over it. The fact is the more remarkable, as unanimity was required in every act of the Tribunes, even after their number was augmented to ten. It proves the irresistible force possessed by that branch of a free government, which has the people on its side.[40]

In fact, even Madison is not wholly correct here. It was not positive unanimity that was required (and was very rarely achieved), but the absence of an actual veto by any of the others. In the absence of a veto, an action by any one, or more, of the tribunes would be effective, even in proposing legislation; but here at least he gives some hint of the factors which marked the turbulent history of the later Republic.

The Founders, perhaps because they were steeped in the conventional history of the Ancient World, were well aware of the troubled political history of the Greco-Roman republics and were wary of what they read about the power of their popular assemblies. Arguments from the geographic scale of the thirteen states on the one hand and from the need for representation, for checks and balances, and (against very strong opposition) for an effective executive all meant that nuclear republics or city-states such as Athens, Sparta, or early Rome would function at least as much as lessons to be avoided than as models to follow. Nonetheless, in the Senate, the Roman Republic was to leave, nominally at least, a permanent imprint on the American Constitution. Although the Senate indeed did owe something to the conception of the Roman Senate as an aristocratic body not wholly dependent on the popular will, as it did also to the British House of Lords, the principle on which it was based differed profoundly, for representation of different geographic units making up a larger federal body was precisely what the Roman Senate had not provided.

From the moment of the adoption of the American Constitution onward, it could be said that, step by step, and sometimes in the form of constitutional monarchies, the future was to lie, first, with republics with defined constitutions, and, second, with the system of representation. Enthusiasm for the model of direct democracy offered by Greco-Roman city states has not been common in the modern world. Furthermore, in the case of no other republic created subsequently has its formation given rise to extended reflections, embodied in major works of political thought, directed to the lessons to be derived from Greece or Rome. In that sense, as regards possible models of political systems, Greece and Rome have become irrelevant, however great their wider (if ever-diminishing) role in the culture of educated people.

The prime symbol of that parting of the ways, and of the general acceptance of a quite different conception of citizenship, could be taken to be the famous speech delivered by Benjamin Constant in 1819, "The Liberty of the Ancients compared with that of the Moderns."[41] The author's central argument is well known. The appeal, especially in the French Revolution, to the virtues of positive citizenship as displayed in the ancient republics was entirely misplaced. First, modern states were too large compared with small ancient republics to which war was endemic. Second, what the contemporary citizen sought was personal freedom, protection from arbitrary mistreatment by the state, and the opportunity to seek personal well-being, above all through commerce. The citizen also could exercise some positive rights, but of a character quite different from those in the ancient republics:

First ask yourselves, Gentlemen, what an Englishman, a Frenchman, and a citizen of the United States of America understand today by the word "liberty."

For each of them it is the right to be subjected only to the laws, and to be neither arrested, detained, put to death or maltreated in any way by the arbitrary will of one or more individuals. It is the right of everyone to express their opinion, choose a profession and practise it, to dispose of property, and even to abuse it; to come and go without permission, and without having to account for their motives or undertakings. It is everyone's right to associate with other individuals, either to discuss their interests, or to profess the religion which they and their associates prefer, or even simply to occupy their days or hours in a way which is most compatible with their inclinations or whims. Finally it is everyone's right to exercise some influence on the administration of the government, either by electing all or particular officials, or through representations, petitions, demands to which the authorities are more or less compelled to pay heed. Now compare this liberty with that of the ancients

The latter consisted in exercising collectively, but directly, several parts of the complete sovereignty; in deliberating, in the public square, over war and peace; in forming alliances with foreign governments; in voting laws, in pronouncing judgements; in examining the accounts, the acts, the stewardship of the magistrates; in calling them to appear in front of the assembled people, in accusing, condemning or absolving them. But if this was what the ancients called liberty, they admitted as compatible with this collective freedom the complete subjection of the individual to the authority of the community. You find among them almost none of the enjoyments which we have just seen form part of the liberty of moderns. All private actions were submitted to a severe surveillance. No importance was given to individual independence, neither in relation to opinions, nor to labor, nor, above all, to religion. The right to choose one's own religious affiliation, a right which we regard as one of the most precious, would have seemed to the ancients a crime and a sacrilege.[42]

It is not Constant's purpose to go into any detail, and he does not elaborate on how, when, and where these conditions had really applied within the ancient world, except to say that they applied less fully in Athens, where personal freedom and commercial pursuits were more evident. He does, however, return later to the role of the censorship at Rome, spelling out that its powers can have been fully effective only in the early period when all Romans lived in a single city:

Roman censorship implied, like ostracism, a discretionary power. In a republic where all citizens, kept by poverty to an extremely simple moral code, lived in the same town, exercised no profession which might distract their attention from the affairs of the state, and thus constantly found themselves the spectators and judges of the usage of public power, censorship could on the one hand have greater influence while on the other, the arbitrary power of the censors was restrained by a kind of moral surveillance exercised over them. But as soon as the size of the republic, the complexity of social relations and the refinements of civilization deprived this institution of what at the same time served as its basis and its limit, censorship degenerated even in Rome. It was not censorship which had created good morals; it was the simplicity of the those morals which constituted the power and efficacy of censorship.[43]

He is thus aware that the model he is using to point a contrast with the modern world derives (as always) from early Rome, and he presumably would not have claimed that it applied equally to Cicero's time. In any case, his thesis is precisely that the appeal to antiquity as a model for an active, martial citizenship, matched by the complete subjection of the individual to collective values, is delusive and inappropriate. Of the "two concepts of liberty,"[44] it was not the positive right to share in the direction of the state which was relevant, but the private exercise of personal freedom. Nonetheless, it is striking that Constant in fact ends with a rhetorical appeal for the exercise of civic virtue, through attention to public issues, through the election of representatives, and through the exercise of their public functions by those who are elected to office. In that sense, he makes a belated attempt to advocate the retention of the "virtue" of ancient republicanism; but essentially his speech can be taken as marking the moment when political thought ceased to contemplate actively the nature of direct popular democracy and when representative government, as in the thought of John Stuart Mill,[45] assumed the role of the model to which democracy could aspire. Neither Constant nor Mill was in a position to imagine the twentieth-century state, which would again frequently demand of its citizens, sometimes before they were of an age to vote, universal military service. So far as I can discover, that development has not been accompanied by any inclination to rethink the possibility of the personal exercise of positive political rights. Nonetheless, although the Roman Republic no longer serves as the universally present model it once was, contemporary political thought has returned to it from various directions—and in ways that share more with the thought patterns of the past than might be imagined.

6   Some Contemporary Approaches

Introduction

Since the late eighteenth century, a vast amount of historical scholarship has been devoted to the ancient world, and our direct knowledge of it, based now not only on literary texts but also on hundreds of thousands of original documents (above all, inscriptions and papyri), on coins, and on archaeological discoveries, has been totally transformed. The same is true of the Roman Republic itself, although perhaps to a lesser extent than many other areas. But the *relevance* of the Republic, as a political system worth analyzing, or as a model to be followed or avoided, has clearly declined. Even if there ever had been in the intervening period constitutional debates on the intellectual level of those that surrounded the formation of the American Constitution, it is extremely unlikely that conceptions of the Roman Republic would have played any significant part. A few ministates that could reasonably be characterized as city-states (Luxembourg, San Marino, Monaco) remain in Europe; but if there are debates about citizen rights within them, they have not entered the mainstream of political thought. Elsewhere, although the major monarchies have been swept away and replaced in each case by states calling themselves "republics," the sheer scale of modern nation-states has made the historical memory of the ancient republics, including Rome, seem irrelevant. As we shall see later (pp. 151–52), at least as regards the last few decades of the Roman Republic, that presumption might be premature, for the area then settled entirely by Roman citizens was not very far short of the territory of the modern Italian state, lacking only the area north of the Po River (until 49 B.C.) as well as Sardinia and Sicily. The Republic of Cicero's time shared (if very uneasily) the characteristics of a city-state and a nation-state (as well as maintaining a somewhat erratic control on an empire that by 49 B.C. stretched from the Atlantic to the Euphrates).

In any case, as we have already seen repeatedly, the "Roman Republic" taken by political thinkers in previous centuries as a model or a warning was precisely not that in which Cicero spoke; rather it was the one enshrined in Livy's narrative, begun a decade or more after Cicero's death in 43 B.C., and completed under the first Emperor, Augustus. It had always been that Republic, along with the portrayals of it in Plutarch's Roman *Lives*, that formed part of the mental furniture of educated men, and that Republic whose story continued to provide reading for schools but no longer seemed relevant in an age of nation-states, which were based on a narrower or wider suffrage (eventually including women) and on representative institutions.

Such interest as there has been in the Roman republican system has therefore been within the context of purely historical treatments, or of occasional comparative studies of particular aspects. The occasion for an actual engagement with, or live debate about, the Roman system, or aspects of it, has hardly arisen. Yet it might be argued that this inattention, or nonengagement, is not wholly justified and that there are features of Roman institutions that deserve some reflection.

As regards the position of women, for instance, in the context of positive political rights, there is nothing to say. The notion of women as voters never arose in the ancient world. But as regards private rights, of inheritance, the ownership of property, property relations as between husband and wife, and the capacity of either party to initiate divorce, many features of Roman law would deserve study from a comparative point of view.[1]

Equally, the institution of slavery has been absent for almost the last century and a half from all modern republics. Here, because of the fundamental significance of slavery in the history of the United States, there has been repeated engagement with the Roman experience.[2] In particular, there is Orlando Patterson's major work on the way in which conceptions of freedom have been conditioned by conceptions of various forms of non-freedom on the part of outsiders, or women, or slaves.[3] A substantial section of the work is devoted to Rome; but even he, while recognizing the important part played in Roman society by the enfranchisement of slaves, does not fully recognize the significance of his own concept of "civic freedom" (positive political rights) in relation to Roman ex-slaves. Uniquely among ancient societies, the Romans, when the slave of a citizen was freed, made that ex-slave a citizen, who could (if an adult male) vote.[4] Combined with the concurrent factor of the lateral extension of citizenship (either to individuals or collectively to the free inhabitants of communities granted the Roman citizenship), this meant that, to a quite exceptional degree, the possession of Roman citizenship did not depend on biological descent, but on successive legal acts. The overwhelming majority of the Roman citizens of Cicero's time did not descend from the inhabitants of the archaic city-state, which was the subject of Livy's first ten books; nor, for that matter, did either Cicero himself or Livy.

The freed slave of a Roman citizen could not himself, it is true, hold elective office, although his descendants could. But the fact that he could vote, combined with the fact that there was no minimum property qualification for the right to vote, meant that Roman male adults (though not female adults) enjoyed universal voting rights in a way that was not true of any of the American states at the time of the Declaration of Independence and became true of modern nation-states only step-by-step in the course of the modern era. Claude Nicolet's classic study of "the world of the citizen" in the Roman Republic would in fact deserve serious study by students of comparative political institutions.[5]

The other disability that the ex-slave suffered was that, in normal circumstances at least, he could not serve in the legions. For freeborn citizens on the other hand, the obligation to undergo military service was universal and was indeed an integral element in citizenship. We see this most clearly indeed in Polybius's account of the qualifications required for standing for elective office:

After electing the consuls, they appoint military tribunes, fourteen from those who have seen five years' service and ten from those who have seen ten. As for the rest, a cavalry soldier must serve for ten years in all and an infantry soldier for sixteen years before reaching the age of forty-six, with the exception of those whose census is under four hundred drachmae, all of whom are employed in naval service. In case of pressing danger twenty years' service is demanded from the infantry. No one is eligible for any political office before he has completed ten years' service.[6]

The requirement for ten years' service thus served as an age qualification, but it also, in a more profound sense, expressed the organic connection between military service and the functions of a citizen. The question of how an individual could acquire the obligation to die in the service of an "imagined community" which he has (normally) not joined voluntarily, but has been born into, and of what, in different political systems, the actual expression of this obligation comes to, is also a topic that might deserve more attention in political thought than (so far as I can discover) it has received.[7] In the Roman case we will return to this obligation later (p. 162), in looking at the Roman/Italian "nation-state" of Cicero's time, when we find that service in the legions somehow has been transferred to function as a qualification for local office in the towns of Italy.

At the same time, that is to say, when looking at the "nation-state" of the mid-first century B.C., we must return to a feature of the Roman system, the beginnings of which in Aristotle's time we already have seen, namely, the absorption into the Roman citizenship of existing city-states that retained their own political identity and local constitutions, producing a dual citizenship. This quite subtle and effective balance, which, however, as Noah Webster had noted (p. 125), never gave rise to anything like a system of representation, would deserve attention again in the context of the partial dissolution of European nation-states (as in the United Kingdom, insofar as it ever has been a nation-state, or in Spain) and their simultaneous absorption into a larger unit, the European Union.

If we turn finally to the working of Roman republican institutions as such, it will be worth looking at how they are treated in what is admittedly a small selection of contemporary works, nearly all of those discussed being (it is regretted) British or American. They include a number of works of exceptional interest, penetration, and significance, and one might wish that in Britain, where what passes for "the Constitution" is in every respect in a state of flux, incoherence, and confusion, such books would be the subject of informed public debate, as equivalent works are in the United States. So, in stressing the very partial and (in my view) distorted view of the Roman Republic to be found in books that in other respects it is a pleasure and an education to read, I am not criticizing them, but rather (in part) reflecting on the strange conceptions of the Republic that were prevalent in historical scholarship through most of the twentieth century—and in part I am drawing attention to the fact that, to quite a large degree, the "Roman Republic" they take into account is (once again) the semi-historical narrative of the early Republic and the "struggle of the orders" (patricians and plebeians).

To repeat briefly points that I have made elsewhere,[8] the distortion arose first from the slim volume published in German in 1912 by Matthias Gelzer on the Roman nobility, which ended with a sweeping conclusion about the role of patronage and *clientela* in Roman society and the effective dependence on the mass of the people on their political leaders in the Senate, or rather on those who were described as *nobiles*, the descendants of previous holders of major elective office. It is worth once again reproducing this conclusion, as it appears in the English translation of 1969:

The entire Roman people, both the ruling circle and the mass of voters whom they ruled, was, as a society, permeated by multifarious relationships based on *fides* and on personal connections, the principal forms of which were *patrocinium* in the courts and over communities, together with political friendship and financial obligation. These relationships determined the distribution of political power. To maintain their rights citizens and subjects alike were constrained to seek the protection of powerful men, and the beginner in politics had need of a powerful protector to secure advancement. Political power was based on membership of the senate, which was composed of the magistrates elected by the people. Thus the most powerful man was he who by virtue of his clients and friends could mobilize the greatest number of voters. From the character of the nobility (the descendants of the most successful politicians) arose the hereditary nature of political power in the great aristocratic families. The forces of political life were concentrated in them, and political struggles were fought out by the *nobiles* at the head of their dependents. It made no difference in what way these dependents had been acquired, or with what means in what field the struggle was being conducted, and if from time to time in the course of events a new man was brought to the fore, the overall picture did not change.[9]

The reader will notice at once that there is a sharp contradiction between the implications of this passage and the presumptions of nearly all writers who have commented on Rome, from Polybius onward, and who are discussed earlier in this book: They took Aristotle's principles of analysis seriously; saw politics as representing real conflicts and tensions between social groups; for the most part believed that there were real dangers in the unfettered domination of the mob, if it were allowed to occur; and advocated constitutional arrangements that represented, in one way or another, a balance of powers. In any case, no normal reader of the standard ancient narratives of the history of the Roman Republic could fail to note a succession of major public issues in which the mass of the people represented a real force that could be kept in check only with difficulty. It was left to P. A. Brunt, in a classic small volume published in 1971, to point out the obvious (which, as so often, was *not* obvious, and needed to be discerned): that the traditional picture was right, and that the history of the Republic was a history of major conflicts of power, interest, and principle.[10] Some years later, in two equally classic chapters, he showed that the evidence provided no support either for the idea of the political dominance of *clientela* or for the influence of established "factions" among senators.[11] Gelzer's picture was an illusion, but one that has proved extraordinarily tenacious, even when its justification in the evidence has been comprehensively disproved. The consequence has been that students of comparative politics or political institutions who duly read "the right books" about Rome in the course of their research found themselves persuaded that Rome was a hierarchical society marked by all-embracing vertical ties of dependence, in which the formal structure of the "constitution" did not matter, in which there was no real political debate, and in which the ordinary citizens had no power.

One further element, which at least has the merit of some support from the evidence, has reinforced this conception: that Rome was a timocratic political community in which power was distributed strictly according to wealth. The source of this idea, however, is one we saw earlier (pp. 42–43), namely, the three retrospective descriptions of the structure of the archaic "assembly of centuries," written by Cicero, Livy, and Dionysius (partially quoted on p. 43), and describing a system that as such no longer existed in the same form and that applied to a period several centuries in the past. Certainly, even the contemporary (for Cicero), late-Republican form of the "assembly of centuries" still was based on census classes, although less sharply graded than the archaic version. The essential point, however, was that, in practice, it rarely met to pass legislation, and in most years seems to have met only for the election of consuls and praetors. The body that regularly passed legislation was the "assembly of the tribes," in which all (adult male) citizens had an equal vote.

To say this is not to prepare the way for any idealistic image of

Cicero's Rome as a perfect democracy; as we will see briefly later, its incoherences were fundamental, and what the exercise of the rights of the people led to was, just as Polybius had indicated, the return of individual power and soon of monarchy. It is to say that misinterpretation by modern historians of the Republic has denied it its proper place in political thought as a particular sort of republic and as one in which, in an erratic and very imperfect way, popular power played a major part.

It may be worth giving one example, admittedly somewhat extreme, of how a respected contemporary ancient historian can represent the role of the popular assembly in Rome:

> The popular assembly, which, in its early stage, had been identified with the sum total of all Roman citizens, increasingly became a mouthpiece of the Roman urban plebs as the entire territory expanded. As a consequence of this, it disappeared from the political scene in the early first century B.C. The democratic element in the Roman constitution had long been a thing of the past.[12]

The point made about the relevance of the extension of the citizenship is, of course, entirely valid; and if anyone wished to argue that, in consequence, votes passed by those citizens who either lived in Rome or were present there on particular occasions could not be regarded, morally, as representative or valid, there would be much to be said for this view. But the empirical question of actual participation, by how many people and from which social or geographic groups, is a significant one in the study of any political system with any democratic features; and in this context late-Republican Rome represents one case among others. But to imply that popular voting on legislation was not fundamental to the history of the late Republic is a total misconception.

So profound a misconception is in fact not common; but far more prevalent is the notion that, even if, formally speaking, the people voted, social and political control was exercised from above, and that consequently it is not worth asking about *what* place, if any, Rome should be allotted in the history of democracy. Before we look at some examples, it is worth recalling that two centuries ago, as M. H. Hansen reminds us, it was simply assumed that Rome, like Athens, was an example of a popular democracy. Hansen quotes the following passage from the first edition of the *Encyclopaedia Britannica*, published in 1771: "Democracy, the same with a popular government, wherein the supreme power is lodged in the hands of the people: such were Rome and Athens; but as to our modern republics, Basil [Basle] only excepted, their government comes nearer to aristocracy than democracy."[13]

Recent Political Studies

If, in the eighteenth century, it could simply be assumed that Rome was an example of democracy, it will be all the more useful to contrast with this the way in which Rome is portrayed in an illuminating modern work, David Held's *Models of Democracy*, to which in a more general sense everything in this book is heavily indebted:

However, if Athens was a democratic republic, contemporary scholarship generally affirms that Rome was by comparison an essentially oligarchic system. Despite the inclusion of Hellenic conceptions of the state in the works of Roman thinkers (notably in Cicero, 106–43 B.C.), and the inclusion of the citizen-born peasants and emancipated slaves in the political community, elites firmly dominated all aspects of Rome's politics. Rome's military history—its extraordinary record of territorial expansion and conquest—helps to explain how and why Rome was able to sustain formal commitments to popular participation, on the one hand, and very limited actual popular control, on the other. Accordingly, from the ancient world, it is the heritage of the classical Greek tradition, and of the model of Athenian democracy in particular, that it is especially important to come to terms with in the history of democratic thought and practice.[14]

For this view to be fully convincing, that is, for it to be reasonable to exclude Rome altogether from consideration of different types of democracy, it would have to be shown that the "elites," or oligarchs, were characteristically united and therefore offered no alternatives to the people. But this was not the case at any stage of Roman history, even if open and fundamental dissension was most characteristic of the last century of the Republic. Moreover, whether we imagine that the level of open disagreement on political choices was low or high, in either case there would be a legitimate subject for comparative study in the methods of public persuasion or propaganda by which the people were led—in short, precisely the propositions about the dependence of the people on political leadership put forward by Joseph Schumpeter in *Capitalism, Socialism and Democracy* and discussed later in the book by Held.[15] In any case, the choices made by the Roman voters in elections were not of "governments" to rule them, but of individuals to fill public posts for one year each, individuals who often came into direct conflict with each other. In consequence, major issues of public policy were in fact debated at public meetings and then voted on.

Similarly, in the volume edited by John Dunn to celebrate the 2,500th anniversary of Cleisthenes's reforms in Athens, *Democracy: the Unfinished Journey*, after two chapters on the Greek world, the discussion moves straight to the Italian city-republics, with no section on Rome. Yet the Roman people had met to hear speeches about proposed legislation (for instance, Cicero's famous speech of 66 B.C., *For the Manilian Law*), had voted in person on legislation, and had elected all the holders of public political office. So what justifies the exclusion of Rome? The answer comes in the editor's conclusion:

Some historians of Rome have recently argued that it too was really a democracy, since the pursuit of a career of public office and political leadership within the ranks of the Roman aristocracy required them at regular intervals to secure election by the popular assemblies of Roman citizens. But the parallel in this respect with the residually aristocratic political and military leadership of Athens' democracy is weak and misleading. Until the Roman armies chose to follow their generals and destroy the political authority of the republic, the consuls and lesser magistrates of Rome may have required a degree of intermittent popularity to pursue their lofty careers successfully. But once they had secured their offices in each instance, they were able to wield the authority which these conferred with massive self-assurance; and they did so, for the most part, with wary attention to the susceptibilities of their fellow members of the senatorial nobility, but with relative indifference to those of the great plebeian majority of Rome's citizens.[16]

The reasons given are very typical. First, there is the assumption that those who were elected to office already came from an "aristocracy" (which was true in a weak sense of nearly all the holders of the two consulships of each year, but much less so of the other elected officials—more than fifty each year). More important is the presumption that election to office was what politics was about. No one will dispute the competitiveness of Roman elections, which has become all the clearer in very recent work.[17] But the picture omits altogether the essential role of the citizens— or rather of some citizens each time—in voting on legislation. The fault is of course not that of John Dunn, but of the curiously aberrant course taken by professional historians of the Republic through nearly all of the twentieth century.

Specifically from the viewpoint of a comparative study of elections, a similar approach to the electoral process at Rome is taken by R. S. Katz in his recent study of democracy and elections. For here again, although the author has very good information on the relevant structures and procedures, the account is informed by presuppositions derived (as they must be) from current scholarship. As a result, clear internal contradictions arise in the very first paragraph in which he speaks of Rome:

Rome was never a democracy in the Greek sense nor, unless one takes communist criticisms of liberal democracy at face value, in the modern sense either. Magistrates (except for the *interreges* required when the terms of one set of magistrates expired before their successors could be elected) could take office only on election by the people. Legislation required the approval of the people and "[i]t was admitted that when the whole People met to legislate, their assent was a command, their refusal to assent a prohibition." Nonetheless, Rome remained an oligarchic timocratic state. Even when a choice was allowed in elections, the choice was tightly controlled by the presiding magistrate. Legislative votes were simply "yes" or "no" decisions on a question with no amendments possible. In addition to the limits on the people's freedom of choice, the presiding magistrate in particular, and the ruling class in general, had a variety of institutional and procedural devices by means of which they could control the outcome of a vote.[18]

As we will see later (pp. 168–82), the question of how Aristotle would have characterized the Roman system of the late Republic, in Cicero's time, is complex. But, as will be seen, there certainly were some features of a pure democracy in Aristotle's terms, which he would not have encountered at Rome. One of these was indeed the opportunity to voice opinions on matters of public policy, where the right to speak at public meetings (*contiones*) does seem to have been controlled by whoever called the meeting, and normally was restricted to officeholders or ex-officeholders. The ability to move amendments from the floor in the assembly, and have them incorporated in the consequent decree, was indeed available at Athens (as surviving inscribed decrees show); but this feature is not as such used as a criterion of democracy by Aristotle. Both democratic systems and voting procedures within them take many different forms, however, and it seems strange to deny the description of "democracy" to a system where all tenure of public office and all legislation depended directly on popular votes (especially in a book published in the U.K., where neither right is enjoyed by citizens). The characterization offered in fact depends on presuppositions about social structure and vertical relations of control; on details about voting procedures, which are highly debatable; and (as so often) on Cicero's account of the "assembly of centuries" as set up by the king Servius Tullius and its rationale in terms of social precedence—and from that, the presumption that this principle was the key to the whole social-political structure.

The description of the various voting structures that operated in Rome that follows in Katz's account (pp. 14–18) is in general accurate and illuminating, but it still seems that the conception of a formal precedence for the richer classes, as in the "assembly of centuries," has overinfluenced the rest: "All Roman voting assemblies were weighted in favor of the rich, but this was particularly true of the centuriate assembly" (p. 15). This, however, is to elide the difference between a formal structure of precedence on the one hand and possible social factors that may have affected voting in the "assembly of tribes" on the other. To repeat, in the formal structure of voting in the "assembly of tribes" (which elected the tribunes and voted on nearly all legislation), there was no precedence for the rich. Certainly, insofar as the results of voting might depend on the presence of voters who had come from places distant from Rome, there must have been a de facto bias in favor of those with the means, and the leisure, to travel. But, first, in the late Republic, about a third of all Roman voters (some 300,000 out of some 900,000) lived either in the city or in the area immediately around it.[19] Second, when voters moved from rural districts to Rome, it does not seem that the censors systematically transferred them to the four "urban" tribes. So a large number of voters formally registered in the thirty-one "rustic" tribes will have been living in or near Rome anyway. If that is so, the growing dominance of the urban plebs in the late Republic can be explained easily (for it contained de facto representatives of all thirty-five tribes, who were in a position to defend their interests, without having to travel to Rome first). In short, the voting patterns exhibited by the "assembly of tribes," and the social factors and influences relevant to them, are matters of historical judgment and debate.

Nonetheless, Katz's account of how Roman voting worked is

clear and pointed, and it is worth reproducing his conclusion to this section:

> Roman voting assemblies never were deliberative bodies analogous to the Athenian Assembly. Instead, they were summoned by a magistrate to answer a specific question put by him—to approve or reject a bill he proposed, to convict or acquit a defendant he charged, or to choose among candidates he recognized. Elections were a trial of strength among rival candidates and their clienteles, rather than tests of the popularity of leaders or of their positions on public questions. The Roman Republic was government with the consent of the people, but in no real sense was it government by the people.[20]

Some nuances in this conclusion might be questioned, but in essence it is correct that in these three major areas—legislation, trials, and elections—the voter simply responded positively or negatively to an option put before him. Certainly, we could not regard this as government *by* the people. But, given that legislation could be preceded both by visible forms of popular pressure and by *contiones* (public meetings) at which the crowds present could and did make their reactions very clear, it could be argued that the word *consent* is not strong enough. Given the open context (primarily the forum) in which Roman public life and debate was conducted, and the highly personal nature of politics, we could regard Rome as providing an example of the "participationist" or "communitarian" democracy discussed by Katz in later chapters (pp. 67–99).

Equally, given the importance of the right to vote on the part of Roman citizens, it would not be right to accept the conception of Roman freedom (*libertas*), put forward in another outstanding recent contribution to political thought, Philip Pettit's *Republicanism*.[21] For he quotes various modern authorities for the view that the Roman plebs sought not public power but private security and protection from oppression. It is indeed true that popular politics contributed directly to the eventual arrival of a monarchic system that offered security and material benefits at the cost of any wider participation in decision making. But while the Republic still stood, this view of Roman *libertas* is clearly inadequate. The proof, as we will see again later (p. 167), is provided by popular reactions after Sulla, as dictator in the late 80s B.C., had removed the right of the tribunes of the plebs to propose legislation directly to the people. It took only a decade for popular pressure to bring about a restoration of that right, with fateful consequences, which Cicero predicted explicitly at the time. Citizenship in Rome did involve the right to active participation, at least in the sense of voting on legislation proposed, or on the selection of one candidate for office as opposed to another, as described already. A far more crucial question is that of how many citizens actually did, or could, exercise those rights.

Finally, we consider the treatment of the Roman Republic in two other modern contributions to political thought, Sanford Lakoff's *Democracy*, published in 1996, and the great posthumous work in three volumes by S. E. Finer, *The History of Government*. If we take Lakoff's *Democracy* first, it should be stressed that the book is a work of great conceptual richness, discussing not only different historical systems but also both contemporary and later conceptions of them, and the degree of continuity (or otherwise) that can be traced from ancient or medieval democratic practice or theory to modern.[22] So, to pick out simply the treatment of the Roman Republic is in no way to do justice to the whole. The discussion of the Republic comes in chapter 4, entitled "Plural Autonomy: Roman and Later Republicanism," and begins by emphasizing that the Republic, as a "form of balanced or mixed government" (p. 65), provided a source for later republican thought in a way that Athenian democracy did not. The author is also entirely correct in seeing that, depending on different interpretations and viewpoints, the Republic could provide material for a variety of different theses: popular sovereignty, "plural autonomy" in the sense of the division of the voters into different voting segments and structures (the various forms of assembly), or, alternatively, aristocratic predominance and the role of the Senate or of magisterial authority. There was also the wider consideration stressed by Machiavelli, that is, military service by citizens and the inculcation of civic virtue.

What is most striking about Lakoff's treatment, which is throughout full of interesting and penetrating observations, is its structure and, above all (once again), its concentration on the semihistorical narrative of early Rome. In a very real sense, in the comparative political thought of today, just as for Machiavelli, "the Roman Republic" is the one constructed in the first decade of Livy's *History*, or in Dionysius of Halicarnassus, whose narrative, now only partially preserved, went only as far as 264 B.C. Thus the history of Rome in Lakoff's *Democracy* is covered in two sections, "From Monarchy to Republic" (pp. 70–75), and "The Struggle of the Orders" (pp. 75–78), taking the story down to the Lex Hortensia of 287 B.C., which secured recognition of the votes of the plebs (*plebiscita*) as binding on all Romans. So far as the evolution of the political structure goes, there is no place for the Rome of the Hannibalic War or for the classical Republic of the first half of the second century, both covered in great detail in Livy's surviving narrative; and there is still less for the last century of the Republic, whose profile in political thought is fatally obscured by the absence of a continuous detailed surviving narrative in Latin, by Livy or anyone else. Yet it is this Rome for which, for the first time, we have a significant range of genuinely contemporary evidence, however fragmentary, partial, or problematic much of it is, on which an interpretation of the system could be based.

In narrative terms, therefore, Lakoff's book pays an astonishing tribute to the dominance of the canonical literary representation. In terms of analysis, however, of course Lakoff goes further than that. First, there is a brief account of Cicero's conception of republicanism (p. 79). Then comes an attempt, not without real interest, to assess the conflicting forces that affected the developed Republic as a political system ("Hierarchy, Pluralism, and the Republican Constitution"). Here, various factors are stressed: for instance, inequalities of wealth, the struggle for plebeian membership of the Senate, the plurality of voting assemblies, the power of the tribunes, and the indeterminancy in the balance of power as between the "assembly of tribes" and the Senate.

This state of balance, taken as characteristic of the period up to the mid-second century (in other words, the time at which Polybius's analysis was written) is seen, in inevitably conventional terms, as having been broken by the "rebellion" of the Gracchi, who are rightly conceived of as having "appealed to the principle of the sovereignty of the people." But there is no account of the important changes in the workings of the system, which did indeed embody an assertion of popular sovereignty and did equally lead subsequently to the reappearance of monarchy. Nor is there any account of the significance of the so-called social war of 90–87 B.C., the "war against the allies," which led the Romans to concede possession of the Roman citizenship to all of Italy south of the Po River. We shall return to this fundamental transformation (pp. 151–52 and 162–63). For the moment, it will suffice to point out that one could hardly find a reference to it in any works of political thought that have sought to analyze what sort of case the Roman Republic represents, or what sort of lessons might be drawn from it. Once again, the Rome of Cicero is essentially invisible, whereas the earlier Rome portrayed in Livy's narrative holds the center of the stage.

In a similar way, although not quite to the same extent, this is true also of the most important and wide-ranging comparative study of governmental institutions, Finer's *History of Government*.[23] This work is of exceptional interest and importance, and all of its vast and sweeping survey of historical political systems is illuminating and rewarding. The same is true of his treatment of the Roman Republic, for a start because this is the only example known to me of a systematic examination of it in the light of, and in comparison with, other systems. As in all such approaches, there are inevitably errors, but these are not worth attention, if only because, here as elsewhere, experts would disagree as to what counts as a significant error, or an error at all. What matters and is significant is, first, the categories of interpretation applied; second, the period on which the work focuses; and third, the conclusions drawn as to the nature of the Roman system.

The categories into which Finer divides states are highly significant, above all because one of them is drawn, or seems to be drawn, directly from the model of the Roman Republic itself. The four main types of polity as proposed by Finer are "Palace," with its direct opposite, "Forum," and cross-cutting these "Church" and "Nobility" (and these may be combined with each other in various hybrid types). "Palace" is of course the symbol of the seat of a monarch. "Church" and "Nobility" are shorthand for the nature of the ruling class, priesthood, or other religious status on the one hand, and lineage or public service (often military) on the other. But for students of the Roman Republic, it is naturally what Finer says about the "Forum" type that is of the greatest interest:

THE FORUM

Another metonomy! Here the place where debate and voting takes place is used to stand for those who take part in this process. The Palace system is a closed little world; the Forum system is open and wide. The Palace system is authoritarian—the right to govern has been conferred from on high; the Forum polity, though not necessarily democratic, is "popular:"

that is, authority is conferred on the rulers from below. The Palace system is monocratic; the Forum is plural-headed.

One essential point must be emphasized here in the most explicit way (it will be used implicitly in all that follows), and it is this. To conform to the Forum type it is not enough that the government has been appointed by popular conferment. If this were all, then a government, once so appointed, could go on ruling indefinitely in the Palace fashion as explained above. Indeed, as will be seen, this is precisely what defines the at-first-sight paradoxical hybrid, the Palace/Forum polity. To conform to the Forum type of polity, the government must be accountable to the people who have conferred on it the right to govern. In practice this means periodic renewal of its mandate by such processes as elections and the like.[24]

What is striking about this definition of a type, which obviously owes its name to *the* Forum in Rome, is that it would be perfectly apposite for any representative system of a relatively public and open character. For instance, it would be valid if the nature of the Roman Senate had been that it was a legislature whose members were elected for limited periods and who then had to give some public account of themselves, or just stand for reelection. But the Roman Senate was not a legislature. Alternatively, all individual holders of public office in Rome (consuls, praetors, quaestors, tribunes, and so forth—more than fifty in all) were elected by the people for a single year. Consuls at any rate had to take an oath, both at the beginning and at the end of their tenure, and could make a speech at the end defending or extolling their conduct in office. They also could be liable to criminal prosecution after the end of their term of office. So in various senses we could say that they were "accountable to the people."

In any case, these considerations are trivial when set against the fact that the Roman system was not a representative one. Not only was the Senate not a legislature, but those elected officials who had the power to propose legislation could do so only by putting their propositions to the voters assembled in the Forum. There, citizens who chose to gathered to hear speeches for and against forthcoming legislation, and there, they assembled in their thirty-five voting units (*tribus*) to vote "yes" or "no" on laws. Paradoxically, therefore, the political system that had the real Roman Forum as its center had been one of direct citizen participation of a far more explicitly democratic nature that the "Forum" type as set out by Finer.

Beyond that, it does seem to me to be true that Finer has not recognized that, not only in fact (i.e., that laws—*leges* or *plebiscita*—could by definition be passed only by popular votes) but also in explicit theory, the Roman system accorded sovereignty to "the Roman people" (*populus Romanus*). We saw earlier (pp. 53, 63–64) how important it was that in the Empire and the Middle Ages the *populus* was construed as having formally transferred sovereignty to the Emperors. So the clear implication early in Finer's first volume (p. 4) that this idea arose only in later periods is surely misleading: "The notion that the state's destinies are decided, in the last resort at least, by the politically significant members of the population, that is, that it belongs to the nation and not the ruler, arises distinctively late outside England, and for the explicit recognition that 'sovereignty resides in the nation' we must wait till the French Revolution. . . ."

It is also perhaps a pity that Finer does not bring in the case of Rome when he discusses (I, p. 44) "the constituents of the Forum polity," namely, who had the vote. The fact that in Athens every adult male citizen had the right to vote is of course mentioned, as is the fact that something approaching this situation was not achieved in Britain until 1884 (when some 60% of male adults gained the vote, with universal adult male suffrage coming only in 1918). But we know of no period in the history of the Republic from the fifth century B.C. onward when any male adults were excluded by low economic status from the right to vote (deliberately limited as to its practical effects by the structure of the "assembly of centuries" but not in the "assembly of tribes"). The semihistorical early Republic, when Rome was a nuclear city-state like Athens (and many other Greek states), is not particularly significant in comparative terms. If we look forward (as students of government rarely if ever do), to the Roman Republic of Cicero's time, the total number of adult male voters was some nine hundred thousand, and the total citizen population living between the Po River and the "toe" of Italy will have been somewhere between three and four million.[25] This figure gains further significance when it is realized that the total population of the thirteen states of America at the time of the Declaration of Independence was some four million[26]—and universal adult male suffrage was not the rule in any of the states.

All these Roman citizens belonged to one of the thirty-five "tribes," and in principle all had the right to come to Rome to vote. Some, indeed, did come, and from not inconsiderable distances. But it was only in Rome, in person, that voting could be carried out, and it was some 350 kilometers in one direction to the Po River, and the best part of six hundred in the other to Rhegium (Reggio). So it can safely be assumed that the overwhelming mass of the people never exercised their right to vote even once. Nonetheless, there are significant issues about Rome, in the mid-first century B.C., and the way in which it exhibited simultaneously various characteristics of a nuclear city-state, on the one hand, and a nation-state on the other; and we will return to these issues later (pp. 162–63). All that needs to be stressed here is that, as regards "the constituents of the Forum polity," the Roman Republic is a case that deserves attention.

Second, as indicated above, we need to examine which period in the history of the Republic provides the material for Finer's analysis. The discussion occupies a substantial section of volume I (pp. 385–441) and, in general, should be acknowledged as providing both a very effective summary of the powers and roles of the various elements, and a balanced attempt to mediate between drastically opposed modern interpretations. Moreover, it takes the story of the Roman constitution further in time than any of the treatments discussed earlier. Thus the analysis starts with the regal period, reasonably enough since all that we can claim to know of the origins of the Roman institutions of the properly historical period is owed to Livy's narrative. But it also brings the story down to the dictatorship of Sulla in 82–1 B.C., seeing his reactionary reforms as "the end of the ancient constitution" (p. 435). Unlike many others, therefore, his treatment covers at least the early part of the fully historical period, that is to say, that from which we have first-hand testimony from participants, as well as a significant scatter of contemporary documents.

However, he does not have space to discuss, for instance, either the ballot laws of the 130s B.C. or still less the vast change in the nature of the Roman political system represented by the extension of citizenship after the Social War, discussed previously. Sulla's reforms, which Finer takes as his terminal point, were indeed very significant, and Finer is wholly correct to say (p. 437) that they amounted to a deliberate rejection of the system of "checks and balances" analyzed in the previous century by Polybius and functioning to produce a sort of creative tension between the "monarchical," the "aristocratic," and the "democratic" elements in the state.

But since, as we have seen, it took a mere decade for popular pressure to bring about a reversal of all the key elements of the reforms, Sulla's dictatorship was not a true terminal point. Particularly as regards the 60s and 50s B.C., we thus miss both the best-attested and the most conflict-ridden period in the political history of the Republic—and miss, as well, the one in which Cicero personally played a major role and formed the ideas that have been so influential in subsequent perceptions of the Republic. But, although Livy did narrate this period, his text is missing for the whole last century and a half of the Republic; so there is no overall ancient narrative to which later observers could relate, or at least none before those written in Greek by Appian in the second century A.D. and Cassius Dio (pp. 46–49 previously) in the third.

Finer's concluding "appraisal" (I, pp. 438–41) hardly does justice either to the Roman system or to his own previous account of it. He notes the level of patriotism and civic virtue (which Machiavelli had stressed) and the ability of Rome to produce something approaching Roman, or Italian, nationhood, as well as the ingrained militarism and brutality of Roman society. But, as his posthumous text stands, he hardly succeeds in appreciating what a truly "Forum-type" polity will have been like: "The Republican constitution was preposterous. Stripped down to the legal provisions only, this constitution was unworkable" (p. 440). In this way he succeeds less well than Polybius in seeing that it was precisely the overt elements of conflict, balance and mutual dependence, along with the continued demonstration and reenactment of these factors in public, literally before the eyes of the people, that allowed the Republic to have more impact on the history of the world than any other city-state.

The Crowd and the Mob

We will return in the final chapter to the evolution of the Republican system in the century between Polybius and the dictatorship of Julius Caesar and will ask how Aristotle might have judged it if he had been a contemporary of Cicero. But before that, and as an appendix to this brief look at modern approaches, it is worth considering one significant modern work of a different type, McClelland's *The Crowd and the Mob*.[27] For Rome, especially toward the end of the Republic, offers a very special case of the power of the crowd, or mob. Many different aspects of Roman public life took place before the eyes of the crowd in the Forum, from the taking of oaths to the conduct of trials in the open air, to gladiatorial shows or political speeches. Violence and organized efforts to assert physical control of the public space of the Forum also were increasingly common, especially in the 50s, the last decade of the Republic proper. But what distinguished the Roman crowd or mob from most of the other urban crowds—which at different periods have acclaimed rulers, or protested, or rioted, or occupied public buildings, or barricaded parts of cities—is that this same crowd or mob, by being redistributed into the subdivisions ("tribes") in which it voted, became, or had the role of representing, the sovereign *populus Romanus*, which alone could pass legislation. The meaning of its presence, as witness, audience, or actor, was therefore entirely different from that of most crowds that in different historical contexts have gathered in city centers at politically important moments.

The assembled Roman voters were all the more closely related to an undifferentiated mob or crowd because legislative meetings of the "assembly of tribes," first, had no fixed timetable during the year (as opposed, for instance, to the Athenian *ekklēsia*, which had forty regular meetings each year) and, second, met in the same place, the Forum, as was the normal focal point for daily life (and for the various public functions mentioned above). The Athenian assembly, on the other hand, normally met in a specially designated area, the Pnyx. It was therefore only the proclamation of an assembly, after a due interval for the public promulgation of the proposed legislation, and the instruction from the presiding magistrate to reassemble into "tribes," that transformed the crowd into the sovereign *populus Romanus*.

McClelland's exceptionally interesting and suggestive book is therefore essential as providing a wider intellectual and interpretative background, "from Plato to Canetti," as the title indicates, for historical attitudes to the power, and danger, of crowds. In structure and purpose, the work is that of intellectual history, of attitudes to crowds in successive periods, not the history of actual crowds (which is in any case rarely possible). Hence when Mc-Clelland comes in chapter 2 to "The Crowd in the Ancient World" the focus is on authors, beginning with Plato. When we come to Rome, however, it is almost unnerving to discover that the treatment divides between three phases and three authors: The latest is Procopius on the Nika riot of A.D. 532 in Constantinople; the second is Tacitus, in the *Histories* and *Annals*, on the "marginalized" people acting as spectators of events in Rome under the Emperors of the first century A.D.; and the first is Livy's *History* to 386 B.C. (pp. 46–50). McClelland is well aware that what he is dealing with is not history but a narrative representation of events from (at best) a semihistorical period and is also of course conscious of the role that this representation was to play in later political thought:

Livy's history allows us to see both Senate and People making themselves a constitution and making it work, though we have to wait for Machiavelli, in the *Discourses on the First Decade of Livy*, and following him, Montesquieu, to draw out the lessons for a theory of balanced government and for an account of the essential part tumults of the people have to play in keeping a free government true to its republican principles . . .[28]

Cicero's Rome has once again vanished from view, which is especially significant in this context, not just because we have direct knowledge of it from contemporary evidence, but because Cicero, who was killed a decade or more before Livy began to write, provides in his speeches, above all the *Verrine Orations* of 70 B.C., the most powerful images of the power of the watching crowd. Moreover, it was he himself who gave the most vivid expression to the idea that popular tumults in the early Republic had been the essential condition of liberty.

The evidence comes from a complex literary context, Cicero's great work *On the Orator* (*De oratore*), which takes the form of a discussion between some major political figures of the previous generation, set in the year 91 B.C., just before the outbreak of the Social War. In it, the great orator Marcus Antonius is made to recall the speech he had made a few years before when defending someone on a charge of treason (*maiestas*). It must be remembered that any such speech would have been made in the Forum, in the open air, before a crowd of spectators surrounding the orators and the jurors. The true audience of such a speech was therefore much wider than those directly concerned in the case. This is what Cicero makes Antonius recall having said:

I gathered together all types of seditions, their wrongs and dangers, and make that oration a survey of all the varied phases of our *res publica*, and concluded in such a way that I said that although all seditions had always been an affliction, some none the less had been justified and even necessary . . . Without dissension among the nobles the kings could not have been driven out from this city, nor tribunes of the plebs elected nor the powers of the consuls so often limited by *plebiscita*—and nor could the right of appeal, that protector of the citizens and champion of liberty, have been granted to the *populus Romanus*.[29]

Even between the lines of our limited evidence, of which too high a proportion comes from Cicero himself, it is possible to see the main elements of a popular tradition of liberty, in terms of which constant reference was made to the legendary struggles of the early Republic.[30] In that sense, the traditional narrative that Livy was soon to mold into his *History* already had an importance that is not affected by uncertainty as to whether the episodes recounted in it ever actually occurred. All the same, Cicero's Rome, even without the benefit of any surviving narrative by Livy, still deserves to receive some of the attention that has been devoted to the Republic in the history of political thought.

7   Cicero's Rome
What Aristotle Might Have Thought

Introduction: The Historical Context

One major theme running through the earlier chapters has been the importance in intellectual history of literary texts to which later thinkers could relate. In the case of the Roman Republic, later perceptions have been dominated by the presence of Livy's narrative and above all—indeed, almost exclusively—by his narrative of early Rome in his first ten books. Why his clear and detailed account of the Hannibalic War and of the first part of the second century, which represented the first stage of Roman general domination of the Mediterranean, has played no such role is hard to explain; but it certainly has not. Another theme has been the overwhelming influence, since the thirteenth century onward, of the categories that Aristotle applied to the analysis of constitutions: the three praiseworthy forms, *basileia* (or *monarchia*), *aristokratia*, and *politeia* (in the special sense of a broad constitution, which, in one way or another, placed some restraint on the power of the *dēmos*); and their perverted forms, *tyrannis*, *oligarchia* and *dēmokratia* (a term that Aristotle used of a constitution in which the *dēmos* was free to exploit its power to its own advantage). From the translation of Aristotle's *Politics* into Latin in the mid-thirteenth century onward, this Greek political terminology was to enter all European languages and influence all political thought.

As a consequence, the question of what sort of balance there should be in any political system between monarchic, aristocratic (or oligarchic), and popular elements had entered political thought, and retrospective reflection on the Roman Republic, even before Polybius's analysis of the Roman *politeia* (in the broader sense of any political system) was rediscovered in the early sixteenth century (just in time for Machiavelli to have had, as is evident, some awareness of it).

Polybius's analysis, quite brief and general as it in fact is, remains the only serious discussion of the Roman *politeia* by a contemporary observer. Aristotle, as we saw (pp. 15–23), might well have commented on the Roman state as it was toward the middle of the second half of the fourth century, and would have found it in an extremely interesting and significant phase of evolution if he had. Evidently, he did not treat it either in the set of Greek *politeiai* collected by his school or among "barbarian customs." Later Greek accounts, if they were seriously interested in institutions at all, looked back, as Dionysius of Halicarnassus did (pp. 39–46), to the origin and early history of the Roman state.

For all these reasons, if our interest is in conceptions of the Republic, and the influence of these conceptions in later political thought, we find ourselves perpetually coming back to early Rome: the degree to which even the monarchy itself was represented in later accounts as having had a constitutional framework; the expulsion of the kings; the "struggle of the orders"; and then—but to a lesser degree than one might suppose—to Polybius's account of the "mixed" or "balanced" Roman *politeia* of the Hannibalic War. Implicitly, as F. W. Walbank has shown, Polybius was concerned to underline also the stresses it had undergone since then and the decline toward demagoguery and the excessive power of the *demos*, which he evidently perceived as having occurred in the decades up to his own time, the middle of the second century (pp. 23–37).

It is paradoxical that, whether in contemporary political thought or in later reflection, the last century of the Republic plays almost no part. The most prominent individual names—Marius, Sulla, Pompey, Caesar—occasionally may appear as examples; but it would be hard to find, from any period, any serious analysis of the late-Republican state as a system. Of course, ideas about the system and its values are scattered everywhere in the speeches and theoretical works of Cicero. His *On Duties* (*De officiis*) is of great importance, as is his *On the Republic*, a dialogue explicitly imitating Plato's *Republic*. But this is given a dramatic setting of 129 B.C., whereas his *On the Laws* (*De legibus*), modeled on Plato's *Laws*, is in essence a proposal for the sort of republic that he would have wished to see.[1] No contemporary Greek observer produced any systematic analysis.

It is not that we cannot, out of the relatively dense mass of contemporary writing and documentation, arrive at conceptions —even if vigorously disputed ones—of the nature of the late-Republican system. What is significant in the history of thought is that no systematic treatment or analysis in any coherent literary form has been available for later thinkers to use.

This may not be surprising, but it is certainly regrettable, if only because there is no other example of a state with the institutions of a nuclear city-state that had so extensive and violent an impact on the rest of the world, with its forces in the 50s B.C. crossing the English Channel in one direction and the Euphrates in the other. With fateful consequences, they had also already captured Jerusalem. So a Polybius, if one had been present in Rome between 67 and 50 B.C. (rather than between 167 and 150 B.C.), would have been presented with a theme of even greater significance.

The fact that there was none is the excuse for the exercise in counterfactual intellectual history that follows, namely, an attempt to ask how the Rome of Cicero's time would have looked if Aristotle had been in a position to apply his categories of analysis to it. In particular, because this author has for the last few years been advancing the view that Rome deserves serious consideration as a type of democracy, discussion will focus on where Rome might have appeared on the scale of different types of *politeia* or *demokratia* if Aristotle's categories were applied to it. It should be stressed that for Aristotle a complete (*teleutaia*) democracy was something undesirable that should be avoided.[2] Equally, to argue that the Roman system had strongly democratic features is not thereby to argue that it did not have profound, indeed fatal, defects. In any case, as we will see subsequently, the answer to the question of whether Aristotle would have characterized late-Republican Rome as a democracy is very mixed: it had some features that he would have seen as clearly democratic and others that corresponded to an aristocratic system, based on personal competition, or to a "timocratic" one, based on distinctions of wealth. Polybius of course had also seen Rome as having a mixed constitution, in which the "monarchic," "aristocratic," and "democratic" elements were balanced (or had been appropriately balanced during the Hannibalic War). However, in a number of ways, which one might understand Polybius as having predicted, and which we will look at later, the system had subsequently evolved significantly in a democratic direction before giving way, once again, to monarchy.

There were, however, some quite fundamental aspects of late-Republican Rome to which Aristotle's categories of analysis could hardly have been applied at all. As we saw earlier (pp. 17–18), even the real Aristotle, if he had paid attention, would have been confronted with a system, which in the 330s and 320s B.C. already was expanding beyond the bounds of the nuclear city-state. By Polybius's time, the combination of colonization and granting citizenship to existing communities had created a zone of citizen settlement stretching from Rome to Campania in the south and to the Adriatic in the north, some 250 kilometers in either direction, with some areas farther north still. Polybius's analysis, for all its immense merits, failed to take explicit account of the geographic dimensions of the Roman state as it was then. He also described the role of the "people" (dēmos) without paying attention either to their subdivision into thirty-five "tribes" on a geographic basis or to the way in which majority voting in the main legislative assembly took the form of thirty-five successive "tribal" votes, with eighteen constituting an overall majority.

As we have seen earlier (pp. 151–52), these features now were reproduced on an even vaster scale, covering the entire peninsula from the toe of Italy to the Po River, and embracing a population that must have considerably exceeded 3,000,000, with some 900,000 adult male voters. This was the result of the "Social War" ("the war of the allies") of 90–87 B.C., by which Rome had been forced to concede citizenship to all of Italy south of the Po.

In the *Politics*, Aristotle twice discussed the possible limits on the size of a genuine *polis*. In the first, he leaves the issue indeterminate:

In the case of a population which inhabits a single territory, we may likewise ask "When should we consider that there is a single city?" For, of course, the identity of a city is not constituted by its walls—it would be possible to surround the whole of the Peloponnese by a single wall. Babylon (which, it is said, had been captured for three whole days before some of its inhabitants knew of the fact) may perhaps be counted a city of this dubious nature: so, too, might any city which had the dimensions of a people [*ethnos*] rather than those of a city [or *polis*]. But it will be better to reserve the consideration of this question for some other occasion.[3]

When he later comes back to the question, he makes a number of observations that are fundamental to his conception of what a *polis* should be:

Experience shows that it is difficult, if not indeed impossible, for a very populous city to enjoy good government. Observation tells us that none of the cities which have a reputation for being well governed are without some limit of population. But the point can also be established on the evidence of the words themselves. Law [*nomos*] is a system of order [*taxis*]; and good government [*eunomia*] must therefore involve a general system of orderliness [*eutaxia*]. But an unlimited number cannot partake in order . . . A city composed of too few members is a city without self-sufficiency (and the city, by its definition, is self-sufficient). One composed of too many will indeed be self-sufficient in the matter of material necessities (as a nation may be) but it will not be a city, since it can hardly have a constitution. Who can be its herald, unless he has Stentor's voice?

The initial stage of the city may therefore be said to require such an initial amount of population as will be self-sufficient for the purpose of achieving a good way of life in the shape and form of a political association. A city which exceeds this initial amount may be a still greater city; but such increase of size, as has already been noticed, cannot continue indefinitely. What the limit of increase should be is a question easily answered if we look at the actual facts. The activities of a city are partly the activities of its governors, and partly those of the governed. The function of governors is to issue commands and give decisions. Both in order to give decisions in matters of disputed rights, and to distribute the offices of government according to the merit of candidates, the citizens of a city must know one another's characters. Where this is not the case, the distribution of offices and the giving of decisions will suffer. Both are matters in which it is wrong to operate by guesswork; but that is what obviously happens where the population is over-large . . .

These considerations indicate clearly the optimum standard of population. It is, in a word, "the greatest surveyable number required for achieving a life of self-sufficiency." Here we may end our discussion of the proper size of the population.[4]

It is true that Aristotle goes on to talk of the proper extent of a city's territory. But even if we take the passage quoted as referring only to the strictly urban population, it is clear that first-century Rome far exceeded the scale indicated. In the earlier passage, in any case, he makes clear that neither a vast city like Babylon nor a whole geographic area like the Peloponnese could satisfy the definition of a *polis*. So the notion of a single *politeia* embracing the inhabitants of the majority of the Italian peninsula would have seemed to him an absurdity.

Indeed, we might well agree that it was; but two aspects need to be taken into account, neither of which could easily be fitted into the presuppositions of Greek political thought. One is that each of the component cities of the Roman/Italian *politeia* retained its character as a self-governing city-state, now without its own military forces, but with a defined body of citizens, elected annual magistrates, and a council. The effect was to produce a sort of dual, or two-level, citizenship; as Cicero remarks in a famous passage from his *Laws* (III.5), each person from such a town now had two *patriae* (native cities), the one from which he came and Rome.

Second, we know from contemporary documentary evidence, in the form of a long inscription on bronze from Heraclea in southern Italy, that Roman citizenship had a specific meaning in three different respects.[5] First, the inscription records a rule that no one who is less than thirty years old shall be a candidate for a local magistracy unless he has served three campaigns as a cavalryman in a legion or six as an infantryman, or he has exemption (ll. 89–94, and 98–104). In a weakened form, therefore, this can be seen as an extension to local communities of Roman citizens of the rule that Polybius had recorded in the previous century (Book VI.19.2), by which military service was a necessary condition for standing for office in Rome. The service in question had to be in the Roman legions; in practice, this meant not universal conscription, but either volunteering or a universal liability to being conscripted when levies were conducted, unpredictably, in different regions of Italy at different times.[6] In this sense, being a Roman citizen was by no means a purely nominal status.

Second, the text shows that when censuses of Roman citizens were conducted, it was the duty of the local magistrates to make up lists of the citizens (both freeborn and ex-slave) in their area, make a record of these, and send to Rome ambassadors from the community to present the lists to the censors (ll. 142–56). How, if at all, the lists, coming from several hundred different communities, then were integrated in Rome defies imagination. In any case, our evidence suggests that in the disturbed conditions of first-century Rome, it was very rare for censuses to be completed. The *principle*, nonetheless, is clear: that every Roman citizen, wherever in Italy he was resident, should be listed through the agency of his local community.

Furthermore, the text is quite explicit as to the requirement that each man should be listed with his full Roman name, *his tribe*, and his property. So, in principle, each one had a place both in the "assembly of tribes" and in the appropriate century in the "assembly of centuries."

The Italy of the mid-first century therefore represented something like a nation-state, occupying a large proportion of the territory of the present Italian state, and enjoying (in principle) universal adult male suffrage (except, of course, for the exclusion of slaves), a stage not reached again in Italy (and even then with some limitations) until 1912.

This remarkable combination of city-state and nation-state might be thought far more worth reflection by modern students of politics than the contents of Livy's early books. Of course, there was a vast gap between the possession in principle of these rights and their actual enjoyment. To vote, the Roman citizen from Italy still had to go to Rome. Some did so, indeed, even from northern Italy; but the vast majority, we can be certain, never did. No arrangements were made for local voting, and the structure had no place either for constituencies or for representation. The sending of ambassadors from communities to appear before the Senate, however, was a (weak) form of representation that did come into play, and Emilio Gabba has emphasized how such embassies played a part not just in delivering lists, but in crucial political episodes in the 50s.[7] On one particular occasion also, the vote for the recall of Cicero from exile in 57 B.C., the leading figures in Rome made a major effort to summon respectable conservative men from Italy to vote through the necessary law passed (for once) in the "assembly of centuries." In light of these factors, the suggestion made by the "Federal Farmer" in the debate on the American Constitution (p. 122 above) that a representative assembly of four to five hundred men from Italy could have provided stability for Rome, although obviously hypothetical, is worth reflection. Almost any system that allowed an organized voice in Rome to the "local nobles" (*domi nobiles* in Latin) of the towns of Italy might indeed have had a chance of creating a moderate and stable *politeia* in Aristotle's sense; but no such step was ever taken.

A Roman/Italian nation-state, on a scale larger than many modern nation-states, thus (in principle) really existed. In any case, such a thing was outside the framework of presumptions that shaped Aristotle's *Politics*, as were also the leagues of cities and the kingdoms (Macedonia and Persia) that played so important a part in the fourth-century Greek world.

It is therefore not worth asking what Aristotle might have made of a citizen-body on this scale. Equally, though the *Politics* makes occasional reference to "tribes" (*phylai*) as constituent elements of Greek *poleis*, it is not likely that he, any more than Polybius, would have made anything of the segmented voting of both the "assembly of tribes" and the "assembly of centuries." Nor, so far as we know, did any Greek *polis* have two voting assemblies, constructed on different lines, functioning in parallel. We would have to assume that, like Polybius, Aristotle would have thought of an undifferentiated "people" (*dēmos*) in relation to the other elements in the system. Differential voting rights determined by economic status, however, are contemplated in the *Politics*, if not in the systematically graduated form displayed in the "assembly of centuries." Overall, we must assume that Aristotle would have viewed Rome, as Polybius did, as a nuclear city-state with a *dēmos*, a Senate, and elected magistrates. What concerned him, like Polybius, was fundamentally, first, what different patterns of the distribution of power between these elements were empirically known and, second, what balance of power was best.

Setting aside the questions of the drastically altered scale of the city-body between Polybius' time and Cicero's (to which in any case contemporaries seem to have devoted remarkably little attention), we do need to take account of a few significant changes in the power structure of Rome over the same period. All of them, given an abortive period of reaction under Sulla's dictatorship in the late 80s, tended to tip the balance further in favor of the "people." With one exception, they can be summarized briefly before we finally turn to Aristotle.

The one exception is the ballot laws of the 130s, which because they are not the subject of standard narratives (like those of Appian or Plutarch), always have tended to be overshadowed by the story of the Gracchi. Taken collectively, these successive laws, substituting a ballot token for public, oral voting, which was clearly vulnerable to pressure from the powerful, were certainly of great importance—as is shown, paradoxically, by the two different interpretations of them that Cicero gives in two different contexts. In his discussion in his dialogue *On the Laws*, a negative view is given, placed in the mouth of his brother Quintus:

But everyone knows that laws which provide a secret ballot have deprived the aristocracy of all its influence. And such a law was never desired by the people when they were free, but was demanded only when they were tyrannized over by the powerful men in the State. (For this very reason we have records of severer condemnations of powerful men under the oral method of voting than when the ballot was used). Therefore means should have been found to deprive powerful leaders of the people's undue eagerness to support them with their votes even in the case of bad measures, but the people should not have been provided with a hiding-place, where they could conceal a mischievous vote by means of the ballot, and keep the aristocracy in ignorance of their real opinions. For these reasons no man of high character has ever proposed or supported a measure like yours. There are indeed four such balloting laws in existence. The first is concerned with the election of magistrates; this is the Gabinian Law (139 B.C.), proposed by a man who was unknown and of low degree. That was followed two years later by the Cassian Law (137 B.C.), which referred to trials before the people; it was proposed by Lucius Cassius, who was a nobleman, but—I say it without prejudice to his family—stood apart from the aristocracy, and, by favoring popular measures, was always seeking the fickle applause of the mob. The third law is that of Carbo (131 or 130 B.C.), which applies to the adoption or rejection of proposed laws; this Carbo was a factious and mischievous citizen, who could not gain his personal safety from the aristocracy even by returning to his allegiance to their party. The method of oral voting, then, appeared to have gone out of existence except in trials for treason, which even Cassius had omitted from his balloting law. But Gaius Coelius (107 B.C.) provided the ballot even for such trials; however, he regretted to the end of his days that he had done an injury to the republic in order to destroy Gaius Popilius.[8]

This negative view is of great importance, not least in outlining the three fundamental types of question on which the people could vote: on elections, on legislation, and on criminal trials. No hesitation is expressed in saying that the damaging consequence was precisely that individuals would now be free from pressure by their betters. In his oration *In Defence of Plancius* of 55 B.C., however, when speaking in public in the Forum, Cicero adopts a different position: The voting tablet was welcome to the people, for others could see their faces but not their intentions, and they were free to vote as they wished, whatever promises they had given.[9] It was not right, therefore, to try to challenge the result of an election in court.

Actual procedures in voting are not discussed in Aristotle's *Politics*, but mechanisms for ensuring a personal vote, by ballot, are described in the Aristotelian *Constitution of the Athenians* as regards the large popular jury counts.[10] Voting in the Athenian assembly (*ekklēsia*), on the other hand, seems to have been by show of hands, with no precise counting of numbers. In this respect, therefore, the Roman system seems always to have given greater emphasis both to the citizen's individual vote and (from the 130s onward) to ensuring its privacy.

We need not dwell on all the "popular" measures of the period from the Gracchi (the 130s and 120s) to the "Social War" of 90–87,[11] except to note the first steps to arrange a fixed-price monthly ration of corn for citizens; the transfer of appointment to public priesthoods to popular election; and the passing of a law on *maiestas* (treason), whose wording explicitly emphasized the sovereignty of the *populus Romanus*. Above all, however, there were public debates, and communal decisions voted in the form of laws (*leges*), which intervened progressively in the sphere that by convention had been left to discussion and decision by the Senate: foreign policy, and the disposition of commands and military forces. By convention, the Senate had decided which would be the *provinciae* (spheres of operation) of the consuls and praetors elected each year, and had also been free to decide which of the current elected magistrates should be left in command as a pro-magistrate for a further year. The newly-elected magistrates, by a remarkable procedure apparently designed to reduce competition, then drew lots for who should occupy each of the available *provinciae*.[12]

It was this annual strategic debate and vote, accompanied by decisions as to how large the forces directed to any one area should be, and the allocation of the relevant resources, along with the custom of receiving all embassies from foreign nations, which more than anything else gives some justification for the established notion that the Senate was Rome's effective ruling body. The reception of embassies indeed was a role that the Senate never lost, and the custom at Athens (for instance) whereby foreign embassies might come before the popular assembly was never adopted. Polybius summed up this aspect of the Senate's role with his usual accuracy:

It also occupies itself with the dispatch of all embassies sent to countries outside of Italy for the purpose either of settling differences, or of offering friendly advice, or indeed of imposing demands, or of receiving submission, or of declaring war; and in like manner with respect to embassies arriving in Rome it decides what reception and what answer should be given to them. All these matters are in the hands of the senate, nor have the people anything whatever to do with them. So that again to one residing in Rome during the absence of the consuls the constitution appears to be entirely aristocratic; and this is the conviction of many Greek states and many of the kings, as the senate manages all business connected with them.[13]

In a formal sense, this pattern was never disturbed, and in the 50s the Senate could still hold debates "on the consular provinces." But before the Social War, tribunes of the plebs had begun on occasion (not every year) to exploit the sovereignty of the people to override the dispositions made by the Senate, and also on occasion to put to the people detailed laws laying down instructions for the conduct of their office by provincial governors.[14]

Sulla himself, the future dictator, was affected by this change as consul in 88, when a law proposed by a tribune took away from him the command against Mithridates in Asia, allocated to him by lot following the determination of the two consular provinces by the Senate. It is thus possible, although pure speculation, that it was this issue of the intervention of popular voting in the sphere of foreign and provincial policy that led Sulla, after gaining power by force in 82 B.C. and being appointed dictator, to put through a measure making impossible the independent proposal of legislation by tribunes (Sulla's legislation is very poorly attested, and the account given here is intended only as the broadest of outlines). But the restoration of this right was insistently demanded through the 70s and was duly brought about by legislation in 70 B.C.

As it happens, Cicero's five orations prosecuting Verres, the former governor of Sicily (the *Verrine Orations*) were written in the summer of this year, the first of them actually delivered and the others not (as Verres had already gone into exile). They happen to provide a more vivid picture than any other source of the presence and pressure of the crowd in the Forum, where trials were held, and they also contain the most pointed expression of the significance of the restoration to the tribunes of the right to propose legislation. It will be worth quoting again the passage in which Cicero speaks of this, alluding also to an important change in the composition of the law courts (where since Sulla all the jurors had been senators):

This city endured, as long as it could, that kinglike domination of yours (the Senators), and it endured it in the law-courts and throughout the *res publica*. But on the day that the tribunes of the plebs were restored to the Roman People, all that, in case you do not understand it, was removed and torn from you.[15]

So, indeed, it was to prove; and through the 60s and 50s, legislation proposed to the people by tribunes on foreign affairs, on the allocation of commands, on the distribution of land to citizens, and on the establishment of a free monthly corn ration for each citizen was to be at the heart of the increasingly contentious and increasingly violent and unstable political process, which was soon to reach a quite new phase when Julius Caesar led his forces into Italy in January of 49 B.C.

The most obvious symbol of the new order is provided by Cicero's own speech *For the Manilian Law* (or *On the Command of Gnaeus Pompeius*) delivered to the people in the Forum, in 66 B.C. in support of a law proposed by a tribune, which transferred the command in the current war against Mithridates to Pompey. It is significant in several ways: in referring back to a similar issue in the previous year, when another tribunician law had given Pompey the command against pirates in the Mediterranean; in rehearsing before the people the strategic, economic and constitutional issues; and in arguing that the necessities of the moment required the concentration of military command in a single pair of hands.

Aristotle's Criteria

It is as regards this brief and troubled final stage in the constitutional history of the Republic, a phase that lasted only two decades before Julius Caesar had himself appointed dictator in 49, that it may be worth, as an exercise, asking how Aristotle would have categorized the Roman system and where he would have placed it on his double scale of *basileia* (kingship), *aristokratia*, and *politeia* (or "polity") on the one hand, and their respective "distortions" (*parekbaseis*), tyranny, oligarchy, and *dēmokratia* on the other.[16]

We have already discussed the problems that would have been presented to Aristotle's definitions by the sheer scale of the Roman system as it now was (pp. 164–65), and we will not return to that, or to the idiosyncratic Roman system of segmentary voting (pp. 18–20). As for the scale of types of regime, Aristotle himself in the *Politics* never thinks of applying the notion of *basileia* to annually elected magistrates in any Greek city; but he does do so in his discussion of Carthage, using the word *basileis* ("kings") of the elected "judges" (*sufetim*).[17] There were, in fact, two of these, elected each year, although Aristotle does not make either of these points explicitly. He therefore might well have done as Polybius did and used this concept of the Roman consuls. But if he had gone into any detail, his account of the role of the consuls would have had to differ significantly from Polybius's analysis. For Polybius had stressed with his usual acuteness that the political role and power of the consuls of each year was essentially, in his time, a matter of a short period before they both went off on campaigns: "The consuls, previous to leading out their legions, exercise authority in Rome over all public affairs . . ."[18] But in Cicero's time, the consuls, although they still received a command (*provincia*) from the beginning, normally stayed in Rome through their year of office and did not go off on campaign until near, or even after, the end of it. Election to office did, however, still lead, once on campaign, to a "royal" status in relation to the troops.

If we are looking at how Aristotle might have regarded Rome as a political system—and through that device at how *we* ought to— no one would take seriously the idea that the importance of the elected consuls ought to make us think of Rome as having been already a sort of monarchy. It soon would be, and the contrast between the two stages is evident. Indeed, the long-term commands voted in the 60s and 50s came about precisely because, in this sense, the power of the consuls was too limited and not "kingly" enough. In what ways these recurrent long-term commands might have affected Aristotle's view of the system is an interesting question.

If we think of the normal presumptions of the system as they had until now affected consuls, then what we see is the consuls of each year as members of a larger group among whom power was on the one hand limited in duration and scope (a large number of separate annual officeholders with different rights and functions) and on the other depended on election. Modern debates tend to focus on the definition of this ruling group on the one hand and on the balance of power between them and the people on the other, with further refinement of whether rights or duties among the mass of the people were allocated according to wealth, in short, the question of whether Rome worked on what Aristotle would have called a *timocratic system*.

One profound problem in relating Aristotle's thought (hypothetically) to the Roman system is that Aristotle uses *aristokratia* as a term for a system based on competition, or merit, but he does not use it in the modern sense of "aristocracy," that is, to refer to a descent group, defined by birth, and perhaps marked out by titles, or by legal privileges, or even by constitutional rights. But how to apply either *aristokratia* or "aristocracy" to Rome without distortion is a major question. The remaining "patrician" families were certainly a defined descent group, but they were relatively few, and whether an individual (like Sulla or Julius Caesar) happened to belong to such a family was of marginal importance. There were no public positions that a patrician could inherit as of right, although there were some places as public priests to which only patricians were eligible for election. If we were looking for an "aristocracy" (like the British House of Lords) as an element in the balance of the state, we will not find it here.

More significant is the fact that the Romans themselves used the description *nobiles* of the descendants of the holders of major elective offices (even relating to quite distant ancestors). But this was a *description*, not a formal title, and terms like *the Roman nobility* are systematically misleading when used in modern languages. No one, however, could possibly deny either that descent played a major part in claims to elective office, especially the consulship (but less so progressively for less prestigious posts), and that the Romans were quite conscious of this, speaking of a consul like Cicero, who was a first-generation senator, as a "new man" (*novus homo*).

There was no peerage at Rome, no titles and no hereditary (upper) chamber. Yet family prestige and descent from officeholding ancestors were extremely important (although *not* absolutely essential) for election to office. As Cicero stresses in his speech *In Defence of Plancius* of 55 B.C., the people had the right to choose and were not obliged to pay heed to the claims of descent if they did not feel so disposed. In Cicero's time, furthermore, entry to the Senate seems to have depended on election to the quaestorship, a relatively junior post in the established succession of offices (*cursus honorum*), all of them elective.

So how do we define the *élite* or *upper class* or *ruling class*, or (even) *aristocracy* or *oligarchy*, at Rome without circularity? The only criterion by which we can know that a person belonged to the élite in question is that of having been elected to office.

That should not be enough to allow us to talk of an "aristocracy," but it would have been enough for Aristotle to talk of *aristokratia*. For the definitions that he gives of *aristokratia* ("the rule of the best") are precisely that office should be filled by election by merit (*aretē*). We see in his discussion of Carthage that *aristokratia* meant that public offices were filled neither by nomination or cooptation on the one hand (which would be *oligarchia*) or by lot on the other. It would also be a step in the direction of *oligarchia* if there were a property qualification for office: "The Carthaginian system deviates most markedly from aristocracy in the direction of oligarchy by following the widely held view that office-holders should be chosen on grounds of means as well as on grounds of merit, because poor men are unable to rule well and have no leisure."[19] We will return to the question of property qualifications for office; but it seems that Aristotle would not have wanted to use the term *aristokratia* of any system where there was not some public process of judging the merits of the rival candidates. In short, it may be suggested that he uses the term of a competitive system or meritocracy. Formally speaking, if the "best" rule, then that is by definition *aristokratia*. But, in practice, he seems to approve of those systems where the will of the people plays a part in judging who is best:

The name "aristocracy" should properly be applied to the form of constitution which has already been treated in our first part. The only constitution which can with strict justice be called an aristocracy is one where the members are not merely "good" in relation to some standard or other, but are absolutely the "best" [*aristoi*] so far as excellence [of mind and character] is concerned. Only in such a constitution can the good man and the good citizen be absolutely identified; in all others the "good" are only so relative to the particular constitution. Nevertheless there are some further forms of constitution, which differ both from oligarchies and from the so-called "constitutional government" and are also called aristocracies. This is the case when elections to office are based not only on wealth but also on excellence. This type of constitution differs from both of the forms [just mentioned]; and is called aristocracy. [This usage is just, because] even in cities which do not make the encouragement of excellence a matter of public policy, there may still be found individuals who have a good reputation and are seen as respectable people. Accordingly, a constitution which pays regard to wealth, goodness, and [the will of] the people, as the Carthaginians' does, may be called an aristocratic constitution; and the same may also be said of constitutions such as the Spartan, which pay regard to excellence and to [the will of] the people, and where there is thus a mixture of the two factors, democracy and excellence.[20]

Thus, although the notion of an aristocracy as a social group defined by descent does not play a part in Aristotle's thought, it is
clear that he might have conceded, like Polybius, that *aristokratia*
was a possible description of the Roman system.

Insofar as an elective system employed a property qualification
for office, that would have caused it, in Aristotle's terms, to tend
toward *oligarchia*. Did the Roman system do so? There is, perhaps
surprisingly, no absolute proof that throughout the Republic it
did. What is certain is only that by the very early imperial period
there was a property qualification for being an *eques* ("knight"),
and a higher one then was imposed for being a Senator. Furthermore, the passage of Polybius about military service noted earlier
(p. 162) continues by saying that no one can be elected to political
office who has not done ten years' military service, which is the
requirement for a cavalryman. It is very likely, therefore, that cavalry service, the mark of the richer classes, was a precondition for
public office.[21] If so, Aristotle would have seen this as an oligarchic feature of the Roman system.

Aristotle's definitions are flexible, however, and he is very ready
to admit that any empirically observable political system may contain a number of elements (which themselves may be combined in
different ways). After talking about the types of *aristokratia* with
an element of popular election in the passage just quoted, he goes
on to define a *politeia* ("polity," or balanced constitution) as a
similar system, but with more democratic elements. There was
room for much variation, for instance as regards property qualifications, not for office, but for voting in the assembly, and in other
aspects:

A second is to take the mean, between the two different systems. Some
cities, for example, require no property qualification at all, or only a very
low qualification. Here we cannot use both practices to provide a common
term; we have, rather, to take the mean between the two. The third way
is to combine elements from both, and to mix elements of the oligarchical
rule with elements of the democratic. In the appointment of magistrates,
for example, the use of the lot is regarded as democratic, and the use of the
vote as oligarchical. Again, it is considered to be democratic that a property qualification should not be required, and oligarchical that it should
be. Here, accordingly, the method appropriate to an aristocracy or a "constitutional government" [polity] is to take one element from one form of
constitution and another from the other—that is to say, to take from oligarchy the practice of choosing office-holders by voting, and from democracy the practice of requiring no property qualification.

This is the general method of mixture. The sign that a good mixture of democracy and oligarchy has been achieved is that the same constitution is described both as a democracy and as an oligarchy.[22]

Aristotle's awareness that there might be more than one valid way of speaking of the same constitution is an important clue to approaching the Roman system (as Polybius of course saw). In this case, one very important criterion must be emphasized, namely, the absence in the case of Rome of any property qualification for voting. This was a fundamental issue. Aristotle had earlier discussed whether laboring men who were (he assumes) disqualified from office could really be citizens.[23] At Rome, although the "assembly of centuries" gave a systematic priority to the richer classes, and sequential voting might on occasion mean that the lowest classes never voted at all (because a majority of centuries had already been reached), no such system applied in the "assembly of tribes," which was the one before which nearly all legislation was placed.

On the other hand, the passage quoted introduces the principle, derived from the practice in Athens, that a truly democratic method of selecting public officials involved the use of the lot. No such principle ever applied in Rome, where election was a matter of competition or personal merit (which here, confusingly, Aristotle calls oligarchical), and probably on a basis of a property qualification (which really was oligarchical in his terms).

The discussion so far has given ample reason why Aristotle, like Polybius, might have been open to the idea that the Roman constitution displayed significant democratic features while equally illustrating his awareness that actual constitutions could easily exhibit mixed characteristics. So it is worth looking in some detail at his discussion of the various types of democracy while remembering that in his view what mattered above all was whether the ruling element in any state sought only its own benefit or the common good. If the people have power but are concerned for the common interest, the result can be called a *polity*; but if they seek the benefit only of the poor, it is a *dēmokratia*.[24]

In looking at his treatment of democracy, it is essential to be aware that in essence he sees states as being marked by conflicts between interest groups (or social or economic groups), and he will always prefer any system that limits the power of any potentially dominant group. He has no disposition to see "democracy" as an unambiguous good that should be preferred.

His main discussion takes place in a long chapter in his fourth book.[25] Various definitions are first offered, and the term *democracy* will apply only when the free-born and poor both constitute an actual majority (of adult males, it is assumed) and are in control. Then, ideally, one should distinguish the inhabitants by their various socioeconomic functions—but in the end, people are either rich or poor and cannot be both, and the rich are normally few and the poor many. So there seem to be only two types of political system: *dēmokratia* and *oligarchia*.

There can be, however, various types of *dēmokratia*. The first is when there is genuine equality, in which all participate in the state in the same way. Because in such a system what the majority wish must be decisive, this will be a *dēmokratia* (this definition, based on the principle of equality, seems more positive than is implied elsewhere in the *Politics*, and it is not clear whether he thinks that there were real-life examples of it). From this ideal condition, he turns to defining other types of *dēmokratia*, steadily moving to those where the popular will, in its turn swayed by demagogues, is sovereign. It is noticeable that a rhetorical and emotive tone enters his discussion here:

This is one variety of democracy; another is that in which offices are assigned on the basis of a property qualification, but the qualification is low; those who lose it are excluded. A third variety is one in which every citizen whose status is not open to challenge can share in office, but the law is still the final sovereign. A fifth variety of democracy is the same in other respects but the people, and not the law, is the final sovereign. This is what happens when popular decrees are sovereign instead of the law; and that is a result which is brought about by leaders of the demagogue type.

In cities which have a democracy under the law there are no demagogues; it is the best of the citizens who preside over affairs. Demagogues arise in cities where the laws are not sovereign. The people then becomes a monarchy—a single composite monarch made up of many members, with the many playing the sovereign, not as individuals, but collectively. It is not clear what Homer means when he says [*Iliad* II.204] that "it is not good to have the rule of many masters": whether he has in mind a situation of this kind, or one where there are many rulers who act as individuals. However, a democracy of this sort, since it is has the character of a monarch and is not governed by law, sets about ruling in a monarchical way and grows despotic; flatterers are held in honor and it becomes analogous to the tyrannical form of monarchy. For this reason both show a similar temper; both behave like despots to the better citizens; the decrees of the one are like the edicts of the other; the popular leader in the one is the same as, or at any rate like, the flatterer in the other; and in either case the influence of favorites predominates—that of the flatterer in tyrannies, and that of the popular leader in democracies of this variety.

It is popular leaders who, by referring all issues to the decision of the people, are responsible for substituting the sovereignty of decrees for that of the laws. The source of their great position is that the people are sovereign in all matters while they themselves, since the multitude follows their guidance, are sovereign over the people's decision. In addition opponents of those who occupy official positions argue "The people ought to decide": the people accept that invitation readily; and thus all offices lose authority.

Those who attack this kind of democracy saying that it is not a [true] constitution (*politeia*) would appear to be right. Where the laws are not sovereign, there is no *politeia*.[26]

If we look at Cicero's Rome in the light of these principles, there does, as we have seen (p. 172), appear to have been a property qualification for office. In that respect, Rome would have appeared oligarchic. More significant, however, is Aristotle's extended disquisition on the type of democracy in which decrees (*psēphismata*) are sovereign, not the law (*nomos*). Unless this is simply a reference to an established attitude of respect for custom, it must be an allusion to an important feature of the fourth-century Athenian democracy, and one that distinguished it from its fifth-century predecessor. This is to say that there was now an established procedure for reviewing changes to the law before accepting them, as opposed to normal votes on current matters.[27] Aristotle's diatribe about demagogues would in fact have been more apposite to the fifth-century democracy in which Socrates had lived and in which Plato had grown up. But it would have applied without qualification to Cicero's Rome, where there was no privileged or entrenched set of laws that amounted to a "constitution" and no procedure that distinguished ad hoc measures voted on by the people, for instance, on distributions of land, from laws altering the rules of the *res publica*. There was no legal requirement for advance validation of a law by the Senate and no procedure for reviewing laws that had been voted on by the "assembly of tribes" and that affected the structure of the state. It was precisely because there were no constitutional barriers to change, and because voting by the people in the Forum followed on the delivery before them (present, on occasion, in large numbers) of speeches for and against the laws, that this was the great age of Roman oratory.

Demagoguery—"leading the people" by oratorical persuasion, as well as by bribery and organized violence—was the core of the political process. It is in that precise sense—the absence of constitutional delaying procedures applying to new laws but not to votes on current matters of policy—that Rome in Cicero's time was an example of a political system in which, in Aristotle's words, "the people, and not the law, is the final sovereign."

On the other hand, Aristotle is quite clear that the opportunity actually to participate depends on economic conditions and on the availability of the necessary leisure. Hence, a couple of chapters later he notes the type of democracy that had arisen recently, in which, owing to the growth in size of cities and the increase of public revenues, "all are able to take a share in the *politeia* owing to the numeric superiority of the masses, and they participate and act politically by virtue of the fact that the poor too have leisure, because they receive pay."[28] The reference is to the system in Athens of pay for acting as jurors and (in the fourth century) for attending the assembly (*ekklēsia*). This was a feature that Aristotle would not have found reproduced in Rome. Just as no steps were taken to facilitate voting, either in elections or on laws, by those who lived far from the city, so no financial inducement was offered to assist political participation. There is no sign that anyone sought any such reform, and it would have been difficult to implement. For whereas at Athens both debate and voting normally took place at regular meetings of the *ekklēsia*, at Rome the vital process of the delivery of speeches on current issues took place at ad hoc meetings (*contiones*) summoned by officeholders. The meetings of the assemblies were formally separate, and involved only voting on candidates, or for or against a bill that was already fully set out (and had to be read out to the assembly by a herald). Due notice had to be given in each case, but there was no fixed cycle of meetings. In any case, this distinction also—between payment and nonpayment for attendance at meetings of the popular assembly—marks an important contrast between the Rome of Cicero and the Athens of Demosthenes. Aristotle would not have regretted the absence of state pay, for, as he says in concluding this section, this too helped to bring it about that "the mass of the poor becomes sovereign in the state, rather than the laws."[29]

Aristotle does, however, have a vision of a type of political system that can produce an appropriate balance between the "élite" and the mass of the people, although admittedly he sees it as practicable only in the context of a farming population, normally occupied with productive toil. Too large a population of people with urban occupations, who might find it all too easy to attend the assembly, was a danger that had to be counteracted by making sure that the rural element was always present. This, too, was a fundamental issue at Rome. All the same, it is worth quoting Aristotle's vision of a balanced system and asking how far it might have applied to the Republic, and if so when:

For these reasons it is both advantageous and the general practice for the variety of democracy we mentioned earlier to have the following arrangements: all the citizens take part in the election of officials, call them to account, and sit in the lawcourts, but the most important offices are filled by election, and confined to those who can satisfy a property qualification. The greater the importance of an office, the greater the property qualification that is required. Alternatively, no property qualification may be required for any office, but only men of capacity are actually appointed. A city which is governed in this way will be sure to be well governed (its offices will always be in the hands of the best of its members, with the people giving its consent and bearing no grudge against persons of quality); and the men of quality and the notables will be sure to be satisfied, under a system which at once preserves them from being governed by other and inferior persons and ensures (because others are responsible for calling them to account) that they will themselves govern justly. To be kept in such dependence, and to be denied the power of doing just as one pleases, is an advantage, since the power to act at will leaves no defence against the evil that is present in every human being. The outcome will be what is most beneficial in any constitution: government will be conducted by men of quality, and they will be free from misconduct, while the masses will not be disadvantaged.[30]

The overtones of this passage certainly would fit better with what we are told of the Rome of the Hannibalic War period (the context to which Polybius's analysis in his Book VI is intended to apply) than to Cicero's Rome. But it is also noticeable that Aristotle here speaks of just two elements, the elected officeholders and the people, whereas Polybius, to do justice to the Roman system, had had to take account of an "aristocratic" element, which did not consist just of individuals but was represented by a collective body, the Senate. It would be best to admit that there is not much in the *Politics* to offer a basis for conjecturing how Aristotle would have characterized a body that, in Cicero's time, had six hundred members, was filled indirectly by election (to the quaestorship),

received embassies, debated matters of public importance brought
before it by consuls or praetors, and could approve legislation to
be put forward by officeholders—but which could not legislate
itself, and whose approval of legislation was not constitutionally
required. Although its centrality in the state cannot be doubted, it
was always a constitutional anomaly that never quite threw off its
origins as a council summoned by the consuls (and perhaps earlier
by the kings). Little would be gained by trying to set against this
the relatively little that Aristotle says in the *Politics* of the councils of Greek cities. The *Politics*, by its nature, is not really about
the detailed working of institutions, but about the political nature
of different types of city regime.

So, if we try to imagine how the later Republic would have appeared if judged by Aristotle's criteria for different types of city
constitution, we cannot reasonably expect any answer that is complete and convincing. First, there are broad sociological questions,
which we cannot answer. In what terms should we characterize
the members of the Senate as they were at any one moment? As an
"aristocracy" or as a "nobility" or a "meritocracy," or simply as
those members of a wider land-owning class who happened to
have been elected to public office? In what sense did the inhabitants of the Italian peninsula function as Roman citizens? How do
we assess the significance of the fact that, on any construction,
those who voted in Rome represented only a tiny proportion of the
total number of Roman citizens? Were the thirty-one "rustic"
tribes in fact each represented by substantial numbers of voters
who had immigrated to Rome and joined the urban crowd?

However, significant conclusions can be drawn from considering Aristotle's criteria. First, some characteristics of what he would
have considered a "complete democracy" were clearly absent.
There was no pay for any form of public function other than service in the army. The lot was not used in the appointment of any
officeholders (although it was in the allocation of some elected
officeholders—consuls and praetors—to particular *provinciae*).
There seems to have been a property qualification for standing for
elective office.

On the other hand, the right to vote as a citizen was extended
to the freed slaves of Roman citizens. There was no property
qualification for the right to vote. The significance of the graduated voting, in descending sequence by groups belonging to differ-

ent property levels, as found in the "assembly of centuries" has been absurdly exaggerated. In most years in Cicero's time, this assembly met only to elect consuls and praetors. In the "assembly of tribes," which passed nearly all legislation, there was no formal discrimination by property level. Formally speaking, Roman citizens enjoyed universal adult male suffrage, meaning the right to elect officeholders directly and to vote on legislation (the suffrage in most modern democracies means solely the right to vote in periodic elections to representative bodies).

Much of the legislation that came before the Roman people had been the subject of a previous decree of the Senate (*senatus consultum*) and was put forward by one of the relevant officeholders (consuls, praetors or tribunes of the plebs) in the terms laid down in the Senate's decree. The people, as we have seen, although they could hear arguments for and against proposed laws at *contiones*, could not debate or amend legislation when meeting in their legislative assemblies, but only vote for or against. If this procedure had had the force of constitutional law behind it, it would have corresponded, in broad terms, to something like one of the range of procedures that Aristotle saw as characteristic of oligarchies:

In oligarchies it is advantageous either to co-opt [to the deliberative body] some members drawn from the populace, or, alternatively, to erect an institution of the type which exists in some cities, under the name of "preliminary councillors" or "guardians of the laws," and then to allow the citizen body to deal only with such issues as have already been considered, in advance, by these people. On this plan the people at large will share in deliberation, but they will not be able to abrogate any rule of the constitution. Another line of policy which is in the interest of oligarchies is that the people should only be free to vote for measures which are identical, or at any rate in agreement, with those submitted to them; or, alternatively, that the people as a whole should be allowed to give advice but that decisions should be taken by those who hold office. In fact they should do the opposite of what happens in [so-called] "constitutional governments" [polities]. The people should be sovereign for the purpose of rejecting proposals, but not for the purpose of passing them; and any proposals which they pass should be referred back to those in office.[31]

What matters here is not Aristotle's speculative reflections on possible systems, but the underlying principle that no legislation should come before the people except on the basis of previous consideration by a deliberative body. Cicero certainly would have subscribed to the notion of the Senate as the "guardian of the laws."

Moreover, even in the Athenian democracy, proposals before the *ekklēsia* had to be considered first by the council (*boulē*) of 500—but this was a body appointed by lot from all the different districts of Attica.

The crucial point is that a previous decree of the Senate was *not* constitutionally required for the valid proposal of a law. Any one (or more) of the two elected consuls, six praetors and ten tribunes of the plebs could propose a law directly to the people, with (as we have seen, p. 175 above) no discrimination as to whether a change in the constitution of the *res publica* was involved or not.

Not surprisingly, therefore, this speculative discussion of how Aristotle might have interpreted the Roman *res publica* of Cicero's time produces an answer that bears a significant resemblance to the conceptions that Polybius had formed a century earlier. There is nothing to suggest that Aristotle would have wanted to use the term *monarchic* of the role of the consuls. But as regards the balance between elected officeholders and the Senate on the one hand, and the people on the other, he would have seen the *res publica* as a complex balance of "aristocratic" or "oligarchic" elements on the one hand and "democratic" ones on the other. How it would be judged would depend very much on whether that balance had been maintained, or whether the people, under the influence of demagogues (pp. 174–75 above), had come to use their power in unrestrained pursuit of their own interests.

To say that Polybius was right, and that the Roman Republic exhibited strongly democratic characteristics, which became more predominant over the last century or more of its existence as a Republic, is neither to praise nor (as was much more common before the twentieth century) to deplore it, but simply to say that by the criteria available to contemporaries those were the features it had. There were other significant features of it, which were hardly discussed by contemporaries, and have been little noticed in modern political thought, such as the creation of a two-level citizenship, or patriotism, or the relatively brief phase when all of Italy south of the Po River could have been seen as a nation-state with universal liability to military service, universal adult male suffrage, applicable to both elections and legislation, and, at its center, the institutions of a city-state.

Of course, this potential nation-state never acquired the institutions that might have made it into a stable, functioning, reality. Instead, there was an ever-increasing level of political conflict in the city of Rome itself, and an increasing readiness to give exceptional powers to favored individuals. In case the attempt to redress the balance in modern interpretations, and to stress the reality of popular power in the Republic, is taken as a blandly optimistic reinterpretation, the last word will be left to the profoundly pessimistic prediction of where Rome's development was leading, which we owe to Polybius, still by far the most profound commentator on the Republic. It sometimes has been denied that his words are meant as a prediction about Rome itself, but it is quite clear that they are:

But when a new generation arises and the democracy falls into the hands of the grandchildren of its founders, they have become so accustomed to freedom and equality that they no longer value them, and begin to aim at pre-eminence; and it is chiefly those of ample fortune who fall into this error. So when they begin to lust for power and cannot attain it through themselves or their own qualities, they ruin their estates, tempting and corrupting the people in every possible way. And hence when by their foolish thirst for reputation they have created among the masses an appetite for gifts and the habit of receiving them, democracy in its turn is abolished and changes into a rule of force and violence. For the people, having grown accustomed to feed at the expense of others, as soon as they find a leader who is enterprising but is excluded from the honors of office by his penury, institute the rule of violence; and now uniting their forces massacre, banish, and plunder, until they degenerate again into perfect savages and find once more a master and monarch.

Such is the cycle of political revolution, the course appointed by nature in which constitutions change, disappear, and finally return to the point from which they started. Anyone who clearly perceives this may indeed in speaking of the future of any state be wrong in his estimate of the time the process will take, but if his judgement is not tainted by animosity or jealousy, he will very seldom be mistaken as to the stage of growth or decline it has reached, and as to the form into which it will change. And especially in the case of the Roman state will this method enable us to arrive at a knowledge of its formation, growth, and greatest perfection, and likewise of the change for the worse which is sure to follow some day. For, as I said, this state, more than any other, has been formed and has grown naturally, and will undergo a natural decline and change to its contrary.[32]

Polybius's predictions for the future of the Republic are all too telling. Nonetheless, given what passes for democracy in the contemporary nation-state, a Republic in which elected officeholders had to function in public, had to persuade those gathered in the Forum (who themselves represented, however imperfectly, the vastly greater total of citizens), and could not pass legislation without the votes of the people, would still deserve a place among the objects of political thought.

Notes

Foreword

1. F. Millar, *Scripta Classica Israelica* 3 (1976–77): 176.
2. E. Schürer, *The History of the Jewish People in the Age of Jesus Christ (175 BC–AD 135)*, revised by G. Vermes, F. Millar, and others (1973–87).
3. As is well known, Menahem Stern wrote comparatively few reviews; for a highly appreciative one of the first volume of the *New Schürer*, see *Journal of Jewish Studies* 25 (1974): 417–24.
4. J. Geiger, *Scripta Classica Israelica* 13 (1994): 198.
5. R. Syme, *The Roman Revolution* (1939): ix.
6. F. Millar, "Empire, Community and Culture in the Roman Near East: Greeks, Jews and Arabs," *Journal of Jewish Studies* 38 (1987): 143–64 at 147.

1. Introduction

1. F. Millar, *The Crowd in Rome in the Late Republic* (Ann Arbor, Mich., 1998), based on the Jerome Lectures of 1993–94.
2. A. Lintott, *The Constitution of the Roman Republic* (Oxford, 1999).
3. P. Pettit, *Republicanism: A Theory of Freedom and Government* (Oxford, 1997), e.g., p. 277.
4. See, for example, the excellent book by S. Katz, *Democracy and Elections* (New York and Oxford, 1997), 10.
5. Note the very significant proposition advanced by L. Siedentop, *Democracy in Europe* (London, 2000), and especially chapter 2, "Where are our Madisons?" noting the total absence of serious public debate about the political character of the European Union compared with the profound arguments put forward on both sides, federalist and antifederalist, in the debate on the U.S. Constitution.
6. Aptly quoted by B. Manin, *The Principles of Representative Government* (Cambridge, 1997), p. 1.
7. M. Stern, *Greek and Latin Authors on Jews and Judaism* I–III (Jerusalem, 1974–84).
8. Carlo Ginzburg's lectures have been published as *History, Rhetoric*

and *Proof* (Hanover, N.H., and London, 1999). So now have Anthony D. Smith's lectures of 1999, *The Nation in History: Historiographical Debates about Ethnicity and Nationalism* (2000).

2. Greek Observers: Aristotle, Polybius, and After

1. See the still invaluable book by T. A. Sinclair, *A History of Greek Political Thought* (London, 1951; 2nd ed., 1967).

2. See J. Boardman, *The Greeks Overseas: their Early Colonies and Trade* (4th ed., London, 1999).

3. For the best historical treatment of early Rome, see T. J. Cornell, *The Beginnings of Rome: Italy and Rome from the Bronze Age to the Punic Wars (c.1000–264 B.C.)* (London, 1995).

4. See esp. E. Peruzzi, *Civiltà greca nel Lazio preromano* (Firenze, 1998).

5. Heraclides Ponticus, Frag. 102, in F. Werhli, *Die Schule des Aristoteles 7: Herakleides Pontikos* (2nd ed., Basel, 1969), quoted from Plutarch, *Life of Camillus* 22.2.

6. See R. Wachter, *Altlateinische Inschriften: Sprachliche und epigraphische Untersuchungen zu den Dokumenten bis etwa 150 v. Chr.* (Bern, 1987).

7. For the most authoritative modern account see A. W. Lintott, *The Constitution of the Roman Republic* (Oxford, 1999).

8. Aristotle, *Fragmenta*, V. Rose (ed.) (Leipzig, 1886), F. 610, also quoted by Plutarch, *Camillus* 22. For profound problems as to who "Camillus" was, if a historical figure at all, see C. Bruun, "'What every man in the street used to know': M. Furius Camillus, Italic legends and Roman historiography," C. Bruun (ed.), *The Roman Middle Republic: Politics, Religions and Historiography c.400–133 B.C.* (Rome, 2000), 41–68.

9. See A. B. Bosworth, *Conquest and Empire: the Reign of Alexander the Great* (Cambridge, 1988), 167.

10. Aristotle, *Politics* V.6 (1305b 1–6). Both for orientation and for the translations quoted later in this book, I have used the excellent World's Classics translation of the *Politics* (Oxford, 1995), with introduction and notes by R. F. Stalley.

11. See Aristotle, *Fragmenta*, Rose (ed.), p. 258f.

12. Fragment 471 (Akragas); 481 (Gela); 510 (Himera); 520 (Kroton); 524 (Kyme); 583–84 (Sybaris); 585–90 (Syracuse); 590 (Taras).

13. The story is told most fully in Dionysius of Halicarnassus, *Roman Antiquities* VII, 2–11.

14. Aristotle, Fragment 607.

15. For this major addition to our knowledge of the ancient world, see the first full edition with commentary by J. E. Sandys, *Aristotle's Constitution of Athens: A Revised Text with an Introduction, Critical and Explanatory Notes, Testimonia and Indices* (London and New York, 1893). The major modern edition and commentary is that of P. J. Rhodes, *A Commentary on the Aristotelian Athenaion Politeia* (Oxford, 1981,

1993). Note also the translation with introduction and extensive notes by P. J. Rhodes, *Aristotle, The Athenian Constitution* (London, 1984).

16. The fourth-century Athenian democracy, incomparably better known than the fifth-century phase ("Periclean democracy"), which has traditionally attracted far more attention, has been the focus of the work of Mogens Herman Hansen. See the distillation of his work in M. H. Hansen, *The Athenian Democracy in the Age of Demosthenes: Structure, Principles and Ideology* (2nd ed., London, 1999).

17. See pp. 28–35 below.

18. For these themes in Aristotle's *Politics*, see IV.3, IV.13, and VI.7.

19. See esp. *Athēnaion Politeia* 29–33 (411 B.C.); 34–40 (404–3 B.C.).

20. For *politeia* in this specific sense in the *Politics* (as opposed to the more normal sense of a neutral term for any constitution), see esp. II.6, III.7, and IV.8–9.

21. See P. A. Brunt, *Italian Manpower* (Oxford, 1971), 13.

22. See Livy I.8.7.

23. See now T. J. Cornell, "The Lex Ovinia and the Emancipation of the Senate," C. Bruun (ed.), *The Roman Middle Republic; Politics, Religion and Historiography c. 400–133 B.C.* (Rome, 2000), 69–90.

24. For Polybius, the standard work is F. W. Walbank, *Polybius* (Berkeley, 1972).

25. Polybius II.37.9–11 (Loeb trans.).

26. For the *Federalist Papers*, see pp. 128–31 below (but focusing entirely on their treatment of the Republic).

27. For Polybius's use of earlier Greek history, see F. Millar, "Polybius between Greece and Rome," J. T. A. Koumoulides (ed.), *Greek Connections: Essays on Culture and Diplomacy* (Notre Dame, 1987), 1–18.

28. Polybius VI.19.2. The text is corrupt. It is clear that Polybius indicated that cavalrymen were liable for ten years and infantrymen for a period of either six or sixteen. It is not likely that the period for infantry was less.

29. Polybius VI.20.4–5 (Loeb trans.).

30. Polybius II.24.10.

31. Polybius XII.5.2.

32. The surviving text of Livy, missing for Books XI–XX, begins again with Book XXI in 218, and a voting system within the "assembly of centuries" based on *iuniores* (and hence also *seniores*) of each tribe appears under 215 B.C., Livy XXIV.7.12. Livy I.43.11 notes that the current system had come into effect "post expletas quinque et triginta tribus" (241 B.C.).

33. Polybius VI.14.7. As will be clear, there remains some doubt as to whether Polybius means to refer to the "assembly of centuries" or the "assembly of tribes."

34. F. W. Walbank, "A Greek Looks at Rome: Polybius VI Revisited," *Scripta Classica Israelica* 17 (1998): 45.

35. Polybius VI.9.8–9 (Loeb trans.).

36. Polybius VI.10.12–14 (Loeb trans.).

37. For an analysis of Polybius's references to the working of the Roman system, see above all C. Nicolet, "Polybe et les institutions romaines,"

in E. Gabba (ed.), *Polybe* (Geneva, 1973), 209–58. Note also C. Nicolet, "Polybe et la 'constitution' de Rome," C. Nicolet (ed.), *Demokratia et Aristokratia* (Paris, 1987), 15–35.

38. See esp. II.12; III.11; IV.13; VI.5. For the role of large jury courts (not however composed of the whole mass of the citizens) in the fourth-century Athenian democracy see Hansen, op. cit. (note 16), chapter 8.

39. The very important role of the lot in the Roman system, which will not be discussed further here, is excellently treated by N. Rosenstein, "Sorting out the Lot in Republican Rome," *American Journal of Philology* 116 (1995): 43.

40. Polybius VI.51.5–8 (Loeb trans.).

41. The ideology and symbolism of Roman funerals and funeral orations are recognized as having been of great importance in Roman society. See, for example, H. S. Flower, *Ancestor Masks and Aristocratic Power in Roman Culture* (Oxford, 1996), and J. Arce, *Memoria de los antepasados: puesta en escena y desarrollo del elogio fúnebre romano* (Madrid, 2000).

42. Polybius VI.57.8–9 (Loeb trans.).

43. See, for example, XXXI.10.7; 25.2–7; 29.8–12; XXXII.13. Positive and negative views of Roman conduct are presented in balance in XXXVI.9.

44. For Plutarch's *Romans Questions*, see the Loeb edition of his *Moralia*. vol. IV, 1f., and H. J. Rose, *The Roman Questions of Plutarch* (Oxford, 1924).

45. For Diodorus, see K. S. Sacks, *Diodorus and the First Century* (Princeton, 1990).

46. For Appian, whose work is of considerable interest both in structure and in the perspective it offers, there is, regrettably, no overall modern interpretation.

47. For Dionysius, see E. Gabba, *Dionysius and the History of Archaic Rome* (Berkeley, 1991).

48. Dionysius, *Roman Antiquities* I.7 (Loeb trans.).

49. Ibid., II.23.3–5 (Loeb trans.).

50. Ibid., II.14.1–3 (Loeb trans.).

51. Cicero, *On the Republic* II.39–40; Livy I.43.

52. Dionysius, *Roman Antiquities* IV.21 (Loeb trans.). The full description of the *centuriae* covers IV.16–21.

53. Ibid., VII.59.1–3.

54. Ibid., VII.59.9–10.

55. Ibid., IX.43.4.

56. For Dio, see F. Millar, *A Study of Cassius Dio* (Oxford, 1964; repr. 2000).

57. Cassius Dio, *Roman History* XXXVII.27.3–28.3 (Loeb trans., with modification).

58. Ibid., IV (Zonaras IV.15; Loeb trans. from vol. I, p. 127).

59. Ibid., IV (Zonaras IV.15; Loeb trans. from vol. I, p. 131).

60. Ibid., XLIV.2; Loeb trans. of 2.4.

61. Ibid., XLVII.39.

62. Ibid., LII.1.1.

3. *Looking Back on the Republic: The Empire, the Middle Ages, Machiavelli*

1. For this concept, and its problems, as used by the social anthropologist, see, for example, J. Monaghan and P. Just, *Social and Cultural Anthropology: A Very Short Introduction* (Oxford, 2000), chapter 3.

2. On Cicero's *On the Laws* (*De legibus*) see Cicero, *On the Commonwealth and On the Laws*, trans. J. E. G. Zetzel (Cambridge Texts in the History of Political Thought, Cambridge, 1999).

3. Cicero, *On the Commonwealth* (*De re publica*) I.29.45; 45.69; II.23.41; 39.65. See Zetzel, op. cit. (note 2).

4. For Cicero's *De officiis* (*On Duties*), see above all the translation, introduction, and commentary by M. T. Griffin and E. M. Atkins, *Cicero, On Duties* (Cambridge Texts in the History of Political Thought, Cambridge, 1991).

5. Pomponius' *Enchiridion* is known only from the extracts of it preserved in the *Digest* of Justinian of the sixth century A.D. The extracts can be read in O. Lenel, *Paligenesia Iuris Civilis* II (Leipzig, 1889), cols. 44–52. The extract quoted comes from *Digest* I.2.2.pr.2.

6. For the formal conferment of powers on the early emperors, see P. A. Brunt, "Lex de Imperio Vespasiani," *Journal of Roman Studies* 67 (1977): 95. For contemporary documents from the early Empire expressing the conception that sovereignty still resided with the *populus Romanus*, see F. Millar, "Imperial Ideology in the Tabula Siarensis," J. González and J. Arce (eds.), *Estudios sobre la Tabula Siarensis* (Madrid, 1988), 11–19.

7. I need hardly stress how much I owe to these outstanding works: Q. Skinner, *The Foundations of Modern Political Thought* I–II (Cambridge, 1978); J. Canning, *A History of Medieval Political Thought 300–1450* (London, 1996); Janet Coleman, *A History of Political Thought* I: *from Ancient Greece to Early Christianity*; II: *from the Middle Ages to the Renaissance* (Oxford, 2000). Note also ed. J. H. Burns, *The Cambridge History of Medieval Political Thought c. 350–1450* (Cambridge, 1988).

8. See Canning, op. cit. (note 7), p. 65.

9. See now the major work by Philip Jones, *The Italian City-State: From Commune to Signoria* (Oxford, 1997).

10. A. D. Momigliano, "Polybius' Reappearance in Western Europe," E. Gabba (ed.), *Polybe* (Geneva, 1974), 347–72, repr. in Momigliano, *Essays in Ancient and Modern Historiography* (Oxford, 1977), 79–98.

11. Sallust, *Catiline* 7.3.

12. [Aquinas], *De regimine principum* I.5.1–2 (trans. Blythe, with modifications). For this text, see *On the Government of Rulers: De Regimine Principum, Ptolemy of Lucca, with Portions attributed to Thomas Aquinas*, trans. J. M. Blythe (Philadelphia, 1997). See also J. M. Blythe, *Ideal Government and the Mixed Constitution in the Middle Ages* (Princeton, 1992).

13. See Blythe, op. cit. (note 12), p. 33ff.

14. *De regimine* IV.1.4–5, my translation, designed to highlight the new Latin vocabulary of political thought, derived from Aristotle.

15. Ibid., IV.19.1–4. By "Chalcedonii," he in fact means (or ought to have meant) not the people of the Greek city of Chalcedon but the Carthaginians ("Karchēdonioi" in Greek).

16. Ptolemy, *De regimine principum* IV.19.5.

17. Ibid., II.9.4, trans. Blythe.

18. On Marsilius, see esp. A. Gewirth, *Marsilius of Padua, The Defender of Peace* I: *Marsilius of Padua and Medieval Political Philosophy;* II: *The Defensor Pacis* (New York, 1951–56). Vol. II contains a translation of the *Defensor Pacis*. See also C. J. Nederman, *Community and Consent: the Secular Political Theory of Marsiglio of Padua's Defensor Pacis* (Lanham, Md., 1995).

19. See Marsiglio of Padua, *Writings on the Empire:* Defensor Minor *and* De translatione imperii, C. J. Nederman (ed.) (Cambridge Texts in the History of Political Thought, Cambridge, 1993).

20. Bartolus, *De regimine civitatis*, D. Quaglioni (ed.), *Politica e diritto nel Trecento italiano. Il "De tyranno" di Bartolo da Sassoferrato (1314–1357). Con l'edizione critica dei trattati "De Guelphis et Gebellinis," "De regimine civitatis" e "De tyranno"* (Rome, 1983). The text of *De regimine* is printed on pp. 149–70. So far as I know, it has not been translated.

21. See Brunt, op. cit. (note 6), and for the bronze tablet itself see A. E. Gordon, *Illustrated Introduction to Latin Epigraphy* (Berkeley, 1983), no. 46 and Pl. 29.

22. Apart from Quentin Skinner's *Foundations* (note 7), I will note only the briefest of selections from the vast bibliography on Florentine history and political thought of this period: F. Gilbert, *Machiavelli and Guicciardini: Politics and History in Sixteenth-Century Florence* (Princeton, 1965); P. Godman, *From Poliziano to Macchiavelli: Florentine Humanism in the High Renaissance* (Oxford, 1983); and of course the work that dominates the study of political thought in this and the following period, J. G. A. Pocock, *The Machiavellian Moment: Florentine Political Thought and the Atlantic Political Tradition* (Princeton, 1975).

23. For the text see *Marii Salamonii De Principatu Libros Septem*, M. D'Addio (ed.) (Milan, 1955), and cf. Skinner, *Foundations* I, 161 (see note 7 above). The quotations are given from the page numbers of D'Addio's edition.

24. For the Arch of Septimius Severus, see E. M. Steinby (ed.), *Lexicon Topographicum Urbis Romae* I (Rome, 1993), s.v. "Arcus: Septimius Severus (Forum)."

25. Apart from the works listed in note 20, see Q. Skinner, *Machiavelli* (Oxford, 1981); G. Bock, Q. Skinner, and M. Viroli (eds.), *Machiavelli and Republicanism* (Cambridge, 1990); V. B. Sullivan, *Machiavelli's Three Romes: Religion, Human Liberty, and Politics Reformed* (DeKalb, Ill., 1996); M. Viroli, *Machiavelli* (Oxford, 1998), and see now the challenging reappraisal by P. Rahe, "Situating Machiavelli," J. Hankins (ed.), *Renaissance Humanism: Reappraisals and Reflections* (Cambridge, 2000), 270.

26. For the Italian text, *Niccolò Machiavelli, Discorsi sopra la Prima Deca di Tito Livio*, C. Vivanti (ed.) (Torino, 1983). For an English translation, Niccolò Machiavelli, *Discourses on Livy*, trans. H. C. Mansfield and N. Tarcov (Chicago, 1996), from which the quotations in this chapter are taken.

27. See R. T. Ridley, "Livy and the Hannibalic War," C. Bruun (ed.), *The Roman Middle Republic: Politics, Religion and Historiography c. 400–133 B.C.* (Rome, 2000), 13–40.

28. See T. J. Cornell, *The Beginnings of Rome* (London, 1995) for a critical account that still attributes a relatively high degree of credibility to the main lines of the narrative.

29. See C. Bruun (ed.), op. cit. (note 23 above).

30. Momigliano, *op. cit.* (note 10 above).

31. See *Discorsi* I.1.3; 37.2; II.6–7; 23.2.

32. See F. Gilbert, op. cit. (note 22 above); Guicciardini, *Dialogue on the Government of Florence*, trans. and com. by A. Brown (Cambridge Texts in the History of Political Thought, Cambridge, 1994).

33. Trans. from Brown, op. cit. p. 151.

4. Three Views from Seventeenth-Century England

1. For discussions of the character of Venice as a republic, see Skinner, *Foundations* I, pp. 139ff. Of Venetian writers, he mentions (p. 141) especially Gasparo Contarini, *De magistratibus et Republica Venetorum* (1543), trans. by L. Lewkenor, *The Commonwealth and Government of Venice* (1599). The most important non-Venetian treatment is Donato Gianotti, *Libro della Repubblica de' Viniziani* (1540).

2. See James Harrington, *The Commonwealth of Oceana* and *A System of Politics*, J. G. A. Pocock (ed.) (Cambridge Texts in the History of Political Thought, Cambridge, 1992). All quotations are taken from this edition.

3. Harrington, op. cit., p. 6.

4. See, for example, Q. Skinner, "The Italian City-Republics," J. Dunn (ed.), *Democracy: The Unfinished Journey, 508 B.C. to A.D. 1993* (Oxford, 1992), 57–69, discussing also the influence of Italian republican thought in seventeenth-century England; id., *Liberty before Liberalism* (Cambridge, 1998).

5. I have used the edition, with introduction by J. C. A. Gaskin, in the World's Classics series, Thomas Hobbes, *Leviathan* (Oxford, 1996). Quotations are taken from this text, which preserves Hobbes's own (very odd) punctuation.

6. Marchamont Nedham, *The Excellency of a Free State* (London, 1767).

7. See Pocock's introduction (note 1 above), vii–xi.

8. See Skinner, *The Foundations of Modern Political Thought* I (Cambridge, 1978), 140–41, and note 1, above.

9. See A. Lintott, *The Constitution of the Roman Republic* (Oxford, 1999), 60.

10. See J. Alvis (ed.), *Areopagitica and other Political Writings of John Milton* (Indianapolis, 1999). References are to page numbers of this edition.

11. *Defence*, chapter III, p. 169.

12. Ibid., chapter IV, p. 207.

13. Alvis, *op. cit.*, pp. 414ff.

14. *Readie and Easie Way*, p. 429.

15. Ibid., p. 430.

16. Ibid., p. 432.

17. Ibid., p. 441.

18. Ibid., p. 442–43.

19. I owe this point to Quentin Skinner.

5. From Restoration to Revolution: Britain, France, and America

1. See, for example, Ph. Ayres, *Classical Culture and the Idea of Rome in Eighteenth-Century England* (Cambridge, 1997); Ch. Gell, *Le Dix-huitième siècle et l'antiquité en France 1680–1789* I (Oxford, 1995); C. J. Richard, *The Founders and the Classics: Greece, Rome and the American Enlightenment* (Cambridge, Mass., 1994).

2. J. G. A. Pocock, "Machiavelli, Harrington and English Political Ideologies in the Eighteenth Century," *Language and Time: Essays on Political Thought and History* (New York, 1971), 104, on p. 114.

3. B. Bailyn, *The Ideological Origins of the American Revolution* (Cambridge, Mass., 1967; enlarged ed. 1992).

4. For an accessible edition, see C. Robbins (ed.), *Two English Republican Tracts* (Cambridge, 1969). References are to the page numbers of this edition.

5. See above all M. Beard, "Priesthood in the Roman Republic," M. Beard and J. North (eds.), *Pagan Priests: Religion and Power in the Ancient World* (London, 1990), 17–48; and in general M. Beard, J. North, and S. Price, *Religions of Rome* I–II (Cambridge, 1998).

6. Quoted in Ayres, op. cit. (note 1), p. 10.

7. Quoted in Ayres, p. 17.

8. See C. Robbins, *The Eighteenth-Century Commonwealthmen: Studies in the Transmission, Development and Circumstance of English Liberal Thought from the Restoration of Charles II until the War with the Thirteen Colonies* (Cambridge, Mass., 1959).

9. For Thelwall's remarkable career, see the entry on him in the *Dictionary of National Biography* XIX, pp. 590–93.

10. The quotations used here are taken from Montesquieu, *The Spirit of the Laws*, A. Cohler, B. Miller, and H. Stone (eds.) (Cambridge Texts in the History of Political Thought, Cambridge, 1989).

11. Montesquieu, op. cit., pp. 156–66.

12. Ibid., p. 160.

13. Ibid., pp. 77–80.

14. Ibid., p. 14.

15. For Rousseau, I have used the edition and translation by V. Gourevitch, *Rousseau, The Social Contract and Other Later Political Writings* (Cambridge Texts in the History of Political Thought, Cambridge, 1997). See also the edition by M. Cranston (London, 1968). For the influence on his thought of observation of local democracy at work in Switzerland, see Cranston's Introduction, pp. 18–19. Note also the invaluable edition by V. Gourevitch, *Rousseau, The Discourses and Other Early Political Writings* (Cambridge Texts in the History of Political Thought, Cambridge, 1997).

16. Gourevitch, *Social Contract*, p. 107.

17. III.15.5, trans. Gourevitch, *Social Contract*, p. 114.

18. See Richard, op. cit. (note 1 above).

19. See John Adams, *Defence of the Constitutions of Government of the United States of America*, originally published in 1787, and republished in Adams, *Works*, C. F. Adams (ed.) (Boston, 1865), IV, 271ff.

20. See H. J. Storing (ed.), *The Complete Antifederalist* I–VII (Chicago, 1981), 4.25.3.

21. I rely on the masterly collection of contemporary material edited by B. Bailyn, *The Debate on the Constitution: Federalist and Antifederalist Speeches, Articles and Letters During the Struggle over Ratification*, vol. I–II (New York, 1993)

22. See the superb edition of the *Papers*, with an excellent Introduction, by I. Kramnick: James Madison, Alexander Hamilton, and John Jay, *The Federalist Papers* (London, 1987).

23. See the collections by Storing and Bailyn, notes 20 and 21 above.

24. *Complete Antifederalist*, 3.3.18–24, para. 3.3.20 (vol. III, pp. 31–32).

25. *Complete Antifederalist*, 2.8.1–230 (vol. II, pp. 214–357). The passage discussed is 2.8.106 (vol. II, pp. 272–73).

26. See *Debate* I, pp. 437ff. For John Stevens, see pp. 1040–41.

27. Ibid., p. 440.

28. Ibid., pp. 129ff. For Noah Webster, see pp. 1049–50.

29. Ibid., p. 136.

30. Ibid., pp. 137–38.

31. Ibid., p. 142.

32. Ibid., p. 144.

33. Ibid., pp. 154–55.

34. Ibid., p. 158.

35. See Paul Rahe, *Republics Ancient and Modern* I. *The Ancient Regime in Classical Greece;* II. *New Modes and Orders in Early Modern Political Thought;* III. *Inventions of Prudence: Constituting the American Republic* (Chapel Hill, 1992). The Roman Republic as such is not the subject of any of these volumes; but my debt to them is far greater throughout than might appear from the very occasional references in which they appear.

36. Quoted from the edition by Kramnick (note 21 above), p. 227; also

printed in *Debate* II, 698ff. (with minor differences of punctuation and spelling).

37. *Paper* LXX is reproduced also in *Debate* II, p. 346ff.

38. Reproduced in *Debate* II, 316ff., omitting the title.

39. See Kramnik's edition, 373; *Debate* II, p. 321.

40. Kramnik, 374–75; *Debate* II, p. 323.

41. See the edition by B. Fontana, Benjamin Constant, *Political Writings* (Cambridge Texts in the History of Political Thought, Cambridge, 1988), pp. 307ff.

42. Trans. Fontana, pp. 310–11.

43. Trans. Fontana, p. 322.

44. I borrow the phrase, as is obvious, from Isaiah Berlin's famous essay.

45. See J. S. Mill, "On Liberty" and "Considerations On Representative Government," first published in 1861. I have used the edition edited and introduced by John Gray: John Stuart Mill, *On Liberty and Other Essays* (Oxford, 1991), 203–467.

6. *Some Contemporary Approaches*

1. See J. F. Gardner, *Women in Roman Law and Society* (London, 1986).

2. Note esp. D. B. Davis, *The Problem of Slavery in Western Culture* (Ithaca N.Y., 1966; repr. Oxford, 1988).

3. O. Patterson, *Freedom* I: *Freedom in the Making of Western Culture* (London, 1991).

4. For comment on this aspect of the book see F. Millar, "The Roman *Libertus* and Civic Freedom," *Arethusa* 28 (1995): 99, published along with other papers discussing aspects of the book, originally delivered at a symposium at Wellesley College.

5. C. Nicolet, *The World of the Citizen in Republican Rome* (London, 1980), originally published as *Le métier de citoyen* (Paris, 1976; 2nd ed. 1988).

6. Polybius VI.19.1–5 (Loeb trans.).

7. One important exception is Michael Walzer, *Obligations: Essays on Disobedience, War and Citizenship* (Cambridge, Mass., 1970), Part Two: "War."

8. F. Millar, *The Crowd in Rome in the Late Republic* (Ann Arbor, 1998), chapter 1. The reader should be warned that the views expressed in this book are far from enjoying universal assent among historians of the Roman Republic.

9. M. Gelzer, *The Roman Nobility*, translated with an introduction by Robin Seager (Oxford, 1975), 139.

10. P. A. Brunt, *Social Conflicts in the Roman Republic* (London, 1971).

11. P. A. Brunt, *The Fall of the Roman Republic and Related Essays* (Oxford, 1988), chapter 8, "*Clientela*"; chapter 9, "Factions."

12. E. Ruschenbush, "Europe and Democracy," R. Osborne and S. Hornblower (eds.), *Ritual, Finance, Politics: Athenian Democratic Accounts Presented to David Lewis* (Oxford, 1994), 189, on p. 191.

13. M. H. Hansen, "The 2500th Anniversary of Cleisthenes' Reforms and the Tradition of Athenian Democracy," Osborne and Hornblower (eds.), op. cit. (note 11), 25, on p. 29. For the place of Athens in the political thought of successive periods see the comprehensive study by J. T. Roberts, *Athens on Trial: The Antidemocratic Tradition in Western Thought* (Princeton, 1994).

14. D. Held, *Models of Democracy* (Cambridge, 1987), 35. The reference is to J. A. Schumpeter, *Capitalism, Socialism and Democracy*, first published in 1942, and many times reprinted.

15. Held, op. cit. (note 14), p. 164ff.

16. J. Dunn, *Democracy: the Unfinished Journey, 508 B.C. to A.D. 1993* (Oxford, 1992), 244.

17. See esp. A. Yakobson, *Elections and Electioneering in Rome: A Study in the Political System of the Late Republic* (Stuttgart, 1999).

18. R. S. Katz, *Democracy and Elections* (New York and Oxford, 1997), 14.

19. Millar, op. cit. (note 8), p. 30ff.

20. Katz, op. cit. (note 18), p. 18

21. Ph. Pettit, *Republicanism: A Theory of Freedom and Government* (Oxford, 1997).

22. S. Lakoff, *Democracy: History, Theory, Practice* (Boulder, 1996).

23. S. E. Finer, *The History of Government* I–III (Oxford, 1997), esp. vol. I: *Ancient Monarchies and Empires*.

24. Finer I, p. 43.

25. For the complex evidence on the numbers of citizens and others (including slaves) in Italy, see above all P. A. Brunt, *Italian Manpower 225 B.C.–A.D. 14* (Oxford, 1971). The table of census figures on pp. 13–14 shows 910,000 in 70–69 (representing adult males), and 4,063,000 in 28 B.C. (representing all free persons of Roman citizen status, and reflecting the extension of citizenship in 49 B.C. to the area north of the Po River). It should be acknowledged that, if these are indeed the meanings of the two figures, the relation between them gives rise to fundamental problems; see E. Lo Cascio, "The Size of the Roman Population: Beloch and the Meaning of the Augustan Census Figures," *Journal of Roman Studies* 84 (1994): 23. Nonetheless, no interpretation of these figures will remove the conclusion that the Roman citizen population of Italy in the mid-first century B.C. was very large, and approached the scale of the population of the thirteen states of America in 1776.

26. For the estimated population in 1790 (just under four million) see H. W. Austin, *Political Facts of the United States Since 1789* (New York, 1986), 461.

27. J. S. McClelland, *The Crowd and the Mob from Plato to Canetti* (London, 1989).

28. McClelland, op. cit., p. 50.

29. Cicero, *On the Orator (De oratore)* II, 198–99.

30. For the best treatment of this tradition see P. A. Brunt, *The Fall of the Roman Republic* (note 11 above), chapter 6, "*Libertas* in the Republic."

7. *Cicero's Rome: What Aristotle Might Have Thought*

1. For accessible and interesting presentations of these works, see Cicero, *On Duties*, by M. T. Griffin and E. M. Atkins (eds.) (Cambridge, 1991), and *On the Commonwealth and On the Laws*, J. E. G. Zetzel (ed.) (Cambridge, 1999), both in *Cambridge Texts in the History of Political Thought*.

2. See, for example, Aristotle, *Politics* IV.12 (1296 b 30).

3. Aristotle, *Politics* III.3, trans. E. Barker in the World's Classics series, with revisions and introduction by R. F. Stalley (Oxford, 1995). This translation has been used throughout this chapter.

4. Aristotle, *Politics* VII.4.

5. See M. H. Crawford (ed.), *Roman Statutes* I (London, 1996), no. 24 (text, translation, and commentary).

6. See P. A. Brunt, "The Army and the Land in the Roman Revolution," *Journal of Roman Studies* 52 (1962): 69, revised in *The Fall of the Roman Republic and Related Essays* (Oxford, 1988), 240.

7. See E. Gabba, "Le città italiche del I sec. a.C. e la politica," *Rivista Storica Italiana* 93 (1986): 653, reprinted in *Italia Romana* (Como, 1994), 123.

8. Cicero, *On the Laws* III.15.34–36, Loeb trans., with the addition of dates.

9. Cicero, *In Defence of Plancius* 6.16.

10. [Aristotle], *Constitution of the Athenians* 68–69. See M. H. Hansen, *The Athenian Democracy in the Age of Demosthenes* 2nd ed. (London, 1999), 202–203.

11. Some developments of this period are sketched in F. Millar, "Politics, Persuasion and the People before the Social War," *Journal of Roman Studies* 76 (1986): 1.

12. See N. Rosenstein, "Sorting out the Lot in Republican Rome," *American Journal of Philology* 116 (1995): 43.

13. Polybius VI.13.6–9, Loeb trans.

14. The most striking instance is the law of 101–100 B.C., known from partial copies in Greek preserved on inscriptions from Delphi and Cnidus, see M. H. Crawford (ed.), *Roman Statues* I (London, 1996), no. 12.

15. Cicero, *Verrine Oration* II.5.68–175, quoted in F. Millar, *The Crowd in Rome in the Late Republic* (Ann Arbor, 1998), 66.

16. For these two scales see esp. Aristotle, *Politics* III.7 and IV.4.

17. *Politics* II.11.

18. Polybius VI.12.1, Loeb trans.

19. Aristotle, *Politics* II.11 (1273 a 21), trans. Barker.

20. *Politics* IV.7, trans. Barker.

21. For this argument see C. Nicolet, "Le cens sénatorial sous la République et sous Auguste," *Journal of Roman Studies* 66 (1976): 20, revised in C. Nicolet (ed.), *Des Ordres à Rome* (Paris, 1984), p. 143, and reprinted in C. Nicolet, *Censeurs et publicans: Economie et fiscalité dans la Rome antique* (Paris, 2000), p. 163.

22. *Politics* IV.9, trans. Barker.

23. Ibid., III.5.
24. Ibid., III.7.
25. Ibid., IV.4.
26. Ibid., IV.4 (1291 b 38–1292 a 28), trans. Barker, with minor emendations.
27. See Hansen, *Athenian Democracy* (note 10 above), chapter 7.
28. *Politics* IV.6 (1293 a 3–7).
29. Ibid., IV.6 (1293 a 9–10).
30. Ibid., IV.4 (1318 b 27–1319 a 3), trans. Barker.
31. Ibid., IV.14 (1298 b 26–38), trans. Barker.
32. Polybius VI.8.5–14, Loeb trans.

Subject Index

Achaean League, Polybius on, 24

Adams, John (*Defence of the Constitutions of Government*), 121

Addison, Joseph, on Republican constitution, 106–7

Antifederalist arguments, 121–23

Aristocracy, problems of definition as applied to Rome, 169–72

Aristotle and his school: *Politics, Constitution of the Athenians, Politeiai, Barbarian Customs,* 15–16; Latin translation of *Politics* by William of Moerbeke, 55, 57; views on possible size of *polis*, 160–61; his criteria for types of *politeia* as applied to the late Republic, 168–80

Assemblies, Roman, 18–21, 26–28; Dionysius of Halicarnassus on, 42–45; Alexander Hamilton on, in *Federalist Paper* XXXIV, 128–29; Cicero, Livy, and Dionysius on, 140; social structure of voting in, 145–46; *see also* ballot laws

Ballot laws of 130s B.C., 164–65

Bartolus of Sassoferrato (*De regimine civitatis*), on Roman Republic, 62–63

Blackstone, Sir William, on Roman voting-rights, 107

Carthage, Polybius' view of, 34–35

Cassius Dio (*Roman History*), on Roman Republic, 46–49

Census, registration of Roman citizens in during first century B.C., 162–63

Cicero (*On the Laws* and *On the Commonwealth*), on Roman institutions, 51, 158

Clientela: disputed significance of in Roman politics, 5; Gelzer's views, 139; P. A. Brunt's views, 140

Cola (Nicola) di Rienzi, republican ideas, 63–64

Comitia Centuriata. *See* Assemblies, Roman

Comitia Tributa. *See* Assemblies, Roman

Constant, Benjamin, "The Liberty of the Ancients compared to that of the Moderns," 132–34

Democracy, varieties of as defined by Aristotle, 173–78

Dionysius of Halicarnassus (*Roman Antiquities*), account of Roman institutions), 39–46

Entrenched clauses, Aristotle's view of importance of, and absence of in Rome, 173–5

Federalist Papers (J. Madison, A. Hamilton, J. Jay), 121; Hamilton, in *Paper* XXXIV, on Roman voting assemblies, 128–9; on executive powers in *Paper* LXX, 129; Madison, in

Paper LXIII, on the need for a deliberative body, and the undesirability of direct democracy, 129–31

Finer, S. E. (*History of Government*), on Roman Republic, 149–53

Florence, political history, 64–65

Forum type of government (S. E. Finer), 149–51

Freedmen, Roman: acquisition of political rights on emancipation, 137

Gelzer, M., views on Republican political relations, 139

Greek world, relationship to Rome, 37–39

Harrington, James (*Commonwealth of Oceana*): on settlement of Jews in Ireland, 81; lessons drawn from Roman Republic, 86–96

Held, D., view of Rome as oligarchic system, 142

Hobbes, Thomas (*Leviathan*), on sovereignty and liberty, 82–84

Italy: Roman system in, 25; in first century B.C., 162–63

Juristic writers, on basis of Empire in popular vote, 53, 63, 65–66, 151

Lakoff, S. (*Democracy*), on Rome, 147–49

Lex de Imperio Vespasiani: used by Cola di Rienzi, 63–64; quoted by Mario Salamonio, 67

Libertas, popular concept of in Rome, 146, 156

Livy, use of by Machiavelli, 68–69

McClelland, J. S. (*The Crowd and the Mob*), on Rome, 154–56

Machiavelli, Niccolò (*Discourses on the First Ten Books of Livy*), on Roman Republic, 67–78

Marsilius (Marsiglio) of Padua, on Roman Republic, 61–62

Military service, Roman: importance as aspect of citizenship, 137–38; in first century B.C., 62

Montesquieu (*On the Spirit of the Laws*), on the Roman Republic, 108–13

Milton, John (*Readie and Easie Way to Establish a Free Commonwealth*), on Roman Republic, 96–99

Moyle, Walter (*Essay upon the Constitution of the Roman Government*), analysis of the Republican constitution, 102–6

Nedham, Marchamont (*Excellency of a Free State*), on Roman Republic, 54–56

Pay (for voting or service as juror), absence of in Rome, 176

Polybius, analysis of Roman constitution, 23–36

Ptolemy (Bartholomew) of Lucca, on Roman Republic, 59–61

Representation, political, particular sense of as applicable to Rome, 6

Rome: early history of to the fourth century B.C., 12–14; in fourth to the second century B.C., 23–25; in second to the first century B.C., 158–60, 164–68

Rousseau, J.-J. (*The Social Contract*), on the significance of the Roman Republic as embodying the principle of popular sovereignty, 113–20

Salamonio, Mario (*De principatu*), on Roman Republic, 65–67

Senate, Roman: early development, 22–23; role of in Polybius' view, 166–67; role in relation to legislation, 179–80
Slavery, significance of Roman,
136

Tribes (*tribus*), Roman, 18

Voting, Roman, nature of, 144. *See
also* ballot laws

Webster, Noah (*Examination into
the Leading Principles of the
Federal Constitution*), on the
principle of representation, and
the comparison between the
Roman and British constitutions, 123–28
William of Moerbeke (Latin translation of Aristotle's *Politics*),
55, 57
Women, position of in Rome, 136

Index of Passages Quoted

Anon., "Essays of an Old Whig"
IV, 122
[Aquinas?], *De regimine principum*
I.5.1–2, 58
Aristotle, *Politics* III.3, 160
Politics IV.4, 174–5, 177
Politics IV.7, 171
Politics IV.9, 172–3
Politics IV.14, 179
Politics VII.4, 161

Cassius Dio, *Roman History* IV
(Zonaras IV.15), 47–48
XXXVII.27.3–28.3, 47
Cicero, *On the Laws* 15.34–6,
164–65
On the Orator II, 198–99, 156
Verrine Oration II.5.68.175, 167
Constant, Benjamin, "The Liberty
of the Ancients compared with
that of the Moderns" (ed.
Fontana), pp. 310–11, 133
p. 322, 133–34

Dionysius of Halicarnassus,
Roman Antiquities I.7, 40
Roman Antiquities II.23.3–4,
40–41
Roman Antiquities II.14.1–3,
41–2
Roman Antiquities IV.21, 43
Roman Antiquities VII.59.1–3,
44
Roman Antiquities VII.59.9–10,
45
Roman Antiquities IX.43.4, 45

Dunn, J., *Democracy: The
Unfinished Journey*, p. 244, 143

Finer, S. E., *History of Government* I, p. 43, 149–50

Gelzer, M., *The Roman Nobility*,
p. 139, 139
Guicciardini, Francesco, *Dialogue
on the Government of Florence*
(trans. Brown), p. 151, 78–79

Hamilton, A., *Federalist Paper*
XXXIV, 128–29
Harrington, James, *Common-
wealth of Oceana* (trans.
Pococke), p. 6, 81
Commonwealth of Oceana
(trans. Pococke), p. 20, 87
Commonwealth of Oceana
(trans. Pococke), p. 23, 89–90
Commonwealth of Oceana
(trans. Pococke), p. 24, 90
Commonwealth of Oceana
(trans. Pococke), p. 135, 93
Commonwealth of Oceana
(trans. Pococke), pp.166–67,
95
Held, D., *Models of Democracy*,
p. 35, 142
Hobbes, *Leviathan* II.21.8–9, 82–83

Katz, R. S., *Democracy and Elections*, p. 14, 144
Democracy and Elections,
p. 18, 146

Machiavelli, *Discourses* I.2.2–4, 73
  Discourses I.6.3, 74
  Discourses I.6.4, 71
  Discourses III, 24, 74
  Discourses III.31.4, 72
Madison, James, *Federalist Paper*
  LXIII, 131
Milton, John, *Readie and Easie
  Way to Establish a Free Com-
  monwealth* (ed. Alvis), pp. 429–
  30, 97–98
  pp. 442–43, 98
Montesquieu, *On the Spirit of the
  Laws* II.2, 111
  XI.6, 109
Moyle, Walter, *Essays upon the
  Constitution of the Roman
  Government* (ed. Robbins),
  pp. 215–16, 103–4
  pp. 236–7, 104–5

Nedham, Marchamont, *On the
  Excellency of a Free State,*
  pp. xiv–xv, 85

Polybius, *History* II.37.9–11, 24
  History VI.8.5–14, 181
  History VI.9.89, 29

History VI.10.12–14, 30
History VI.13.6–9, 166–67
History VI.51.5–8, 35
History VI.57.8–9, 35
Pomponius, *Enchiridion* (*Digest*
  I.2.2, *pr.* 2), 52–53
Ptolemy (Bartholomew) of Lucca,
  De regimine principum I.1.4–5,
  59–60
  De regimine principum IV.19.5,
  60–1

Rousseau, J.-J., *Social Contract*
  III.10, 115
  Social Contract III.12, 115
  Social Contract III.14, 116
  Social Contract III.15, 116
  Social Contract IV.3, 117
  Social Contract IV.4.24, 11718
  Social Contract IV.4.356, 118

Webster, Noah, *Examination into
  the Leading Principles of the
  Federal Constitution,* p. 136,
  124–25
  p. 142, 125
  p. 144, 126
  p. 158, 127